THE
SCOTTISH REFOR

**BASED ON THE
BIRKBECK LECTURES DELIVERED IN THE
UNIVERSITY OF CAMBRIDGE
IN 1957-8**

THE SCOTTISH
REFORMATION

BY

GORDON DONALDSON

CAMBRIDGE UNIVERSITY PRESS

CAMBRIDGE

LONDON NEW YORK NEW ROCHELLE

MELBOURNE SYDNEY

CAMBRIDGE UNIVERSITY PRESS
Cambridge, New York, Melbourne, Madrid, Cape Town, Singapore, São Paulo

Cambridge University Press
The Edinburgh Building, Cambridge CB2 8RU, UK

Published in the United States of America by Cambridge University Press, New York

www.cambridge.org
Information on this title: www.cambridge.org/9780521086752

First published 1960
Reissued 1972
Reprinted 1979
This digitally printed version 2008

A catalogue record for this publication is available from the British Library

Library of Congress Catalogue Card Number: 60–16183

ISBN 978-0-521-08675-2 hardback
ISBN 978-0-521-07284-7 paperback

CONTENTS

PREFACE

THE preparation of this book was the outcome of an invitation to deliver the Birkbeck Lectures in Ecclesiastical History in the University of Cambridge in 1957–8, and its publication comes at a time when the approaching quatercentenary of the events of 1560 has revived interest in the Scottish reformation. A comprehensive history of a movement which had so many ramifications would be little less than the history of Scotland in the sixteenth century, because, apart from the ecclesiastical reformation, there was a diplomatic revolution which reversed Scotland's traditional foreign policy, there were changes in the institutions and the balance of forces in the country which meant little less than a constitutional revolution, and all must be seen against a background of social change. The subject of this book is ecclesiastical history, and even in that field it has little to say about some of the more familiar topics. My own work, pursued intermittently over a period of more than twenty years, has been primarily on record evidence, and my interest has been to determine how ecclesiastical institutions developed and operated, which they often did in ways which differed from the plans of contemporaries and differed still more from the theories of later controversialists. It is in this factual and realistic study that I hope the evidence assembled in this book will be principally of value.

I would record my gratitude to Trinity College for the honour of its invitation to deliver the lectures. I owe much to the encouragement and counsel of the Very Reverend Norman Sykes, Dean of Winchester, and to the many colleagues and other friends with whom I have discussed various problems of interpretation and from whom I have received valuable suggestions: especially to Professor W. Croft Dickinson and the Rev. Thomas Lothian, who read the typescript of the lectures before they were delivered, and to Mr I. B. Cowan, who read the typescript of this book.

EDINBURGH   G. D.

LIST OF ABBREVIATIONS

A.P.S.	*Acts of the Parliaments of Scotland.*
B.U.K.	*Acts and Proceedings of the General Assemblies.* Bannatyne and Maitland Clubs, 1839–45.
Calderwood	David Calderwood, *The History of the Kirk of Scotland.* Wodrow Society, 1842–9.
Cal. S. P. Scot.	*Calendar of State Papers relating to Scotland and Mary, Queen of Scots.* H.M.S.O.
Dickinson	W. Croft Dickinson, *John Knox's History of the Reformation in Scotland,* 1949.
E.H.R.	*English Historical Review.*
Formulare	*St Andrews Formulare.* Stair Society, 1942–4.
H.M.C.	Historical Manuscripts Commission.
Laing	David Laing, *The Works of John Knox,* 1846–64.
Reg. Ho.	H.M. General Register House, Edinburgh.
R.M.S.	*Registrum Magni Sigilli Regum Scotorum.* H.M.S.O.
R.P.C.	*Register of the Privy Council of Scotland.* H.M.S.O.
R.S.S.	*Registrum Secreti Sigilli Regum Scotorum.* H.M.S.O.
R.S.S.	Registrum Secreti Sigilli. [MS.].
Reg. K. S. St A.	*Register of the Kirk Session of St Andrews.* Scottish History Society, 1889–90.
Reg. Pres.	Register of Presentations to Benefices.
S.H.R.	*Scottish Historical Review.*
S.H.S.	Scottish History Society.
S.R.S.	Scottish Record Society.
S.T.S.	Scottish Text Society.

NOTE ON REFERENCES

Citations of Knox's History of the Reformation refer to both Laing's edition and Dickinson's, and the proceedings of the general assembly are likewise cited from both the *B.U.K.* and Calderwood.

References to the works of English reformers are to the Parker Society editions.

MSS. referred to are in H.M. General Register House, Edinburgh, except when another location is specified.

CHAPTER I

KIRKS AND KIRKMEN UNREFORMED

JOHN KNOX called his great work 'The History of the Reformation of Religion', but his ablest opponent, Ninian Winyet, was no less concerned for 'reformation of doctrine and manners'. Nor was it only the challenge of radicals which provoked the more conservative to an interest in reform. It is true that the provincial council of the Scottish church which in 1559 adopted measures directed at 'the reformation of church discipline' was acting in response to somewhat novel proposals put forward by certain 'temporal lords and barons'; but in so far as those lords and barons were concerned with the need for churchmen to seek 'reformation of their lives' they were asking no more than another provincial council had declared to be its own object a decade earlier, when it passed statutes 'for the reformation of morals in the Church of Scotland'. Demands for reform had indeed come still earlier from Scottish laymen, but from those of impeccable orthodoxy: in 1541 a Scottish parliament which legislated against 'heresy' also passed an act 'for reforming of kirks and kirkmen'; the impulse to pass that act is to be related to King James V's exhortation to his bishops, a short time before, to reform their manner of living; and that exhortation in turn was prompted by a performance of the earliest version of Sir David Lindsay's *Three Estates*, a satire which had as its sharp and persistent theme the need for 'reformation'.

All could see that much was in need of reform. But it was of 'discipline', of the 'lives' of the clergy, of their 'manners' and their 'morals' that reformation was all but unanimously craved. Such reformation meant primarily the reform of ecclesiastical polity, and already before 1560 there can thus be discerned that emphasis which was to determine so much of later Scottish church history, in which the interest has so seldom been either theological or liturgical. Certainly the preoccupation of any historian of the Scottish reformation must be, as the preoccupation of contemporaries was, with church order, with systems of administration, with organisation and even with finance. And he must start where contemporaries started, with the structure of the late medieval church. Sixteenth-century writings, some of them with a popular appeal in their own day and later, and some of them of great literary merit, have done much to make the discreditable state of the late medieval church the familiar topic it has remained ever since. But the amount of criticism of ecclesiastical institutions which survives from the period of the reformation may mislead in more than one way. Few, if any, Scottish works in which similar material could be found are extant from earlier generations; if they were, they might disclose that it is as true of Scotland as it is of England that an awareness of abuses and an anxiety to remedy them were no novelty in the sixteenth century,[1] and it might emerge that the impression of a sharp deterioration in the hundred years or so before the reformation is very largely an illusion. In any event, the writings of reformers, whether moderate or radical, are not the place to look for a cool and balanced verdict; they must at least be analysed and tested like any other historical material to discover how far their evidence is consistent in itself and how far it is corroborated or refuted by other information, or they may be used mainly as a commentary on the truths disclosed by an examination of more objective sources. If this is done, and if—facile simplification being set aside—it is once appreciated that the structure of the late medieval church was a complex structure, embracing institutions of diverse origins, multifarious purposes and varying qualities, it emerges that, while the picture is a dark one, the gloom is not wholly unrelieved.

The houses of monks and canons regular had nearly all been founded more than three centuries before. Not only had the foundation of new houses long ceased, but the further enrichment of existing houses had become exceedingly rare, and these facts, while undoubtedly arising partly from mere changing fashion, do suggest that the value of monasteries was no longer apparent. Nor is it difficult to cite a whole series of incidents generally indicative of decline. Before the fourteenth century was out, the bishop of Glasgow had received a papal mandate to visit monasteries in Scotland and

---

[1] Cf. W. A. Pantin, *The English Church in the Fourteenth Century*, p. 238.

Ireland, 'they being in many ways deformed and broken down'.[1] When, early in the fifteenth century, James I censured the Benedictine and Augustinian orders,[2] he may have been doing no more than imitating Henry V of England,[3] whose prisoner he had lately been, but his foundation of Scotland's only house of the strict Carthusian rule—the Charterhouse at Perth—looks like a practical commentary on the laxity of the older orders. The 'Charturis monkis' were able to maintain their own fervour, for, in the words of an admiring friar a century later, 'be giding of the halie gost [they] ay remanit without fall', and in 1500 their austerity drew into their ranks an Augustinian abbot who despaired of his own order.[4] In general, however, the dominant characteristic of a sixteenth-century monastery was that it was a property-owning corporation.[5] The abbot was now primarily a landed magnate, and too often a secular cleric, a layman or even a minor who could be only a titular head of a religious community. The monks, losing sight of one of the essentials of their rule, now lived in comfort and at leisure on their individual 'portions', and the 'portion' approximated so closely to a benefice that it could even be assigned to a person who was not a member of the conventual body.[6] When efforts were made to deal with this and other abuses they were unwelcome. It may have been no more than courtesy when, in 1531, the Scottish council sent an officer of arms with the abbot of Glenluce to 'assist him in his visitation' of the Cistercian abbeys;[7] but there was no ambiguity in the following year, when the abbot of Soulseat, faced with the task of visiting the Premonstratensian houses, applied to the crown for 'supply, help, maintenance and assistance' because he dreaded that the abbots 'wald nocht obey, bot be the contrary resist and withstand to the

---

[1] *Calendar of Papal Registers*, IV, 251.
[2] *A.P.S.* II, 25 (translated in Dickinson, Donaldson and Milne, *Source Book of Scottish History*, II, 97–9).
[3] Wylie and Waugh, *Reign of Henry V*, III, 283–4.
[4] Abell's Chronicle (Nat. Lib. Scot. MS. 1746), fo. 79b; John Bellenden, *Hystory and Cronikles of Scotland* (1821), II, 299.
[5] Cf. *Letters of James V* (H.M.S.O.), pp. 174–5 (A.D. 1530).
[6] *Formulare*, II, No. 444; *R.S.S.* V, 220, 1007; *Melrose Regality Records* (S.H.S.), III, 154, 162–3; *Acts of the Lords of Council in Public Affairs* (H.M.S.O.), p. 611; *R.S.S.* VII, 2491.
[7] *Acts of the Lords of Council in Public Affairs*, p. 348.

sammyne'.[1] Another visiting abbot, sent by the chapter general of the Cistercians to inspect their Scottish houses, confined himself to an attack on the violation of the rule forbidding private property, against which he fulminated censures and then 'promptly departed', leaving the Scottish monks indignant at an attempted interference with what they regarded as 'the immemorial manner of monastic life' and some of them ready to desist from the 'offices of prayer', in protest.[2] There was at least one other occasion when Scottish monks went on strike, by desisting from the recitation of the offices, but then it arose from a refusal to increase their portions.[3] One can only speculate whether a preoccupation with the size of portions led to a deliberate policy of restricting entry and whether monks who wanted to leave a house, at the sacrifice of their portions, would have any obstacle put in their way. The evidence does on the whole suggest that in many houses the number of monks declined appreciably in the two or three decades before 1560,[4] and—unless, indeed, an entrant paid a heavy premium[5]—it is hard to believe that the convent would welcome recruits.

It is equally hard to believe that either abbot or monks would put before their own immediate financial advantage the duty of husbanding the resources of the house or the expenditure of money on the fabric, and easier to believe the allegation that an abbot would build a palatial residence for himself and allow the church and the domestic quarters of the brethren to go to ruin.[6] Yet, while records

[1] R.S.S. II, 1349.
[2] Letters of James V, pp. 210–11; James Campbell, Balmerino and its Abbey, pp. 110–12.
[3] Formulare, I, No. 261; cf. Melrose Regality Records (S.H.S.), III, 176–7
[4] The principal evidence about the personnel of the houses lies in the signatures to charters granted by abbots with the consent of their convents. While a single charter is never conclusive proof of the number of monks at a particular date—for not all the members of the community necessarily signed—the examination of a series of charters may be relied on to give the names of all the monks over a period. Corroborative evidence is sometimes available: e.g. at Melrose, where twenty-seven monks signed a charter in 1527 and only eleven signed one in 1557 (Morton Papers, Box 54), the number of monks alive in 1555 was sixteen (Melrose Regality Records, III, 192) and in 1562 was thirteen (Thirds of Benefices [S.H.S.], pp. 134, 157).
[5] Robert Richardson, Commentary on the Rule of St Augustine (S.H.S.), p. 174; cf. p. 10 below. [6] Ibid. pp. 54–5, 98–9.

provide evidence about monastic finance and about the state of the buildings,[1] it is none too easy to form a clear picture of life in a Scottish monastery on the eve of the reformation. There is little real proof that the monks were other than respectable in character. It would be unsound to attach much importance to doggerel verse, where the attractions of facile rhyme were the first consideration, but it should be noted that while the writer of the notorious lines beginning 'The paip, that pagane full of pryde' castigates the secular clergy for sexual immorality, he makes no such accusations against the monks. The abbot, indeed, he classes with the bishop, who 'wald nocht wed ane wyfe',

> Thinkand it was ane lustie lyfe
> Ilk day to have ane new ane,

but of the monks of Melrose he has nothing worse to say than that they

> maid gude kaill
> On Frydayis quhen thay fastit.[2]

Sir David Lindsay, in *The Tragedie of the Cardinall*, refers generally to the 'gret abhominatioun in mony abayis' which would be seen by their founder, King David I, were he to return, but in *The Three Estates* he excludes men's houses from his indictment and makes the king see only 'the great abominatioun amang thir abesses and thir nunries'. His only specific allusion to immorality in monasteries is in the lines

> Speir at the monks of Bamirrinoch
> Gif lecherie be sin,

which may easily have been a topical reference to some isolated scandal; elsewhere he makes a distinction between the abbot, who says of himself

> My paramours is baith als fat and fair
> As ony wench into the toun of Air

and, on the other hand, the monks, who

> leif richt easelie
> Thair is na monks from Carrick to Carraill
> That fairs better and drinks mair helsum aill.[3]

---

[1] P. 21 below. [2] *Gude and Godlie Ballates*, ed. D. Laing (1868), pp. 178–81.
[3] Lindsay, *Works* (S.T.S. ed. D. Hamer), I, 142; II, 51, 281, 315, 317.

Knox indeed tells of an 'ancient matron' who called the monastery of Scone 'a den of whoremongers',[1] but even she singled out the abbot as especially vicious, and of his evil life there is ample supporting evidence.[2] Ninian Winyet, again, who was not sparing in all the criticism that was needed, says nothing worse of the monastic life than that it was 'abusit amang mony in idilnes and welthy lyfe, and cloikit with glistering ceremoneis . . . mair than in trew religioun'.[3] There was assuredly no austerity about a system which permitted Adam Chatto, subprior of Kelso, to have a 'double portion', consisting of £40, thirty bolls of bear and twelve bolls of wheat, with 'twa corne yairdis and the fruit yaird occupyit be the said Adam and his servandis, lyand besyid the said abbay, with ane chalmer in the dortar thairof'.[4]

Possibly the most damning fact about the monks is simply that they played hardly any part in the reformation, on either side. Monkish resistance to reform, from purely selfish motives, was not indeed unknown, but it is difficult to name a monk who made a notable stand on any higher ground.[5] On the other hand, not a great many monks took an active part in the work of the reformed church,[6] and the only one who achieved any distinction as a reformer was the Cistercian John Mackbrair, who left Glenluce so early as 1550 and entered the ministry of the Church of England.[7] It was very different with the canons regular. At an early stage the Augustinians had produced Alexander Alane or Alesius, a reformer of international reputation, and a little later Thomas Forret, canon of Inchcolm, who was put to death for 'heresy' in 1539, while in John Winram, subprior of St Andrews, they gave a superintendent to the reformed church.[8] Robert Richardson, a canon of Cambuskenneth, had been early in the field as a more conservative reformer, and wrote a commentary on the rule of his order in 1530; but

---

[1] Laing, I, 362 (Dickinson, I, 191).   [2] P. 104 below.
[3] *Certane tractatis* (Maitland Club), p. 110.   [4] *R.S.S.* VII, 1888.
[5] Quentin Kennedy is no exception, for he was a secular before his appointment to the abbacy of Crossraguel.
[6] See G. Donaldson, 'The parish clergy and the reformation', in *Innes Review*, X.
[7] *Dumfries and Galloway Nat. Hist. and Antiq. Soc. Trans.* 3rd ser. IX, 158 f.
[8] *D.N.B.* (Alesius); Laing, I, 63 (Dickinson, I, 26); p. 126 below. See in general Peter Lorimer, *Patrick Hamilton*, pp. 166–76.

he, too, seems to have ended his days in the reformed church, though south of the Border.[1] The canons regular, who had all along been in the habit of serving as vicars in churches appropriated to their houses, found it easier than monks did to take part in the work of the reformed church as ministers and readers.[2]

The general opinion seems to have been that the monasteries, at least in their traditional form, could simply be disregarded. The efforts of the occasional zealous abbot or of the provincial councils[3] seem to have been directed mainly towards the fostering of intellectual pursuits and the raising of educational standards, and Winyet, defender of the old order though he was, does not seem to have envisaged the monasteries continuing as they had been constituted of old: 'of the quhilkis monasteriis every ane, be a godly reformatioun, besydes a cumpanie to waik on prayar, micht haif bene a college of godly leirning to the support of puir studentis'.[4] When tumult arose in the realm, the monasteries suffered fewer and less destructive attacks than the friaries, but a possible explanation of this is that as the monasteries were mostly in rural areas they were not ready targets for zealous burghers. The sacking of Scone was the work of an urban mob from Dundee and Perth, and the Charterhouse shared the fate of the Perth friaries not because it was corrupt—the evidence is all to the contrary[5]—but because it was situated within the burgh. The pattern of the attacks hardly permits any inference either about the state of the monasteries or about the popular attitude to them.

Yet in spite of all the obscurity and uncertainty there are two things to be said for the standards maintained by the monasteries: legitimations of the offspring of monks below the rank of abbot and prior are very hard to find—and to that extent some of the verses

---

[1] If he is to be identified with the Scottish clerk naturalised in England in 1540 (*Letters and Papers of Henry VIII*, xv, p. 292) he was probably associated with English influence on the Scottish government's experiment in a reforming policy in 1543 (*ibid.* xviii (1), Nos. 478, 696; (2), No. 392). See also G. G. Coulton, *Five Centuries of Religion*, iv, 420–1.

[2] See *Innes Review*, loc. cit.   [3] Pp. 32–3 below.

[4] *Certane tractatis*, p. 110.

[5] It should be noted that the prior, at least, took the conservative side (*R.S.S.* vi, 297).

7

quoted above are substantiated;[1] and right down to the reformation the monks continued to receive an education which at least taught them to sign their names.[2]

It is impossible to say as much for the nunneries, where the inmates were illiterate. With the exception of the sisters of the house of St Katharine of Siena in Edinburgh (founded in 1517), it is hard to find a Scottish nun, or even a prioress, who could sign her own name.[3] The sisters of this recent foundation—which may have had a pre-eminence among women's houses comparable to that of the Charterhouse among men's—were exceptional in other ways as well, for in Lindsay's *Testament of the Papyngo* it was among them that Chastity found a refuge after she had been repulsed by other nunneries.[4] In general, the breakdown of discipline seems to have been almost complete. In 1549 we find a nun of Haddington suing the prioress for a payment due to her,[5] and in the same year the provincial council ordered all prioresses to gather together the dispersed nuns of their houses and maintain them either in their own houses or others:[6] reading the two pieces of evidence together one concludes that prioresses were prepared to let their nuns depart and so be relieved of the cost of maintaining them. Of the unchaste lives of the nuns there is a lurid account in a report made at Rome in 1556,[7] and that the nunneries had gone further in decay than any other organisation in the church is in any event suggested by the fact that three or four of them were among the very few foundations which had been suppressed before the reformation.[8]

[1] It may be argued that this evidence is not significant, on the ground that the children of men who had no private property had no reason to seek legitimation: but (a) one would still expect to find legitimations after 1560, when the former regulars could hold private property, and (b) the principal advantage of legitimation was that it avoided the escheat of the bastard's goods to the crown should he die without lawful heirs of his body or disposition of his goods.

[2] Not quite invariably: John Rig, canon of Whithorn, could not write (Register of Deeds, II, 170).

[3] D. Hay Fleming, *Reformation in Scotland*, pp. 95–8; Morton Papers, 18 Aug. 1560; Books of Assumption, I, 195v; *East Lothian Antiq. and Field Naturalists' Soc. Trans.* V, 15.

[4] Lindsay, *Works*, I, 83.   [5] *Acts of the Lords of Council in Public Affairs*, p. 595.

[6] Patrick, *Statutes of the Scottish Church* (S.H.S.), p. 96.

[7] Pollen, *Papal Negotiations with Queen Mary* (S.H.S.), pp. 528–9.

[8] D. E. Easson, *Medieval Religious Houses: Scotland*, pp. 120, 121, cf. pp. 125, 127.

The oldest Scottish friaries dated from the thirteenth century, and belonged to a phase which had immediately followed the main period of monastic foundations. But, while several Dominican and Franciscan houses were thus as old as some of the monasteries, the Carmelite friaries mostly originated after 1300, and a series of foundations of Observant Franciscan friaries extended through the late fifteenth century and even into the beginning of the sixteenth. Not only were new friaries thus being founded, but some of the older ones were still, in the middle of the sixteenth century, increasing their property by bequest and gift,[1] and it may be inferred that institutions which continued to attract fresh endowments must have been in a fairly healthy state. The friars were still known as preachers, and indeed so far as preaching was provided at all the burden seems to have fallen on them instead of being shared by the secular clergy:

> War nocht the precheing of the beggyng freris
> Tynt [lost] war the faith among the seculeris[2]

As usual, it was the recent foundations—among the friaries those of the Observants—which were most faithful to their ideals, and the Observants of Jedburgh attracted to their rule a pious chronicler who had formerly been a canon of the Augustinian house of Inchaffray.[3] With the onset of the reformation, friars were prominent on both sides. Knox's aversion to them arose less from any corruption in their orders than from the strong opposition which some of them offered to his party. On the other hand, not only did many friars become ministers or readers after 1560, but for a generation before that the Blackfriars especially had made conspicuous contributions to the furtherance of the reformed cause and several had been exiled or put to death.[4] As to their morals, even the industrious Hay

---

[1] E.g. Moir Bryce, *Scottish Grey Friars*, II, 41, 42, 103, 138, and *Black Friars of Edinburgh*, pp. 85–91; *R.M.S.* III, 575; *R.S.S.* IV, 442, 1620.

[2] Lindsay, *Works*, I, 86; cf. 139, 276, 332, II, 89, 313.

[3] Abell's Chronicle (Nat. Lib. Scot. MS. 1746), fos. 82b, 113a. Investigation might disclose that the Observants in general declined to accept the reformation and that some of them took refuge overseas, but there is no evidence to support the tale of a wholesale exodus. A Carmelite of Linlithgow, too, was a recusant who went into exile (*R.S.S.* VII, 632).

[4] See in general Peter Lorimer, *Patrick Hamilton*, pp. 177–91.

Fleming could not find a single legitimation of a child of a friar, and the catalogue of clerical misdemeanours in *The Paip that Pagane full of Pryde* has little ill to say of friars except that they resorted to flattery in order to obtain alms and that with 'babbling' they 'blerit our ee' [blinded our eyes]—which suggests preaching in support of the traditional theology.[1] Although John Major, a generation earlier, had been critical of the sumptuous churches of the friars,[2] their houses were not, as a matter of fact, wealthy.[3] It is true that it was worth while to pay a premium for admission,[4] and that as professional mendicants the friars acquired a reputation for greed which became proverbial;[5] yet the worst that Knox could say of the Greyfriars of Perth was that they possessed fine linen and had a large store of salt beef in the month of May,[6] and it may be significant of their standards that the payments made to friars after the reformation amounted to only a third or less of those made to monks, even although the monks, unlike the friars, were still entitled to free quarters.[7] However, the revenues of the friars were derived largely from annuals payable from tenements in burghs,[8] their houses were situated in burghs, their way of life open to the constant observation of the burgesses. Thus even the slightest deviation from their professed ideals would arouse immediate criticism, and, whenever feeling ran high, their properties were ready targets for zealously protestant burghers as well as for riff-raff in search of loot.[9] The attacks on the friaries do not provide conclusive evidence either of grave delinquency within them or of a serious popular aversion, any more than the looting of Italian ice-cream shops in 1940 indicated the previous existence of anti-Italian feeling in Britain or any defects in the Italians as citizens.

[1] *Gude and Godlie Ballates*, pp. 179–80. Cf. Lindsay, *Works*, II, 89, 91.
[2] *Greater Britain* (S.H.S.), p. 297.
[3] See the tables in Moir Bryce, *Scottish Grey Friars*, I, 140, and in Easson, *op. cit.* The Dominicans were better off than the Franciscans.
[4] Moir Bryce, *op. cit.* I, 184; II, 36.
[5] M. Anderson, *Proverbs in Scots*, Nos. 535, 739, 1712.
[6] Laing, I, 322–3 (Dickinson, I, 162–3).
[7] See *Innes Review*, *loc. cit.*
[8] The Observants did not possess annuals, and were quite the poorest order.
[9] Cf. John Lesley, *History of Scotland* (Bannatyne Club), p. 275; and see p. 48 below.

But while it was true that friaries had continued to attract fresh endowments until so late as the sixteenth century, the bulk of fresh endowments had long been going elsewhere. The typical foundations of the fifteenth and early sixteenth centuries were collegiate churches and university colleges, and in the same period there was conspicuous enrichment of burgh churches, some of the finest of which date substantially from that period. Lay magnates, in short, now gave their money to collegiate churches which were not under the sway of an order with headquarters overseas but which the founder and his successors were able to dominate at least to the extent of retaining the benefices in the family; bishops established university colleges over which they retained powers of direction; and burgesses gave their annuals to proprietary chaplainries in their own town churches, for which the town councils could frame regulations.[1] These developments do indicate, in a general way, something of a movement away from the religious orders; they may suggest a strengthening of national and local patriotism; and, if only in the retention of a measure of lay control over the work and the moral standards of the priests serving chaplainries, may even demonstrate an element of anti-clericalism. Almost equally suggestive are the fortunes of the cathedral establishments. All but two of the Scottish cathedral chapters were secular, and, while there were few fresh endowments for monasteries, the enrichment of the cathedrals continued by the erection of additional prebends, the corporate organisation of the vicars choral became progressively stronger, and concurrently new chaplainries were founded at the various altars.

The most casual acquaintance with the organisation of the pre-reformation church reveals its variety, one might almost say its versatility. More than that, if it is permissible to regard the changes from monks to friars and from friaries to collegiate churches as something more than mere changes of fashion, they indicate a series of attempts to adapt the church's organisation and methods to

---

[1] For examples of the control of town councils over chaplainries, see John Ferguson, *Ecclesia antiqua*, pp. 40, 46, 151–2; James Paterson, *Obit Book of Church of St John Baptist, Ayr*, x; *Charters and Documents of Peebles* (Burgh Record Soc.), pp. 50–1; *Extracts from the Records of the Burgh of Edinburgh*, I, 130.

its tasks and to improve them. But it can be readily observed that in every phase of development there had been neglect of that essential part of the church's organisation, the parish church. Not only, indeed, did the successive developments neglect the parishes, but they were actually detrimental to their welfare, for the whole structure of abbeys, cathedrals, bishoprics, collegiate churches and universities was to a very large extent financed at the expense of the parishes, through the appropriation to those institutions of an overwhelming majority of the parish churches. It has emerged from recent investigations that in over 85 per cent[1] of the parishes of Scotland the bulk of the parochial revenues was being diverted to some institution or other, while the service of the parish was committed to an underpaid vicar.

From quite early times it had been realised that appropriation was potentially an evil and required regulation. The first step had been to provide that vicars with security of tenure should be appointed and the second had been to prescribe a minimum stipend. A provincial statute of the thirteenth century had laid down that a vicar's income should be not less than ten merks, free of burdens, and in the middle of the sixteenth century the minimum was tardily raised to twenty and twenty-four merks.[2] These provisions were not rigidly observed, and even in 1560, despite the great fall in the value of money, there were a few vicarages with less than the statutory minimum fixed in the thirteenth century and many with very little more; but even had they been observed they would have been inadequate, because, although ten merks had been satisfactory at one time, by 1560 a reasonable competence for a professional man was somewhere in the region of £80 to £100 a year in the Scots money of the time. Very few vicars had a living wage.[3]

[1] This is the finding of Mr I. B. Cowan, who has made an exhaustive study of the subject (*The Parishes of Medieval Scotland* [S.R.S.], p. v).

[2] Patrick, *op. cit.* pp. 11–12, 112, 169.

[3] The values of the vicarages are to be found in the *Thirds of Benefices*. While teinds of course fluctuated in value, and were therefore related to the changing cost of living, it would seem that by this period practically all benefices were in tack or lease for a fixed annual sum, so that the vicars' stipends remained unchanged from year to year. On the other hand, the figures given in the *Thirds* do not include offerings, which supplemented stipends considerably (see p. 14 below). Scots money was worth about a fifth of sterling in 1560.

An act of parliament of 1471, re-enacted in 1488,[1] annulled appropriations made since 1460 and forbade any in future except to collegiate churches, but as it was predominantly to collegiate churches that appropriations were now going this would have been a somewhat lame prohibition even had it been observed, which it was not. The process went on, not only through the fifteenth century,[2] but into the sixteenth. The stage had now been reached of what may be termed secondary appropriation: the existing vicarage was in its turn appropriated, so that the bulk of the vicar's revenues, as well as those of the parson, was diverted from the parish, and a new vicarage—a vicarage pensionary or portionary—was created, for which the provision could not be other than meagre.[3] Thus the situation constantly deteriorated, for every collegiate church which was founded, every university college which was founded, every new canonry in a cathedral, drained off more and more money which should have supported parsons in the parishes. When the resulting structure is surveyed, it becomes plain that one great indictment of the medieval church is that it was top-heavy, for its resources were concentrated at the higher levels, which were maintained at the expense of the service of the parishes. Plainly, the virtues of houses of canons regular, of friaries, of colleges and cathedrals—virtues which, even in the middle of the sixteenth century, were still undeniable—had to be weighed in the balance against the flagrant defects in the parochial ministry and the secular clergy generally which arose from the starvation of the parishes.

The underpayment of the parish clergy resulted in many conspicuous evils. The most direct consequence was that the vicars had to supplement their inadequate stipends by one means or another. One way of making ends meet was to accumulate several livings. Robert Auchmouty, for example, held concurrently the vicarage of Stirling, the vicarage of Dun, the vicarage of Arbroath and the

---

[1] *A.P.S.* II, 99, 209.
[2] A. I. Cameron, *Apostolic Camera and Scottish Benefices*, p. lxxiv.
[3] E.g. *Scottish Supplications to Rome* (S.H.S.), I, 270, 271; *Formulare*, No. 430; *Reg. Episcopatus Aberdonensis*, I, 224–5; *Munimenta Universitatis Glasguensis*, I, 493 f.; *Letters of James V*, pp. 368–9.

chaplainry of Bannockburn, which together yielded him an income of upwards of £100 a year.[1] An alternative way of making ends meet was for the priest to engage in some secular calling, and few pieces of ecclesiastical legislation had to be more frequently enacted than the prohibition of clerics engaging in secular affairs or in trading.[2] These two methods of achieving a competence seem to have been ably combined by William McDowell, who held three vicarages and two or three chaplainries and was besides master of works to the queen.[3] In one way or another, a priest inevitably neglected his vocation, and the sacred functions were bound to be imperfectly performed.

Financial necessity likewise led the parish clergy to insist on their right to 'offerings' when they administered the sacraments and rites of the church to their people. The misery caused by the exaction of mortuary dues is one of the best known of the grievances against the ecclesiastical system, because of the vivid impression conveyed by Lindsay in his *Three Estates*.[4] Lindsay alleges that the clergy detained the corpse at the kirk-stile until they received surety that the dues would be paid,[5] but the statutes of the church themselves suggest the more appalling picture of the priest at the altar-rail withholding the sacrament until he received the Easter offering.[6] The abolition of mortuary dues had been proposed as early as 1534,[7] but, although a statute of the provincial council of 1559 laid down that they should be restricted, and by the very poor no longer paid at all,[8] their exaction continued as long as the clergy could enforce it: on 22 May 1559, in the very month when the ecclesiastical revolution began, the vicar of Ayr obtained a decreet in his favour for payment of 40s. as 'corspresand' [corpse-present] with 4d. to 'Sanct Mongois work' and 2s. for 'his service' in conducting a funeral.[9]

If these were the more direct consequences of the financial position of the parish clergy, there were more subtle effects on their

[1] R.S.S. III, 2475–6, 2578, 2591, IV, 517, 1129, 2041; *Thirds of Benefices*, p. 236; Reg. Pres. I, 54, 151, II, 76, 177.
[2] Patrick, *op. cit.* pp. 15, 16, 36, 65, 71, 92, 166.
[3] *Dumfries and Galloway Nat. Hist. and Antiq. Soc. Trans.* 3rd ser. xxx, 56–7.
[4] Lindsay, *Works*, II, 196–9, 260–1.   [5] *Ibid.* I, 339.
[6] Patrick, *op. cit.* pp. 42, 185.   [7] *State Papers of Henry VIII*, IV, 667.
[8] Patrick, *op. cit.* pp. 178–9.   [9] Ayr Burgh Court Book, 1549–60, fo. 32v.

intellectual and moral standards. Priests could hardly be other than ill educated—and their congregations in consequence ill instructed —for no man of ability or learning was likely to accept the starvation wage which was all a conscientious vicar could expect. It is very true that academic competence is not, even now, an essential qualification for effective pastoral work, and it was perhaps even less essential in the middle ages, when congregations had poorer intellectual equipment than they have today; and we simply do not know to what extent Scottish priests may have been furnished, as English priests were, with manuals of instruction to guide them in their work. Yet the concern of contemporaries is indicated in the complaint by the Scottish provincial council of 1549 about clerical 'ignorance of literature and of all the liberal arts', in the directions issued in 1552 that priests were to rehearse a new vernacular catechism carefully in private before they ventured to read it in public, and in a remark by a Scottish priest to the archbishop of St Andrews in 1540, that men were admitted to the handling of the Lord's holy body who hardly knew the alphabet.[1]

A direct connection between the poverty of the vicars and their moral standards may be less immediately obvious, but it is likely that their poor educational level itself meant that they would be likewise men of poor ideals who would seek relaxation in carnal rather than intellectual pursuits. At any rate, the provincial council of 1549 complained of the 'profane lewdness of life' of the clergy, and a Jesuit, reporting in 1562, described the lives of priests as 'extremely licentious and scandalous'.[2] It may be further observed that if human fertility is high where economic security is low, the poverty of the vicars and chaplains may go some way to account for the hundreds of legitimations of clerical offspring recorded in the Registers of the Great and Privy Seals. Hay Fleming calendared them down to 1559[3] and had he proceeded further he would not have failed to note the conspicuous slump in legitimations which followed the recognition of clerical marriage in 1560.[4] In the period

---

[1] Patrick, *op. cit.* pp. 84, 146; Archibald Hay, *Ad illustrissimum . . . Davidem Betoun . . . panegyricus* (Paris, 1540), fo. 34r; *Cal. S. P. Scot.* I, 144.
[2] Patrick, *op. cit.* p. 84; Pollen, *op. cit.* p. 138.
[3] Hay Fleming, *Reformation in Scotland*, App. B.   [4] *R.S.S.* v, Intro. p. xvii.

1548–56, for example, the legitimations of the offspring of priests stand to those of the offspring of laymen in the ratio 2:5, and, even although the scandal is palliated by the fact that the clergy, unlike the laity, were disqualified from having lawful children, the proportion is remarkable, since the number of clergy can hardly have much exceeded 3,000[1] in a population of about 800,000 or 900,000. The characteristics of 'drunken sir John Latinless'[2] are not the groundless allegations of a satirist, nor was it a protestant pamphleteer who remarked that priests came to the Holy Table who had not slept off the night's debauch.[3]

These were some of the evils which followed from the poverty of the parochial clergy. But evils flowed equally from its counterpart, the wealth of the dignitaries. It was not the lowly-paid vicars who were most conspicuous as pluralists, but careerists who piled one fat canonry or dignity upon another until they accumulated an income surpassing that of some bishops.[4] One consequence of the inflation of cathedral establishments had been the creation of additional sinecures: as the canon, already relieved of parochial duties by a vicar in his parish, was relieved of cathedral duties by a vicar choral for the services and a procurator for chapter meetings, the canonry lent itself to pluralism and non-residence. The holding of several canonries and dignities in plurality was of course no novelty in the sixteenth century,[5] nor are the examples found in Scotland peculiarly flagrant. But in the era of the reformation we find John Thornton holding at once 'the chantourie of Murray with the parroche kirkis of Alves and Langbryde, baith personage and vicarage, annexit thairto, the subdenrie of Ros with the kirkis of Thayn and Athirtayn pertening thairto, the personage of Forteviot and kirk of Malar annexit to the samin, the personage of Benholme and the personage and vicarage of Ancrum'.[6] Thornton was something of a connoisseur of benefices, and had selected a group which

---

[1] Higher estimates have left out of account the prevalence of pluralism and the duplication arising from such causes as the holding of vicarages by canons regular.

[2] Lindsay, *Works*, I, 126.   [3] Archibald Hay, *op. cit.* fo. 34r.

[4] Cf. Lindsay, *Works*, II, 271, 353.

[5] E.g. *Scottish Supplications to Rome*, I, 26, 56–7, 70–2, 97, 262–3; II, 36, 38, 43.

[6] *R.S.S.* v, 2036.

yielded him upwards of £1,100 a year in the Scots money of the time. John Stevenson held the chantory of Glasgow, the vicarage of Mochrum, the parsonage and vicarage of Thankerton and the parsonage and vicarage of Muckarsie, which made him nearly half as wealthy as Thornton,[1] and Abraham Crichton had the provostry of Dunglass, the parsonages of Chirnside and Upsetlington and the vicarages of Aberlady and Strageath,[2] which were worth rather less than a third of Thornton's collection.

The activities of such adventurers in their pursuit of offices of profit would of itself have led to much litigation,[3] but conflicting claims in any event arose because, with the growing complexity of the papal rules of reservation, rights in the disposition of a benefice could often be claimed by two or three parties—pope, lay patron and ordinary. The many disputes were commonly settled not by a judgment which recognised the exclusive right of one or other claimant, but by the simpler expedient of dividing the spoils. The successful candidate obtained the title, but enjoyed the revenues only subject to the deduction of a substantial pension assigned as a consolation prize to his rival.[4] The guiding principle was that no one should suffer financial loss, and dismemberment of the fruits of benefices was carried out wholly without regard to the sacred functions properly pertaining to the offices concerned.

Again, while vicarages did sometimes remain in a family and even pass from father to son,[5] this abuse too was more conspicuous in the higher ranges of ecclesiastical office. 'The kin' has always been a potent element in Scottish life, and the richer the benefice the stronger was the desire to keep it in the family. When, about 1542, John Thornton proposed to resign three of his many benefices, he nominated as his successors John Thornton *junior*, James Thornton and John Thornton *natu minimus*, described as his brothers and nephews,[6] and on his death, many years later, all his benefices went to a James Thornton about whose relationship to John the records

---

[1] *Thirds of Benefices*, p. 87.
[2] *Ibid.* pp. 88, 147, 283; *R.S.S.* v, 2314, 2371, 2721.
[3] Cf. *Letters of James V*, p. 354.
[4] E.g. *Formulare*, I, Nos. 31–3, 36–7, 39–41, 97, 120, 262; II, Nos. 363–5.
[5] Cf. pp. 20, 45 below.   [6] *Formulare*, II, No. 443.

are reticent.[1] Cardinal Betoun himself resigned Arbroath in favour of his nephew, reserving a pension to one of his sons.[2] Quentin Kennedy succeeded his brother in the vicarage of Penpont and then his uncle in the abbey of Crossraguel. The Glasgow prebend of Ballinrik seems to have been held by four successive members of the Baillie family during eight decades of the sixteenth century, and another Glasgow prebend—Ashkirk—passed from Richard Bothwell to his nephew, William, and then to William's brother, Adam. Moreover, in a bishopric or an abbey, we often find that during the tenure of office of any bishop or abbot several men of his surname were promoted to positions of dignity and emolument;[3] in Dunblane, where the bishopric had been held by successive bishops of the name of Chisholm since 1487, we find that the archdeaconry, the deanery, the chancellory and the subdeanery, as well as three prebends, were all held by Chisholms.[4]

It is abundantly clear that extremes of wealth and poverty alike led to irregularities. But they would not have done so had they not been accompanied by a general relaxation of discipline.

At the initial stage of admission to benefices, existing practice was defective at every level. The right to appoint to the greater benefices had long been contested between the pope on one hand and the king or local magnates on the other, and at one stage the assertion of papal rights had been beneficial by excluding undue lay influence. Since 1487, however, while papal provision remained formally the method of appointment, the crown's recommendations for benefices worth more than 200 florins, gold of the *camera*, had nearly always been accepted. The result of this collusion between crown and papacy had been a series of scandalous appointments, beginning in the reign of James IV, who appointed first his brother, aged twenty-one, and then his illegitimate son, aged eleven, to the archbishopric of St Andrews, the primacy of Scotland. Worse was to come. James V, at the age of twenty, wrote to the pope, remarking on the frailty of human nature and intimating that he had three small sons, for whose welfare he was, out of his paternal affection, much concerned. He asked the pope to grant

[1] *R.S.S.* v, 2036.   [2] *Formulare*, II, No. 540.
[3] Cf. Robert Richardson, *op. cit.* p. 157.   [4] Cf. Archibald Hay, *op. cit.* fo. 35v.

them a dispensation to be promoted to any office whatever in the church; the only limitation he suggested was that they were not to become bishops or archbishops until they reached the age of twenty.[1] The pope, as it happened, was Clement VII, in whom some would have us see the upholder of Christian morality against Henry VIII of England; but this same Pope Clement gave James of Scotland a free hand to distribute Scotland's wealthiest abbeys among his illegitimate sons, one of them the offspring of an adulterous connection. The disastrous effects of crown nomination were generally acknowledged,[2] but there is no reason to suppose that papal selection would in that period have produced better results, for in the years after Flodden, when Leo X for a time tried to reassert papal authority in the disposal of the Scottish prelacies, he proposed to allot some of them to Italians.[3]

Other benefices, below the level of the prelacies, were affected by the papal rules of reservation and by the practice of *resignatio in favorem*, which facilitated hereditary succession. But even when the normal machinery of presentation by the patron and collation[4] by the bishop still operated, there is little evidence that the examination of candidates was such as to exclude the unsatisfactory. The investigation of the qualifications of ordinands lay properly with the archdeacon, but there were complaints that either because this duty was disregarded or because the archdeacon was more stupid than the examinees entrance to the church was in practice open to all without selection. There is no reason to doubt the truth of the complaints that orders were conferred not only on the ignorant but even on boys not yet capable of reasoning and that benefices were constantly bestowed on children and unworthy persons.[5]

[1] *Letters of James V*, p. 235. For reference to the situation which the Scots king was exploiting, see p. 37 below.
[2] Winyet, *Certane tractatis*, 7; Lindsay, *Works*, I, 85; Quentin Kennedy's 'Tractive', in *Wodrow Soc. Misc.* I, 151–2.
[3] *Letters of James V*, pp. 8, 41, 49, 50.
[4] In Scots usage, 'collation' is the act of the bishop whereby he confers a benefice on the nominee of a patron and orders institution to be given at the church concerned. Thus Scots 'collation' = English 'institution' and Scots 'institution' = English 'induction'.
[5] Archibald Hay, *op. cit.* fos. 33r, 34v; cf. Lindsay, *Works*, I, 49, 86, 141–2; Winyet, *op. cit.* p. 6; Pollen, *Papal Negotiations with Queen Mary*, p. 138.

There were equally grave weaknesses in the operation of the machinery for the oversight of clergy and churches. It is all too plain that the episcopate was sometimes ineffective through the personal shortcomings of the men appointed to sees, and the lists of Scottish bishops in the sixteenth century show many instances of prolonged vacancy and of the appointment of unconsecrated 'administrators' who could not perform the spiritual functions of a bishop. But even if a bishop was capable and conscientious his authority was undermined by exemptions and dispensations. Rome could, and—partly from financial motives—did, issue dispensations for all sorts of irregularities—non-residence, plurality, defect of birth, defect of age—and so encouraged the promotion of unqualified men and other breaches of the law of the church. Relaxed discipline did not mean simply that the law was not being observed; worse than that, the law was being constantly set aside. Every abuse, every violation of canon law, could be covered by a dispensation from Rome. Any bishop who might have wanted to suppress irregularities in his diocese and remedy the great and growing evils in the church would have been thwarted by such dispensations and frustrated by papal action. His control over the appointments in his diocese had been largely taken from him through the system of reservation; no attempt to keep unsuitable clergy out of the diocese could succeed; any effort to check non-residence or pluralism could be defied by those who could flourish papal dispensations in his face and flout his authority.[1] Equally, it is hard to see how concubinage could be effectively dealt with as long as a priest's bastard could obtain a dispensation enabling him to succeed his father in his benefices.[2] Thus local attempts to deal with abuses were bound to be nullified when Rome was not upholding canon law.[3]

In a period when self-seeking, apathy and indiscipline were rife, it was impossible that church buildings could be adequately maintained. There are, indeed, some considerations relevant to this subject which are sometimes forgotten: the ambitions of medieval builders sometimes outran their skill, sometimes outran their

---

[1] It is only fair to say that Scottish archbishops were themselves granting dispensations for irregularities (e.g. *Formulare*, I, Nos. 14, 15, 111–12, 183–4, 275).
[2] E.g. *Scottish Supplications to Rome*, II, 69. [3] Cf. pp. 44–5 below.

financial resources, with the result that some buildings were structurally unsound, others (notably collegiate churches) were never completed; secondly, anyone familiar with the care of churches knows how constant attention and expenditure are required even in normal conditions, and how rapidly deterioration sets in if there is a period of neglect; and, thirdly, in earlier days the task was a harder one because of the recurrent effects of war and tumult and the greater danger from fire and lightning. But, while such considerations would affect any attempt to assign responsibility, they do not alter the fact that there is a constant stream of evidence, from the fourteenth century onwards, about the damaged or decaying state of Scottish monastic buildings.[1] The two or three decades before 1560 went a long way to complete the ruin of the monasteries. Apart from advancing secularisation and consequent negligence, there was a series of military campaigns in which sacred buildings were treated with little respect—Hertford's devastation of the Border abbeys and of Holyrood, and the operations at St Andrews in 1547, Haddington in 1548 and Leith in 1560.[2] Very often in this period the need to repair the buildings was given as a reason for feuing abbey property,[3] and while this was something of a pretext, in the sense that the money raised would often go elsewhere, the statements can hardly have been without some foundation. As there is supporting evidence, there is every reason to accept the remark of the commendator of Melrose, in 1550, that the monastery had been

---

[1] E.g. Scone, 1369 (Reg. Ho. Calendar of Charters, No. 150); Arbroath, 1418–21 (Scottish Supplications to Rome, I, 18, 270); Kelso, 1420 (ibid. 177); Dryburgh, 1420 (ibid. 196); Iona, 1421, 1428 (ibid. 264–5, 268, 271; II, 193); Paisley, 1423 (ibid. II, 30); St Andrews, 1479 (Morton Papers, No. 184); Melrose, 1506 (Letters of James IV [S.H.S.], p. 38); Coldingham, c. 1516 and 1552 (Formulare, I, 169–70; Acts of the Lords of Council in Public Affairs, p. 614); Balmerino, 1530 (Morton Papers, 27 Oct. 1530, Box 36); Tongland, 1529 (Letters of James V, pp. 153, 162); Dundrennan, 1529 (ibid. p. 160); Culross, 1531 (ibid. p. 195); Peebles, 1532 (ibid. pp. 204–5); Inchmaholm, 1537 (ibid. p. 338); Fearn, 1541 (ibid. pp. 420–1); Cambuskenneth, c. 1540 (Formulare, II, 93); Monymusk, 1549–58 (Easson, op. cit. p. 79).

[2] Cf. Hay Fleming, op. cit. pp. 329 f.

[3] E.g. Culross (R.M.S. IV, 27, 746); Newbattle (ibid. 31, 1351, 1386, 1642); Melrose (ibid. 159); Scone (ibid. 1473); Coldingham (ibid. 1613, 1761); Coupar (ibid. 1699, 1741); and Holywood (ibid. 1773). Cf. Melrose Regality Records, III, 155, 165.

burned and destroyed by the old enemy of England during the late war,[1] and that of the commendator of Holyrood, in the same year, that his abbey had been burned by the English when they invaded the realm with fire and sword.[2] Even if the evidence of supplications and feu charters is not to be regarded as the literal truth, the fact that allegations of ruin and decay could so readily be made and accepted is sufficiently significant. All our knowledge substantiates the generalisation, in 1556, that 'very many churches and monasteries had been established of old in stately buildings, but within the last ten years or thereabouts had been reduced to ruins by hostile inroads, or through the avarice and neglect of those placed in charge were crumbling to decay'.[3]

As to rural parish churches, it is somewhat remarkable that such a high proportion of the really good pre-reformation work which still survives is Romanesque and that a fine example of fourteenth- or fifteenth-century date, apart from collegiate churches, is very rare. It was different in the towns, where the burgesses readily devoted their own means to the upkeep of their churches, but it does seem that after the initial effort of the twelfth century had spent itself there were no funds to spare for the embellishment of the ordinary country churches, many of which must in consequence have been as bleakly utilitarian as the worst of the 'heritors' kirks' of the eighteenth and early nineteenth centuries.[4] Once more, the appropriation of parishes may be part of the explanation, for institutions drawing parsonage teinds were responsible for the upkeep of the chancels of appropriated churches, and, while there is far too little evidence to show how consistently they performed their duty,[5] any 'avarice' and 'neglect' on their part would certainly explain the poverty and simplicity of rural churches.[6] A thirteenth-

---

[1] Morton Charters, Box 54; cf. *Melrose Regality Records*, III, 160, 217–19.

[2] *R.S.S.* IV, 752.   [3] Pollen, *op. cit.* p. 529.

[4] See George Hay, *The Architecture of Scottish Post-reformation Churches*, pp. 13–14.

[5] That a conscientious bishop did not spare expense on the upkeep of appropriated churches is demonstrated by *Rentale Dunkeldense* (S.H.S.), e.g. pp. 91, 140, 148.

[6] When the parsonage teinds were set in tack, the parson's responsibility passed to the tacksman (e.g. Barnbarroch charters, 11 July 1549), and as his whole interest was financial profit he was unlikely to treat the duty seriously.

century bishop of St Andrews had thought it necessary to issue an ordinance to the effect that churches must be roofed, the walls not ruinous and the windows unbroken, and when the last provincial council before the reformation 'decreed that all ruinous and dilapidated churches within the realm of Scotland shall be rebuilt and repaired'[1] its legislation was not mere common form. A report on the churches in the Merse (Berwickshire) in 1556 notes that twenty-two of them were in a particularly bad state. The walls of some were levelled to the ground, in others the walls or roofs were ruinous or threatening collapse, they were without windows, without fonts, without altar vestments, without missals or manuals, with the result that mass could not be celebrated.[2] A detailed account of the situation at Ayton states that in 1555 the choir was thatched with turf and that it was intended to add straw to the turf after the following harvest, but that it was not thought worth while to put on a better roof, 'for fear of the Englishmen'; the temporary covering was 'apparently watertight', and the roof was as good, so it was said, as that of any of the churches pertaining to the priory of Coldingham—but the new roof fell in the following spring, whereupon a canopy was erected over the high altar sufficient to shelter the priest and the clerk in wet weather, and when it was fine, mass was said 'whiles at the Lady altar and whiles in the kirk yaird'.[3] No doubt there were peculiar difficulties in a Border county like Berwickshire, and Ayton lay on the main route into Scotland from the south; after all, in 1529 it had been alleged that Border reivers boasted of having destroyed fifty-two parish churches in Scotland,[4] and the English invasions of the 1540s must have discouraged expenditure of labour and money on buildings of any kind. Yet the whole picture can be presented in Hay Fleming's remark that 'the tacit assumption that all the ecclesiastical buildings of Scotland were in fair or good condition when that outburst [of 1559–60] took place is preposterous'.[5]

Those isolated reports on the churches in the Merse are among

[1] Patrick, *op. cit.* pp. 57–8, 168. Cf. *Cal. S. P. Scot.* I, 144; *R.S.S.*, IV, 641.
[2] Reg. Ho. Ecclesiastical Documents, No. 8 (9 April 1556).
[3] *Ibid.* No. 10.   [4] *Letters and Papers of Henry VIII*, IV, pt. iii, No. 5289.
[5] Hay Fleming, *op. cit.* p. 353.

the very few documents directly bearing on the conditions in which worship was conducted, and any attempt to form an impression of the general level of church life in the parishes is mainly a matter of inference. Church attendance and the standard of instruction and devotion had probably all along been adversely affected in some rural areas by the distance of many homes from a place of worship. No doubt chapels of ease did a certain amount to supplement the parish churches, but, even so, parts of Scotland suffered from a chronic shortage of churches until so late as the nineteenth century, when intense ecclesiastical competition at last produced a more than adequate supply. When a supplication for the division of a parish refers to parishioners who scarcely come to church even at Easter and then 'come like beasts', or the erection of a new parish proceeds on the narrative that the people in a certain area, severed from their church by a river, are unable to attend at Christmas, are dying without the sacraments and run the risk of drowning when they come with funerals,[1] the statements may be overdrawn by interested parties, but they must represent a foundation of fact. Again, the remark of the provincial council of 1552 that 'very few indeed out of the most populous parishes deign to be present at the sacrifice of holy mass on the Sundays and the other double festivals appointed by the church'[2] can be paralleled in almost any century; but when that council criticised those who 'have fallen into the habit of hearing mass irreverently and impiously, or who jest or behave scurrilously in church at time of sermon, or who presume at such times to make mockery or engage in profane bargainings in church porches or churchyards',[3] it was not alluding either to a novel situation arising from the advance of the reformation or to the slack habits resulting from the many uses to which a church was inevitably put when it was the only public building in the parish. The truth seems to be that even in earlier days the interior of a church had commanded little respect, for before unorthodox opinions about the Eucharist began to circulate in Scotland narratives of

---

[1] *Scottish Supplications to Rome*, I, 122; *Formulare*, II, No. 511. For references to similar difficulties in the seventeenth century, see P. Hately-Waddell, *An old Kirk Chronicle*, pp. 48–9, 59.
[2] Patrick, *op. cit.*, p. 138.   [3] *Ibid.* p. 139.

deeds of violence in churches already had as their stock phrases such words as 'with no honour to the most holy sacrament', or 'in presence of the most holy sacrament but with no reverence towards it'. Neither persons nor property had secured safety by seeking the protection of the sanctuary, and it was not unknown for a priest to be dragged from the very altar in pursuance of some private feud.[1] It was, therefore, with only the milder manifestations of irreverence that the authorities were concerned when they forbade 'carreling and wanton synging in the kirk' and condemned those who, 'beand in the kirk in the tyme of Goddis word or service, occupeis thame self in vaine, evil or ony warldly talking, lauchhing, scorning or ony siclik doingis',[2] or when they instructed the clergy not to permit their people to 'come to the blessed sacrament misorderly' but to make them 'hear you read without noise or din, and to sit still so in devotion, with devout heart and mind, until they be orderly served of the said blessed sacrament'.[3]

If standards were low throughout the country generally, they were worse in the Highland areas.[4] Not only were many of the parishes there of enormous extent and intersected by mountainous wastes and stretches of water, but there was a dearth of religious establishments of every kind. There was not a single friary in the Highlands except a Carmelite house which had a brief existence at Kingussie in the early sixteenth century, there was no collegiate church except at Kilmun, on the Firth of Clyde, and—apart from the insular houses of Iona and Oronsay—there were only three monasteries: the Cistercian abbey of Saddell in Kintyre (which was in decay in the early sixteenth century), the small Valliscaulian house of Ardchattan, and the smaller and poorer Augustinian priory of Strathfillan. It is significant, too, that the cathedrals for

[1] *Formulare*, I, Nos. 83, 87; II, Nos. 340, 352. For other examples of violence against clergy, cf. *ibid.* Nos. 80, 81, 82, 86, and Act Book of Commissariot of Dunblane, 1551–5. For disturbances in churches, see *Protocol Book of Gavin Ross* (S.R.S.), No. 727, *Protocol Book of John Christison* (S.R.S.), No. 171, and Pitcairn, *Criminal Trials*, I, pt. i, 56–7, 376.

[2] *Archbishop Hamilton's Catechism*, ed. T. G. Law, pp. 68, 69.

[3] Patrick, *op. cit.* p. 190.

[4] It is not always realised that the 'Highland line' excludes not only the coastal plain south of the Moray Firth but also a good deal of the territory between Inverness and the Dornoch Firth.

the Highland dioceses were all situated on the fringe of the Lowlands, except in the west, where they were on islands. If the aim was security, it was not achieved. In 1390 the cathedral of Elgin was burned by the 'Wolf of Badenoch', and at the end of the following year the canons were 'in remotis agentes, propter malum regimen Moravie'.[1] The cathedrals of Dunblane and Dornoch were said to be ruinous in the 1420s.[2] At Dunkeld, when the bishop was celebrating mass one Whitsunday, the cathedral was attacked by armed men and he had to take refuge in the beams above the choir, and it was for a time the custom to hold the synod not at Dunkeld but in the safety of the Carmelite priory of Tullilum, on the outskirts of Perth, *propter roboriam catheranorum* [caterans] *contra ecclesiasticos*.[3] Bishops who ventured into the western dioceses were likewise apt to receive rude treatment: in 1452, 'when the native-born Chancellor and Treasurer of Argyle wished to insult their Lowlands Bishop, they "halsit him in errische [Gaelic], sayand bannachadee" ', and this bishop obtained leave for seven years to administer his diocese not, like his brother of Dunkeld, from a safe place within it, but from the more remote security of Glasgow.[4] The see of Argyll was without a consecrated bishop from 1523 until after the reformation, except for a few years in the 1530s, and it is doubtful if the see of the Isles had a consecrated bishop after 1513. The result of such long vacancies was, we are told in 1529, that those born in the more remote islands had not had baptism or other sacrament, not to speak of Christian teaching; while Argyll, it was said ten years later, was mountainous and barren and the manners of the inhabitants savage and uncivilised, so that it would be a herculean task to bring under ecclesiastical discipline a people long unrestrained by law.[5] The facts provide but a slender foundation on which to build the romantic picture of a pious Catholic populace who maintained their faith uncontaminated by the reformation. The truth is that the Highlands never had adequate spiritual ministrations until the nineteenth century, when the Free Kirk took the task in hand.

---

[1] Nat. Lib. Scot. MS. 34.7.2.   [2] *Scottish Supplications to Rome*, II, 100, 188.
[3] Mylne, *Vitae episcoporum Dunkeldensium* (Bannatyne Club), pp. 21–2, 23.
[4] A. I. Dunlop, *Bishop James Kennedy*, pp. 141 n., 251, 370.
[5] *Letters of James V*, pp. 162, 364; cf. *Cal. S. P. Scot.* I, 144.

The strength of the medieval system may perhaps be summed up by saying that it made sufficient provision for the saying of prayers and masses for the living and the dead at countless altars and for the worship of God in cathedrals, abbeys and collegiate churches (though it would be a mistake to think that services even there were conducted with the splendour or indeed the decorum customary in great churches today). Equally, its weakness may be summed up by saying that it could not provide adequate ministrations for the congregations of the parish churches. Not only did the people generally lack the instruction which a properly trained secular clergy could have provided, and not only did they lack a sufficient amount of preaching—defects which were all the more serious when the ability to read was not universal; but they did not even enjoy satisfactory administration of the sacramental services to which contemporary thought attached the greatest importance. Any twentieth-century reader who reviews the evidence will assuredly agree with the general consensus of sixteenth-century opinion that 're-formation' was necessary. He will very likely go further and conclude that for a situation so desperate the remedy could hardly be other than drastic. But if there is rather less unanimity today than there was four hundred years ago, the reason is that reformation history, or what passes for reformation history, is apt to be the plaything of ecclesiastical polemic, and that identification with, or repudiation of, the reformers and their work is apt to be something of a party or denominational label. Thus, while well-informed Roman catholics admit the abuses in the unreformed church, those less well informed appear to assume that criticism of the medieval church is criticism of their own present system and feel obliged to try to palliate the evils and defend the indefensible. Some Anglicans take much the same line, and rejoice in identifying themselves with the corrupt prelates of the old regime rather than with the reformers who ousted them. There may be a certain justification for such attitudes in a country where, as the prevailing opinion was long ultra-protestant, the readiness of some writers to allow their opinion of the modern Roman church or the modern Anglican church to colour their view of the medieval church tended to vitiate their work and imported unnecessary emotion into historical discussions. But Roman catholics, it seems, sometimes need to be reminded that their own church is a reformed church; Anglicans must face the fact that their church was transmitted through the first generation of reformers and that believers in continuity cannot repudiate half a century of their history; and zealous protestants must realise that some of the features which they find objectionable in the modern Roman church are innovations, arising through the developments in doctrine and worship and the modifications in organisation which have taken place during the past four centuries, and were not characteristic of the medieval church. 'The reformed church' and 'the reformed churches' are terms with varying meanings, but used in their widest sense they include the Roman catholic church no less than the Anglican church, as well as the churches which are not ashamed to be called protestant. Only the last group are the children of the reformation, and of the many denominations in Scotland only one, and that almost the smallest, bears the term 'reformed' in its title; but all the others are none the less clearly marked by the effects of the revolution of the sixteenth century.

CHAPTER II

ANTECEDENTS OF REVOLUTION, 1525-59

THE Scottish reformation, in the sense of a formal change in the ecclesiastical system, came late in the day. By 1560 over forty years had passed since Luther's denunciation of indulgences and the beginnings of the reformation in Germany, and nearly a generation had passed since Henry VIII's breach with Rome and since the establishment of a reformed church in Denmark and Norway. Reforming opinions had therefore had ample time to penetrate to Scotland. Evidence of a direct influence of continental developments on Scotland begins with an act of parliament of 1525 generally against the import and circulation of Lutheran works.[1] As the Scottish east coast ports were in constant communication with Germany, the Low Countries and Denmark, it is not surprising that the bishop of Aberdeen at once took steps to have the new statute proclaimed in his diocese, on the ground that several strangers and others had in their possession heretical books and were propagating the errors of Luther;[2] but before many years had passed the archbishop of Glasgow, on the other side of the country, learned that in his diocese, too, men were expounding Lutheran opinions both privately and publicly and were reading the New Testament in English.[3] The burning of Patrick Hamilton in 1528 initiated a series of executions for 'heresy', and there were other incidents, such as the decapitating of an image of the Blessed Virgin in the church of the Greyfriars of Ayr in 1533 and the hanging of an image of St Francis in 1537,[4] which suggest that, while the new theology was making headway among educated men, the movement was not

[1] *A.P.S.* II, 295 c. 4.
[2] *Extracts from Council Register of Aberdeen* (Spalding Club), I, 110–11.
[3] *Formulare*, I, No. 185. The date is probably earlier than 1531. For evidence of the importation of Tyndale's translation of the New Testament, see *Letters and Papers of Henry VIII*, IV, II, No. 2903.
[4] Calderwood, I, 104; *Formulare*, II, No. 367; Pitcairn, *Criminal Trials*, I, 286*.

confined to a small group of intellectuals. A royal letter to the council in 1534 discloses that 'divers tractatis and bukis' of Lutheran origin were still finding their way into the country through the east coast ports, and in 1541 there were acts of parliament generally against 'heresy' and the casting down of images.[1]

In 1543 it seemed for a brief space that Scotland was going to have a reformation carried through with official countenance. James V had died in December 1542, and negotiations were opened for the marriage of his infant daughter to Prince Edward of England, son of Henry VIII. As a concomitant of its Anglophile policy, in March 1543 the Scottish government had an act passed (despite the dissent of the clerical estate) which permitted the lieges to possess the scriptures in Scots or English.[2] The line taken was plainly Henrician rather than protestant, for in June there was an act of council in support of sacramental orthodoxy,[3] yet there are indications not only of popular support for the concession of the vernacular scriptures but also of the existence of radical and iconoclastic elements: Knox gives us a lively and appreciative account of 'the Bible lying almost upon every gentleman's table' and of 'works in our own tongue, besides those that came from England, that did disclose the pride, the craft, the tyranny and abuses of that Roman Antichrist';[4] the magistrates of Aberdeen acceded to the government's request that they should appoint two friars as official preachers of 'the true word of God';[5] and there were attacks by mobs on friaries in Perth and Dundee and on the abbey of Lindores.

For political reasons the experiment in official action was not enduring. But the popular movement which had supported and welcomed it continued to find expression in iconoclasm;[6] and the mission of George Wishart in 1544 and 1545 was remarkable for the comparative freedom with which he was able to preach in churches and for the size of the following which he attracted. After his execution and the murder of Cardinal Betoun, popular and radical

[1] *Acts of the Lords of Council in Public Affairs*, p. 423; *A.P.S.* II, 370–1.
[2] *A.P.S.* II, 415.
[3] *Acts of the Lords of Council in Public Affairs*, p. 528.
[4] Laing, I, 100–1 (Dickinson, I, 45).
[5] *Extracts from Council Register of Aberdeen* (Spalding Club), I, 189.
[6] *Ibid.* 211; Calderwood, I, 171; Pitcairn, I, 335*, 353* (cf. *R.S.S.* IV, 1919).

feeling must once again have threatened ecclesiastical properties, for there was an act of council expressing the fear that 'evill disponit personis will invaid, distroy, cast doun and withhald abbays, abbay places, kirkis, alswele paroche kirks as utheris religious places, freris of all ordouris, nunreis, chapellis and utheris spirituale mennis houssis'.[1] The brethren of religious houses can have felt anything but secure, and their consciousness of their peril is demonstrated by protections issued in 1554 to the Blackfriars and the Charterhouse[2] —the very institutions which were to feel the first blast of the Knox-ian reformation a few years later. Throughout the 'forties and the 'fifties proceedings against 'heretics' continued intermittently, though there were few executions, and it is significant of the spread of reforming opinions that even in far-away Orkney a chaplain had to obtain a remission for his 'tenacity and pertinacity' in heresy in 1550.[3] Plainly, the most cursory review of the progress of the re-forming movement demonstrates that it was confined neither to a single social group nor to one or two parts of the country, and that from an early stage it contained certain radical and destructive ele-ments.[4]

As reform had already proceeded so far in other countries, and reforming opinions had become so strong in Scotland itself, it must have been apparent before 1560 that a period of decision had been reached and that affairs could not simply drift. If the traditional ecclesiastical constitution was to continue, in communion with Rome, it could do so only in a purified and more efficient form; the alternative would be to repudiate Rome and accept schism, where-upon a further choice would have to be made—or perhaps dictated by circumstances—among a number of reformed models. The issue was not reform or no-reform, but rather reform or revolution. And revolution came only after a series of earnest but ineffective attempts at reform.

The church in Scotland was exposed to no sudden and unfore-seen shock. There had been ample opportunity to fortify the exist-ing structure against such assaults as had already been made on the

[1] *R.P.C.* I, 28-9.   [2] *R.S.S.* IV, 2390, 2799.   [3] *Ibid.* 916.
[4] For a list of references to 'heresy', some of them associated with failure to take part in expeditions against England, see *R.S.S.* III, xl (1542-8).

church in other lands. The evidence hardly warrants the belief that all was lost, in any part of the ecclesiastical structure except possibly the nunneries. We await a history of later Scottish monasticism, but it does appear that, desperate though the situation in the abbeys was, efforts at reform were made. Robert Bellenden and Robert Richardson both had hopes, for a time, that the Augustinians might be reformed, and a certain amount seems to have been achieved at Cambuskenneth by Abbot Alexander Myln.[1] The Premonstratensians and the Cistercians were both under some pressure from their continental headquarters to accept a restoration of discipline, and, while there is little or no evidence of any response among the Scottish Premonstratensians,[2] the aims of Cîteaux[3] did receive a certain amount of support from the Scottish houses of the order. As late as 1553 the monks of Coupar Angus recorded their resolve 'to lead a regular life and to order our manners according to the reformers of the Cistercian order; and specially that all the fruits . . . be possessed and used in common by us';[4] and the abbey of Kinloss was fortunate in having as its head first Thomas Chrystall and then Robert Reid, who took a real interest in at least the material and intellectual wellbeing of the house.[5] But possibly more promising than the spasmodic and somewhat half-hearted efforts in the monasteries was the fact that the last phase in the changing fashions of ecclesiastical endowment, that of collegiate churches and university colleges, continued until the middle of the sixteenth century. The last of the collegiate churches, Biggar, was not founded until 1546; St Mary's college at St Andrews was not finally organised until 1554; and Robert Reid, bishop of Orkney as well as commendator of Kinloss, who died so late as 1558, left funds to be devoted to educational purposes—funds ultimately applied to the endowment of the post-reformation university of Edinburgh. Those whose piety ran on traditional lines were still, in the 1550s, endowing new chaplainries

---

[1] Pp. 3, 6–7 above; Easson, *op. cit.* p. 31.

[2] P. Norbert Backmund, *Monasticon Praemonstratense*, II, 94–6; cf. p. 3 above.

[3] See *Charters of Coupar Angus* (S.H.S.), II, 284; Morton, *Monastic Annals of Teviotdale*, p. 238; *Formulare*, I, 56; *Letters of James V*, pp. 187, 210–11; James Campbell, *Balmerino and its Abbey*, pp. 110–12; Easson, *op. cit.* p. 24. Cf. pp. 3–4 above.

[4] *Charters of Coupar Angus*, I, lxiv.   [5] Easson, *op. cit.* p. 31.

or annexing vicarages to collegiate churches, besides making gifts to the Blackfriars.[1] If the institutions of the existing ecclesiastical system were thus still inducing fresh endowment it may be deduced that there was enough vitality in that system, and enough attachment to it, to give reform without revolution considerable support.

An appeal was made to Archbishop David Betoun of St Andrews (1538-46) to reform the evil lives of the clergy,[2] but it was Betoun's successor, John Hamilton, who initiated the policy of reform from within. Three provincial councils, in 1549, 1552 and 1559, passed a whole code of reforming statutes, designed to check irregularities of every kind—concubinage, non-residence, pluralism, intemperance and even unbecoming dress. Each bishop was to visit his whole diocese every two years, and to preach in person in his see. Not only were the morals and learning of ordinands to be more strictly scrutinised, but the parish clergy already in possession, if found wanting in 'learning, morals and discretion', were to be suspended or persuaded to resign, and appointments to benefices were to be null unless the presentee was found by the bishop to be fit for his duties. Episcopal authority was further strengthened by legislation that ordinaries were to visit monastic houses whether or not they had previously been exempt from the bishop's inspection, and were to assist in the recall of apostate monks. The system of oversight was to be intensified by the activity of archdeacons and rural deans, and church buildings were to be repaired. Sermons were to be provided by parsons and by corporations holding parsonages in appropriation, and provision was made for the instruction of the people by the issue of Archbishop Hamilton's *Catechism* and of a brief Exhortation on the Eucharist known as the 'Twopenny Faith'.[3] Detailed regulations were made by the councils for the better education of priests and monks, and Hamilton's awareness of the need to raise educational standards is further illustrated by his completion of the organisation and endowment of St Mary's College at St Andrews, with a view to 'defending and confirming the Catholic

---

[1] E.g. *R.S.S.* IV, 1912, 3240; p. 9 above.
[2] Archibald Hay, *op. cit.*; cf. Hay Fleming, *op. cit.* p. 43.
[3] Patrick, *op. cit.* pp. 94-5, 101-2, 109-12, 114, 136, 143, 167, 168, 171-3, 176, 188.

faith' and opposing heresies and schisms;[1] it may be, too, that there was a connection between the archbishop's policy and the action of the crown in 1556 in providing for lectures at Edinburgh not only in the laws but also in Greek.[2]

The archbishop of St Andrews was not the only reforming prelate. Robert Reid, bishop of Orkney, one of the outstanding churchmen of the century, had drawn up a new constitution for his cathedral chapter in 1544.[3] It provided for the endowment of seven dignitaries and seven canons, thirteen chaplains and six choristers. The chancellor was to read a public lecture on canon law, every week, and one of the chaplains was to act as master of the grammar school. While the scheme illustrates the bishop's zeal for efficiency and his interest in education, it shows his limitations as well as his capacity. The new chapter was to be financed only by further stripping the parishes of revenues which would have been better applied to the maintenance of competent parish priests able to instruct the people in the faith; and lecturing in Kirkwall on canon law was not the way to cope with imminent revolution.

Other bishops supported Hamilton, at least to the extent of furthering the programme of his reforming councils. Archbishop Betoun of Glasgow, in April 1559, issued a series of mandates to implement the legislation of the last provincial council,[4] giving instructions for preaching, the repair of monastic and parish churches, the residence of vicars in their parishes and the wearing of the clerical garb, and condemning pluralism, concubinage and the endowment of clerical offspring from the patrimony of the church. In the diocese of Aberdeen, where the bishop himself was conspicuously in need of reform, it was the dean and chapter who, in January 1559, drew up corresponding proposals: the clergy were to remove their 'open concubines', the bishop setting an example by 'removing and discharging himself of the company of the gentlewoman by whom he is greatly slandered'; in order that 'the people be not in danger because of the lack of preaching of the true Catholic faith', two sermons were to be provided in each parish church within the next few months—one before Ash Wednesday and another

---

[1] Thomas McCrie, *Andrew Melville* (1899), p. 351.   [2] *R.S.S.* IV, 3144, 3268.
[3] *R.M.S.* III, 3102.   [4] *Melrose Regality Records* (S.H.S.), III, 167–87.

between that date and Easter; the 'statute of residence' was to be put in execution; 'heretics' were to be prosecuted and action taken against those involved in 'burning the church of Echt' or in casting down images.[1]

The proceedings of Archbishop Hamilton, his advisers and supporters, might suggest that in Scotland a counter-reformation preceded the reformation, but this Scottish movement lacked several of the characteristics of the counter-reformation known in other countries. It owed nothing to the papacy, and was indeed anti-papal to the extent that the pope, when not altogether ignored—as he often was—was regarded critically;[2] and, while it was not unconnected with the proceedings of the council of Trent, its whole theological tendency was not in the direction of Tridentine rigidity but along the more liberal line of modification in accordance with reforming thought. Archbishop Hamilton's *Catechism* demonstrates how thoroughly the new doctrines had penetrated into Scotland, for it framed its expositions of the Eucharist and of justification in such a way that they would have satisfied many protestants. Further, in so far as Archbishop Hamilton's policy was aimed at the restoration of discipline, the strengthening of the system of oversight of the parishes, the education of the clergy and the instruction of the people, it was not only in accordance with the programme of the reformers, but even in accordance with some of the schemes which they were later to put into operation. The programme of the reformers—or perhaps rather of the revolutionaries—was indeed more comprehensive than anything proposed by bishops or councils, but its more radical character lay less in its recommendations for discipline, oversight and education than in its financial projects. The most serious defect of the archbishop's policy, on the other hand, lay not in any deviation from the principles of the reformation, but in an essentially practical matter—failure to do anything towards that redistribution of endowments which was so plainly necessary. There was agreement, up to a point, between the more conservative reformers and the revolutionaries that the balance

[1] Keith, *History of Church and State in Scotland* (Spottiswoode Soc.), I, cxx-cxxiii; *Spalding Club Misc.* IV, 57.

[2] Pp. 44-5 below.

should be redressed in favour of the parishes, but only if the balance should be redressed in a financial sense could the improvements in clergy and people be effected for which Archbishop Hamilton and the reformers alike looked. The simplest arithmetic showed that, should the top-heavy superstructure of the church be drastically pruned, there would be ample funds available to provide more than adequate stipends for all the parish clergy the country needed, and to make generous provision for education and the poor. If the monasteries, cathedrals and collegiate churches were stripped of their wealth, and the parishes regained the revenues which properly belonged to them, then a competent ministry could be maintained throughout the land, ministers and their flocks could be educated, church buildings could be decently maintained, the word of God could be preached and the sacraments duly administered in every congregation in the land. The total annual revenues of the church must have been in the region of £400,000. This sum could have yielded far more than enough to pay a minister and a schoolmaster and provide for poor relief in each of the thousand parishes and still leave ample for central and regional administration.

It is true that occasional instances may be found before the reformation of the suppression of an ineffective or decadent institution and the transfer of its endowments to one possessing greater vitality.[1] But such instances were all too rare, the foundations affected were mostly of negligible importance, and in the main the older institutions, however moribund, retained their wealth. Among observers on the conservative side, we find the clearest grasp of the need for redistribution of endowments in a report made at Rome in 1556 by Cardinal Sermoneta, no doubt under direction from the Scottish government: besides suggesting in general terms that after suitable provision had been made for monks the monastic revenues should be applied to the restoration of decayed churches and other buildings, he offered the specific plan of compelling all 'rulers, abbots and heads of churches' to spend a fourth part of their fruits on the repair of buildings.[2] Even this was

---

[1] E.g. Easson, op. cit. pp. 66, 90, 91, 92, 98, 135, 137, 151, 152, 154; cf. p. 8 above.

[2] Pollen, op. cit. pp. 528–30.

not enough. And all that Archbishop Hamilton's councils proposed as a contribution towards the solution of the vast problem of reform of endowments was that the minimum vicar's stipend should be increased to twenty or twenty-four merks.

During the generation which passed between the first impact of the Lutheran reformation on Scotland and the revolution of 1560, reforming opinions had become firmly rooted in the country and attempts had been made to fortify the existing structure of the church. But the course which the Scottish reformation took was not determined by those facts alone or by the reformers' proposals for the remodelling of the ecclesiastical polity. Changes had meantime been taking place which were only indirectly and in part due to the progress of the reformation, but which in themselves involved the decline, and in some respects the collapse, of the medieval system.

The most conspicuous of the developments which thus helped to shape the situation in 1560 was the increase of royal control over the church, at the expense mainly of the papacy. In the 1530s the pope, faced with the defection of England, was resolved to retain the allegiance of Scotland even at the cost of virtually abdicating his authority in that country. It was in 1535 that the pope finally conceded the king's right not merely to recommend, but to nominate, to vacant prelacies. As a result of papal complaisance, the houses of Kelso, Melrose, Coldingham, St Andrews priory and Holyrood were appropriated to the illegitimate sons of James V, and the Scottish parliament ordained that the surplus revenues, beyond what was required for the boys' maintenance, should be diverted to general crown purposes.[1] These abbeys were, by 1560, treated as simply part of the patrimony of the crown, which disposed not only of the abbatial revenues but even of monks' portions. Apart from such special cases, the government had, by immemorial usage, the disposal of the temporality of vacant bishoprics, and its claim to the disposal of the spirituality, though not exercised regularly since early times and expressly relinquished in 1450, had recently been revived. At this stage, moreover, the right to dispose of temporality, at least, clearly extended beyond the

[1] *A.P.S.* II, 424.

bishoprics to the other prelacies, and it became a common practice for the crown to appoint an *oeconomus* to administer the revenues of a religious house during a vacancy. For some years before 1560 the crown seems to have regarded the property of abbeys and bishoprics alike as at its full disposal, for it frequently, during vacancies, granted pensions for life from the fruits. Nomination of a new abbot or bishop, too, was commonly followed immediately by the grant of at least the temporality in anticipation of papal provision.[1] There would be hardly any change in practice should the crown turn its power of nomination into a power of appointment, or should the *oeconomus* to whom it committed the administration of a vacant prelacy remain in office to become indistinguishable from a commendator, or should the gift to a nominee embrace spirituality as well as temporality. Some strange things had happened before 1560, perhaps none more remarkable than the gift, in 1548, of the priory of Eccles, spirituality and temporality, to Marion Hamilton, wholly without reference to nomination at Rome but with a direction to the vicars general of the see of St Andrews to put her into possession.[2] Clearly, the papacy could thus be eliminated.

Bishoprics, unlike abbeys, could hardly be turned into mere lay commendatorships, and even the practice of appointing 'administrators'—usually with the expectation, not always realised, that they would subsequently qualify for consecration—could not become the general rule without bringing ecclesiastical machinery to a standstill. The device adopted was therefore to nominate a genuine bishop but to accompany his nomination with the reservation to laymen of pensions amounting to a very large part, sometimes the major part, of the revenues. The term 'tulchan', to describe the holder of a see who drew its revenues for the benefit of others, is applied—with what justification will appear later—to the bishops appointed in the 1570s, but the most glaring examples of 'tulchanism' are to be found before the reformation. Thus, when Robert Stewart was provided to Caithness in 1541, pensions were reserved

---

[1] These developments are discussed in the Introduction to *R.S.S.* v.

[2] *R.S.S.* III, 2823. As early as the reign of James V a style had been composed for a provision to an abbey by the king (*Warrender Papers* [S.H.S.], I, 6–7).

of five hundred merks to a natural son of the earl of Moray (himself a natural son of James IV), and of two hundred merks and forty merks to two other persons; and when William Gordon was provided to Aberdeen in 1546, pensions were reserved of one thousand merks to John Hamilton, son of the earl of Arran, and of five hundred merks to the queen's secretary.[1] The see of Orkney provides a particularly flagrant instance: when Robert Reid was provided in 1541, a pension of eight hundred merks was reserved to Lord John Stewart, one of James V's natural sons;[2] and when Adam Bothwell succeeded in 1559 it was to a see saddled with pensions of £400 to Lord John, another £400 to Sir John Bellenden, £200 to the son of Lord Ruthven and possibly a further one hundred and sixty merks to Adam Murray, with the result that the bishop was left with a mere pittance and was in serious financial difficulty.[3]

While the crown was thus displacing the papacy and improving its own financial position and that of its lay nominees at the expense of the prelacies, the nobles carried on their own campaign of secularisation. To have a member of the family appointed as commendator of an abbey or priory was a profitable device, and already some years before 1560 the office of abbot or commendator was in some cases becoming the perquisite of a particular noble house: thus Dryburgh tended to be at the disposal of the Erskines, Paisley and Kilwinning[4] of the Hamiltons, Whithorn of the Flemings, Crossraguel of the Kennedies, Culross of the Colvilles and Jedburgh of the Humes. A principle of heredity was not only in operation but was openly recognised and sometimes rigidly observed. An act of council passed on the eve of the battle of Pinkie, in 1547,

---

[1] *Formulare*, II, Nos. 415, 548; *Letters of James V*, p. 432. Cf. *Scottish correspondence of Mary of Lorraine* (S.H.S.), p. 413.

[2] *Letters of James V*, p. 423.

[3] *Thirds of Benefices*, pp. 83-4, 115; John Dowden, *Bishops of Scotland*, p. 267; G. Donaldson, 'Bishop Adam Bothwell and the Reformation in Orkney', in *Scot. Church Hist. Soc. Records*, XIII. For discussion of another example of such transactions, see 'Alexander Gordon, bishop of Galloway', in *Dumfries and Galloway Nat. Hist. and Antiq. Soc. Trans.* 3rd ser. XXIV.

[4] Alexander Hamilton, abbot of Kilwinning, had entered into an obligation, sometime in the 1530s, whereby the nominee of the earl of Arran and Sir James Hamilton of Finnart was to succeed him in the abbacy, but the obligation had been rescinded as illegal (*Formulare*, II, No. 356).

ordained that in the event of the death of the holder of a benefice in the course of the campaign his next of kin should have the right to nominate his successor and that the benefice should fall to his nearest qualified heir.[1] When hereditary succession was thus admitted in law, it could be asserted with the utmost candour: the nunnery of Haddington had been held by prioresses of the house of Hepburn, and in 1566, after the fruits had been granted by Queen Mary to Maitland of Lethington, a petition was received from James Hepburn, earl of Bothwell, stating that the nunnery had been 'a lang tyme broukit [enjoyed] be his freindis, promovit from tyme to tyme at the nominatioun of his predecessouris' and 'wes his maist native roume and kyndlie possessioun'.[2] In the same way, Sir Walter Scott of Branxholm claimed that the kirk of St Mary of the Lowes was his 'auld kyndlie roume and possessioun'.[3] When it is asked why the Scottish crown did not follow English example and dissolve the monasteries, one answer is that it was already profiting sufficiently from the church, without interfering with its existing structure; but another is that the abbey property was already to a large extent in the hands of laymen other than the sovereign, and the failure of post-reformation attempts to annex the monastic temporalities to the crown suggests that a pre-reformation experiment in dissolution would likewise have been of little benefit to the crown.

Even in the absence of such quasi-proprietary rights in benefices, ecclesiastical revenues could be diverted from the clergy to the nobility by feu charters of lands and by tacks or leases of teinds. This development was facilitated in more than one way by the pope's surrender to the king and his abandonment of effective control in Scotland, and it was fostered by the general breakdown of ecclesiastical discipline and the growing sense of insecurity among the clergy. One of the ways in which the Scottish king had turned to account the papal apprehensions arising from Henry VIII's proceedings had been to obtain from Clement VII a grant of a tenth of

---

[1] *A.P.S.* II, 599–600. There was a similar clause in an act of 1571 (*A.P.S.* III, 63).
[2] *R.S.S.* v, 2686. The adjective 'kindly' is associated with 'kin' and is almost equivalent to 'hereditary'.
[3] *Ibid.* VI, 61.

all ecclesiastical revenues for three years and the imposition of a regular tax of about £10,000 Scots annually. (The three tenths were ostensibly for the defence of the realm and the £10,000 ostensibly for the endowment of a College of Justice, and the pope did exact an undertaking from the king to remain faithful to Rome.) The prelates compounded for the 'great tax' of £10,000 annually by undertaking to pay some £72,000 in four years and to assign benefices in their patronage to bring in £1,400 yearly in perpetuity. There were further impositions on the church, similar in principle though smaller in scale, in the later years of James V and during the regency of Mary of Guise, now as a rule on the pretext of the defence of the realm against England, and in the same period the clerical proportion of a general taxation was increased from two-fifths to one-half. Meantime, when the clergy were faced with this new and heavy expenditure, they were finding it increasingly difficult to collect their revenues. The normal proceeding against those in debt to the church for rents or teinds was by way of an action in a church court—the court of an official or commissary—followed by a 'monition' and threat of excommunication or 'cursing'. But it had become the practice to issue 'cursings' for offences so trivial that the threatened censures were mocked and despised and the whole system brought into disrepute.[1] John Major had already remarked that 'men too lightly entangle themselves with ecclesiastical censures. No one, unless he commits mortal sin, ought to be excommunicated'. And in the 1530s it was being said that the church's censures were of no moment, but designed only to terrify the simple and extort their goods.[2] Those who accepted the teaching of the reformation naturally ceased to be impressed by the fulminations of the spiritual courts, and the churchmen began to find that they could secure their income only by calling in secular aid in one form or another. They could indeed resort to process in the civil courts;[3] but it was more effective to appoint a local lay magnate as a bailie, pay him a salary and leave it to him to employ his own

---

[1] Laing, I, 38–9 (Dickinson, I, 16). Erroll Writs, No. 553, is an example of a monition for the removal of a march cairn in 1555.

[2] *Greater Britain* (S.H.S.), pp. 172–3; *Formulare*, II, No. 370.

[3] E.g. R.S.S. V, 282, 285.

methods of exaction.[1] The tack or lease was likewise a useful means of ensuring a steady income and placing the onus of collection on a layman. When we recall that an east coast fisherman had been sent to the stake for casting every tenth fish back into the sea[2] we can appreciate why the vicar of the Fife coastal parish of Kilrenny, complaining that conditions were so gloomy that churchmen could not defend themselves and their goods without the succour of good and faithful laymen, set his fish teinds in tack to a local laird.[3] (It must not, of course, be thought that the initiative in setting a benefice in tack was always that of the incumbent: in 1555 the patron of the parsonage of Parton agreed to present Charles Geddes to the benefice, which was valued at fifty-three merks yearly, on condition that he would set it in tack to the patron for twenty merks.)[4] A device more convenient than the tack, to clergy faced with the need to find large sums of money, was the feu charter, but it had hitherto been surrounded by certain legal difficulties, for canon law forbade alienation, and the papacy looked unfavourably on a feu, which was a grant in perpetuity for a fixed payment. With the 'great tax' of the 1530s, however, the churchmen could plead 'urgent necessity'; in granting a charter they could exact a lump sum towards their share of the tax and by stipulating for a feu duty slightly in excess of the rent previously paid they could represent the transaction as being to their 'evident advantage'; they thus fulfilled the requirements of the letter of canon law, and, although the alienation of property in return for a duty which could never be increased was manifestly not to the advantage of the church, the papacy, which had sanctioned the taxation from which the entire proceeding had originated, could hardly withhold its approval. As the reformation came nearer, the growing sense of insecurity among the clergy gave a further stimulus to secularisation. In 1549 the bishop and chapter of Aberdeen granted letters of bailiary over the temporality of the bishopric to the earl of Huntly, who 'hes oblist him . . . to

---

[1] E.g. Lord Hume was appointed bailie of the nunnery of Coldstream in 1551 (R.M.S. IV, 1709). In the nunnery of Haddington the earl of Bothwell was bailie, with a salary of £100 per annum, and Hepburn of Benestoun bailie depute with £40 (Books of Assumption, I, 166).
[2] Laing, I, 58 (Dickinson, I, 24).   [3] Formulare, II, No. 497.
[4] Register of Deeds, I, 195; Thirds of Benefices, p. 22.

us . . . and kirkmen within the said dyosy, to caus us to be obeyit of all . . . oure fruictis . . . and to fortifie and manteine the Christiane fayth within the said dyosy and libertie of haly kirk'; and other ecclesiastical institutions sought protection by granting feu charters on condition that the grantee would support the church.[1] But, whatever undertakings were entered upon, it had become a sufficient motive for granting feus that they enabled the clergy in possession to raise large capital sums in anticipation of the deluge. It should, however, be said that, strong as the inducements to feuing were, churchmen were not unanimously behind its reckless and ill-considered extension: the monks of Melrose might be unwilling accomplices when they appended their signatures to charters, but they could hardly resist, for the commendator 'grew crawbit' at their reluctance to give their consent; and the prebendaries of Lincluden protested that they were compelled by their provost, through fear of bodily harm and of loss of their pensions and livings, to agree to certain charters.[2]

The pope, who had already abandoned any control over the admission to Scottish prelacies and had authorised taxation which could be paid only by alienation of church property, however disguised, went a step further when he relinquished his power, previously jealously reserved, of confirming feu charters. The desirability, from the point of view of the crown and the nobility, of having within the realm a source of authority for such confirmations, was one motive for seeking legatine powers for the archbishops of St Andrews—a privilege persistently requested by the king of Scots,[3] but one which the pope understood the situation too well to grant with alacrity and which was given, first to David Betoun and then to John Hamilton, only with great reluctance. There were, of course, many other reasons for seeking legatine powers—one of them the advantage of having a local authority to give matrimonial dispensations[4]—and a study is required of the ex-

---

[1] R.M.S. IV, 763; Formulare, II, No. 464; Reg. Ho. Bulls, 65a.
[2] Melrose Regality Records, III, 155-6; Protocol Book of Mark Carruthers (S.R.S.), No. 190; Reg. Honoris de Morton (Bannatyne Club), I, 44.
[3] E.g. Letters of James V, pp. 349, 358, 377, 384, 386-7, 400, 406, 422.
[4] Cf. Liber officialis S. Andree (Abbotsford Club), pp. xxv-xxvi.

tent to which the faculties granted to Betoun and Hamilton, as legates, obviated the need for recourse to Rome for absolutions from censures, dispensations for irregularities, transactions in benefices and appeals from local judicatories.[1] So far as the confirmation of feu charters was concerned, disregard of the papacy was reflected not only in the use made of the legatine powers, but in the development of the practice of resorting for confirmation not to any ecclesiastical authority but to the crown, in implied acknowledgment of its comprehensive rights over ecclesiastical property.[2]

Developments which thus led in practice to the virtual elimination of papal authority in many fields were, if not associated with, at least paralleled by, various features in the principles of the reformers. The reformation as a protest against relaxed discipline in general and as a reaction in favour of efficient oversight in particular would on these grounds alone, if for no other reason, have been anti-papal, because papal dispensations had undermined discipline and because papal encroachments had depressed and frustrated the local organs by which the work of the church should have been supervised. The papacy was such an obstacle to good government that it put a severe strain on the constancy of even its most loyal supporters.[3] Thus the chronicler Abell, an Observant friar, deeply moved by the resistance of the English Observants to Henry VIII, expressed himself as strongly in favour of the papal supremacy in theory: 'how peralus it is to rebell aganis the heid of halie kirk and Christis vicair and wald anull his power gevin be Christ to Sanct Petir and his successouris'; yet, loyal papalist as he was, he was ready to deny that the pope had power to grant dispensations enabling seculars to hold abbacies.[4] Contemporaries became fully aware that efforts at reform were bound to be ineffective as long as papal dispensations were current in Scotland: James V, writing to the pope in 1535, intimated that he proposed to deprive certain

[1] The commission to John Hamilton summarised in *Warrender Papers* (S.H.S.), I, 25–9, should be compared with Edinburgh Univ. Lib., Laing MS. III, 21, fo. 100b (dated 6 March 1555). Cf. Pollen, *op. cit.* p. xcii.

[2] See *R.S.S.* v, Intro. p. xii.

[3] Sir David Lindsay's *The Monarche* is a tremendous indictment of the papacy, and elsewhere in his works he attacks clerical transactions at Rome.

[4] Nat. Lib. Scot. MS. 1746, fos. 113b–14b, 120a–2b.

priests suspected of homicide, and asked the pope not to grant dispensations;[1] articles presented to the provincial council in 1559 asked for the restriction of appeals to Rome and for the putting into execution of statutes against the purchase of benefices at Rome, besides complaining—perhaps a little needlessly—of the necessity for recourse to Rome for confirmation of feus;[2] and that same provincial council, which decided to petition both crown and papacy not to promote to benefices men unfit in morals, learning or age, also implored the regent to supplicate the pope to grant no more dispensations whereby the offspring of clergy could be promoted in their fathers' churches.[3]

If there was thus ample justification for opposition to the papacy on purely practical grounds, such opposition was accompanied, in the last years before 1560, by an almost universal tendency to disregard the papacy even in theory. The silence of Archbishop Hamilton's *Catechism* on the subject of papal authority is not the only illustration of the trend of contemporary thought. The articles specified by the provincial council of 1549 on which inquisitors of heresy were to found their inquiries refer to the authority of general councils but say nothing of the pope; the provincial council of 1559 laid down that faith should extend to what is communicated by the scriptures and also to what is defined by the 'holy catholic church or a general council', but was again silent about the papacy; and Quentin Kennedy, in his *Compendious tractive* (1558), although specially concerned with the question of authority in the church, concentrated on the weight to be attached to the early general councils and completely ignored the popes.[4] The papal supremacy had few friends in Scotland, even among those otherwise conservative in their thought.

In summing up what it is not too much to call the anti-papal tendency in pre-reformation Scotland, it may be said firstly, and most obviously, that there was no financial temptation for the Scottish crown to proceed to a formal breach with Rome, because it was already exploiting the church's wealth with sufficient success. But it

---

[1] *Letters of James V*, p. 301.   [2] Patrick, *op. cit.* p. 159.
[3] *Ibid.* pp. 165, 176–7.
[4] Patrick, *op. cit.* pp. 126, 173 and n.; *Wodrow Soc. Misc.* I, 95–174.

is possible to go further, and say that the apparent suddenness of the reformation of 1560 and the apparent absence in Scotland of an episode corresponding to Henry VIII's proceedings in England are very largely an illusion, arising from the fact that the Scottish crown was content with the substance of control over the church, especially in a financial sense, and refrained only from any formal claim to supremacy.

Changes in the relations between Scotland and Rome and in the control and distribution of the wealth of the church within Scotland can be traced with some precision, and their part in shaping the situation in 1560 is calculable. But in the background of those more conspicuous developments, and partly in consequence of some of them, there had emerged in Scotland a social situation which cannot be so fully defined but which had in itself all the elements of revolution, or at least of revolt. There are a good many indications that in the late fifteenth century and the early sixteenth, which had been a period of comparative freedom from destructive invasions, the country had grown more prosperous and the burghs wealthier. The burgesses, although they gave freely of their substance to their own town churches, seem to have had much less affection for the prelates and the monastic orders, possibly because they regarded them as unprofitable consumers of material resources. This in itself might not have disposed the burgesses to support the reformation, but they also resented the continued drain of money to Rome,[1] and they must have been attracted to a movement which, with its Anglophile tendencies, offered a guarantee against the recurrence of the destruction which the towns of south-eastern Scotland had suffered in the 1540s.

The secularisation of so much church property, while undoubtedly beneficial to the great magnates, also raised the status and increased the prosperity and influence of many of the smaller lairds. It is easy enough to understand why the lesser barons insisted that they should be heard in the parliament of 1560,[2] but there is no reason why they should have been peculiarly influenced by the exhortations of the reforming preachers, and not too easy, therefore, to define the considerations which prompted their zeal for 'true

[1] Lindsay, *Works*, II, 271.   [2] Pp. 66–7 below.

religion'. They had, however, benefited from the insecurity of the ecclesiastics in recent years, and while their titles to their feus and tacks were no doubt sound in law they may have felt that their gains were more likely to be perpetuated should transactions in ecclesiastical property cease to be subject to control from outwith the realm and should the crown's right to grant and confirm holdings of church land be formally conceded.

While magnates and lairds, and anyone else possessed of capital enabling him to put down a large sum of money, might benefit from the feuing of church lands, and were concerned principally to ensure the permanence of their gains, men further down the social scale were in a different position. The tenants of church lands appear on the whole to have enjoyed favourable conditions in earlier generations, with moderate rents and a security of tenure which was often in practice hereditary. When the churchmen resorted to feuing, however, the tenants could not in general afford the terms demanded, and they found themselves at the mercy of the middlemen who had acquired the feus and who now proposed to recoup themselves for their outlay by rack-renting or evicting the old tenants. This grievance, which is one of the best documented of all,[1] did not of course arise from the introduction of feu tenure in itself, for that was generally regarded as desirable, nor could the churchmen be justly blamed for resorting to feuing to meet taxation imposed by pope and king; but the disregard of the claims of the old tenants, and the failure to use feus to give them security of tenure, clearly fostered an aversion to the prelates. The provincial council of 1559, recognising that the letting of church lands to others than the existing occupiers had been detrimental to the church, forbade lands to be granted in future 'save to tenants and tillers of the same',[2] but by that time the damage had been done. All the humbler members of society, and not only the evicted tenants, in any event suffered from the extortionate exaction of offerings, especially the mortuary dues,[3] and also from the unreasonable exaction of teinds.[4] While

---

[1] Lindsay, *Works*, II, 249, 255, 267, 349; Winyet, *Certane tractatis*, p. 8; *Cal. S. P. Scot.* I, 143.
[2] Patrick, *op. cit.* pp. 179-80.
[3] P. 14 above.   [4] Lindsay, *Works*, II, 197-9, 261.

there were thus financial grounds for the unpopularity of the existing clergy, the schemes of the reformed church professed an especial tenderness for 'the poor labourers of the ground'[1] which must have won support from this oppressed class.

At a still lower social level, there is ample evidence in the legislation of the period, both before and after the reformation, that pauperism and begging were a constant problem, though it is impossible to guess its dimensions. From the paupers came a special antipathy to the friars, who professed poverty but whose worldly comforts could be only too easily contrasted with the misery of the genuine poor, who thought they had the best right to alms. The 'Beggars' Summons',[2] which in 1559 gave the friars notice to quit their houses in favour of the poor and infirm, can hardly be regarded as the spontaneous outcome of this antipathy, but that the attitude it represents was real enough cannot be doubted:

> And thocht the corne war never sa skant,
> The gudewyfis will not let Freirs want.[3]

And when Lindsay applies to 'great fat freiris . . . quhilk labours nocht and bene weill fed' St Paul's dictum *Qui non laborat non manducet*,[4] he was anticipating another line of thought in the 'Beggars' Summons', which concludes 'Lat hym therfore that before hes stollin, steill na mare; but rather lat him wyrk wyth his handes, that he may be helpefull to the pure.' This was a thought which affected the popular attitude to churchmen of all categories. Scotland was not a wealthy country, and a livelihood could hardly be gained by a layman of the middle or lower class save by hard work: this fact bred resentment against clerks who lived well without exerting themselves and sometimes without even attending to their nominal duties. Apart from the rather special case of the mortuary dues, the objection to clerical exactions was not so much to the exaction itself as to the fact that the clergy did so little in return for it.[5] Scotsmen felt, in short, that they were not getting value for

---

[1] Laing, II, 221 (Dickinson, II, 303).
[2] *Ibid.* I, 320–1 (Dickinson, II, 255–6). It was a further grievance that self-seeking clergy neglected almshouses and hospitals which they should have maintained (*Cal. S. P. Scot.* I, 144).
[3] Lindsay, *Works*, II, 91.   [4] *Ibid.* 251.   [5] *Ibid.* 275–9.

the £400,000 or so which the church cost the country each year. The last of the developments which helped to shape the situation in 1560 was one arising directly from the proceedings of the reformers. The earlier labours of protestant preachers had been intermittent and spasmodic, but from about 1555 there was something like a consistent and sustained effort, and as the reformed faith was spread and fostered throughout the Lowlands by a number of energetic preachers, regular protestant congregations came to be formed, at first more or less in secret. These were the 'privy kirks' which existed before there was 'the face of a public kirk' in Scotland. Such congregations existed certainly in Edinburgh, St Andrews, Dundee, Perth, Brechin, Montrose, Stirling, Linlithgow, Ayr and very probably in other towns.[1]

There is little enough precise information about the activities of those congregations, but there are some indications that when they met for worship their service consisted of a general confession, lections followed by exposition (or discussion or preaching) and 'common prayers'. It is beyond dispute that the confession of sins, the lectionary and the intercessions were normally supplied by the English Book of Common Prayer, for no other reformed service book was as yet available in print in the English tongue, at least in any quantity, though it is possible that other forms may have circulated in manuscript. At the same time as reformed worship was thus developing in the 'privy kirks', some of the beneficed clergy who were favourable to the reformation appear to have started to use new orders of service from the Prayer Book or perhaps other sources, and the provincial council of 1559 had to ordain that Baptism, the Eucharist and marriage should be administered only according to the accustomed forms and not according to a 'new unaccustomed method'.[2] There is altogether a good deal of evidence that reformed worship, usually according to the forms of the Prayer Book, was fairly well established in Scotland by 1560.[3]

The reformers' meetings for worship necessitated a certain

---

[1] Laing, I, 300; II, 151 (Dickinson, I, 148; II, 277); VI, 22, 78.
[2] Patrick, *op. cit.* pp. 186–7; *Melrose Regality Records,* III, 179–80.
[3] See in general G. Donaldson, *The Making of the Scottish Prayer Book of 1637,* pp. 5–7.

E

amount of organisation, and Knox tells us that the 'privy kirks' found it expedient to elect preachers and to appoint elders and deacons:

Men began to exercise themselves in reading of the Scriptures . . . and variety of persons could not be kept in good obedience and honest fame without overseers, elders and deacons. . . . And they did elect some to occupy the supreme place of exhortation and reading, some to be elders and helpers unto them, for the oversight of the flock, and some to be deacons for the collection of alms to be distributed to the poor.[1]

In thus appointing elders and deacons to conduct their affairs, the Scots were pursuing a course exactly parallel to that taken by the congregations which at that very time Anglican refugees from the Marian persecution were forming in various centres on the Continent and in which elders and deacons were likewise appointed. This procedure was at that time regarded as normal for non-established churches, and in adopting it the Scots were not committing themselves to any specific form of ministry or to any particular system of church order.[2]

By 1559 a reformed church organisation, though still only at congregational level, was remarkably active. The Register of the Kirk Session of St Andrews, for example, begins with an entry dated 27 October 1559 and records the names of the elders and deacons who held office for the year 1559.[3] In some towns the new organisation, and its worship, began to receive official countenance from the local authorities, which were already accustomed to legislate for the clergy in the burgh churches. At Ayr the town council had evidently accepted the reformation as an accomplished fact as early as May 1559, for on the 22nd of that month John Sinclair, a chaplain and chorist in the parish church, protested that he had on the preceding Thursday and Sunday desired Robert Legat, vicar of Ayr, to lend him vestments for mass, but met with refusal because the bailies and dean of gild had 'dischargit the schaplandis [chaplains] of the said kirk and thair service'.[4] On

[1] Laing, II, 151 (Dickinson, II, 277).
[2] Cf. pp. 80, 107–8 below.   [3] *Reg. K. S. St A.* I, 3, 5.
[4] Ayr Burgh Court Book, 1549–60, fo. 31v.

20 November 1559 the town council of Ayr appointed John Or as schoolmaster and assistant minister: in the absence of Christopher Goodman, the minister, he was to 'say and reid the commoun prayaris and minister the sacrament'; and on the same date a church officer was appointed who was to ring the bells 'on ilk day neidfull to the commoun prayaris and precheing'.[1] At Dundee, the town council, which as early as January 1558/9 had begun to pass acts against immorality which suggest the influence of the reformers' demand for discipline, on 2 October 1559 passed an act against contempt of the reformed church and its officers.[2] It is suggestive of the spread of the reformation beyond the burgh churches that already by 3 February 1560 the provost of the collegiate church of Lincluden scandalised his prebendaries by intimating that he intended to 'mary ane wif'.[3]

Thus, as the old church system, undermined by secularisation, was crumbling, a new system had arisen alongside it, and it would not be too much to say that by the end of 1559 there were already two ecclesiastical structures in Scotland. A measure of peaceful co-existence between the two is suggested by the fact that in April 1560 the publication of banns of marriage in their respective churches was certified by William Cornwell, reader of the word of God in Linlithgow, and Mr Alexander Hamilton, vicar of Carriden.[4] Something of the same duality was to persist for several years to come.

Many changes had thus been taking place, officially or unofficially, in theory or in practice, before 1560. Some of them, such as the legislation of the reforming councils, the trend towards the elimination of the papacy and the beginnings of reformed worship, were in accordance with the principles of the reformers. Others, again, were not, and much subsequent history arose from the conflict between the programme of the reformers and some of the developments which had taken place in the years before 1560, not least the inroads made on the church property through the appoint-

[1] Ayr Burgh Court Book, 1549–60, fo. 53v.
[2] Alexander Maxwell, *History of Old Dundee*, pp. 72, 77–8, 81–2.
[3] *Protocol Book of Mark Carruthers* (S.R.S.), No. 190.
[4] *Protocol Book of Nicol Thounis* (S.R.S.), No. 10.

ment of lay commendators, direct taxation in the interests of the crown, and the feuing of church lands. Through these proceedings there had indeed been taking place a redistribution of the church's wealth, but it was a pattern of redistribution quite irreconcilable with the financial proposals presently to be made by the reformers.

CHAPTER III

AN UNSTABLE SITUATION, 1560-7

ECCLESIASTICAL developments, however far-reaching, could not by themselves bring about the reformation. The regent was a Frenchwoman, Mary of Guise, acting for the absent Queen Mary, whose husband Francis became king of France in July 1559, and before there could be a formal alteration in the ecclesiastical system there had to be a political change which would liberate Scotland from the domination of the French and Guisian interest. Military operations by the 'Lords of the Congregation' had begun in the summer of 1559, and by 21 October the insurgents had felt strong enough formally to 'suspend' Mary of Guise from the regency and transfer authority to a 'great council of the realm'. But their next experiences were discouraging, while the French troops of the regent, based on a strongly fortified position at Leith, were admirably placed for operations against the reformers' forces in Fife and for the maintenance of communications with France, until an English fleet appeared in the Firth of Forth on 23 January 1559/60. A little over two months later an English army entered Scotland to undertake the siege of Leith, but that fortress was still holding out when the death of Mary of Guise, on the night of 10–11 June, opened the way to a pacification. English and French commissioners on 6 July concluded the treaty of Edinburgh, which provided for the withdrawal of foreign forces from Scotland and was accompanied by certain concessions from Francis and Mary to their Scottish subjects, *inter alia* authorising the summoning of a parliament, which met in August.

The pattern according to which polity and endowment should be reformed had already been discussed, for as early as 29 April the great council of Scotland had commissioned the ministers then present in Edinburgh to draw up a 'book' containing their 'judgments touching the reformation of religion', and such a book had been completed by 20 May.[1] A 'book of common reformation', no

[1] Laing, II, 183, 257 (Dickinson, II, 280, 323).

doubt as thus compiled in May, was reported at the time of the parliament of August to be 'translating into Latin' for submission to the judgment of experts overseas, but it was apparently not considered by the parliament.[1] The precise contents of this 'book of reformation' are uncertain, but it may be suspected that it was a briefer document than the 'Book of Discipline' preserved by Knox in his *History*, for the latter incorporates additions made as late as January 1561 and may very well include the results of revision undertaken in the later months of 1560.[2]

Whatever had been proposed in a 'book of reformation', it did nothing to shape the course of events when parliament met in August 1560, and the whole issue of polity was at that time an open question. In particular, the relationship of the reformed church to the bishops and to the existing clergy generally was undefined. Sir David Lindsay had foreseen the king and the parliament depriving the prelates,[3] but political conditions in 1560 were such that there was no possibility of either compelling the clergy to accept the reformation or dispossessing them if they declined to accept it. The Scottish reformers, so far from having crown support, had carried through a revolution in defiance of the crown, and were a mere faction, with their main strength in lairds and burgesses and with the support of few nobles who would allow religious considerations to outweigh their own material advantage and the interests of their kin. In the structure of which they proposed to take possession, kinsmen of the most powerful magnates in the land were entrenched in the benefices. The primate was John Hamilton, half-brother of the duke of Châtelherault, who was the leading noble in Scotland and heir presumptive to the throne, and who was, besides, titular head of the reforming party. Therefore an attack on John Hamilton might have cost the reformers the support of the somewhat unstable duke and of the whole house of Hamilton. There was another Hamilton in the see of Argyll; there were members of the great house of Huntly in Aberdeen and Galloway; there was a Stewart of the blood royal in Caithness; there was a Hepburn of the line of the earls of Bothwell in Moray; there was

[1] *Cal. S. P. Scot.* I, p. 472.
[2] Pp. 61–3 below.   [3] Lindsay, *Works*, II, 339.

a dynasty of Chisholms in Dunblane. The structure of Scottish society and government being what it was, such men could not be coerced into acceptance of the reformed Confession of Faith which the parliament approved; neither could they be deprived if they refused to conform. A strong Scottish king could hardly have ventured to deprive them; still less could they be deprived by what was at best a provisional government in a dubious legal position.[1] It was because of the accident that the Scottish bishops could not, at this point, be forcibly dispossessed that the development was so different in Scotland from what it was in England. 'The [Scottish] bishops could be forbidden to say mass; some of them had no desire to be troubled with that or any other duty. But the decent Anglican process, which substitutes an Edmund Grindal for an Edmund Bonner, could not be imitated.'[2]

'Forbidden to say mass' the bishops were; for the parliament forbade the celebration of the Latin rite. But there was no compulsion on the bishops—or, indeed, on anyone[3]—to subscribe the new Confession of Faith. Compulsion being impossible, persuasion alone could be tried. And persuasion was tried, though with only imperfect success. Of this episode we get no hint in Knox's *History*, except possibly his suggestive remark at this point that 'divers men were of divers judgments';[4] but Randolph, the English representative in Edinburgh, and Maitland of Lethington, secretary to the Scottish government, reported to William Cecil on the negotiations with the bishops in August 1560.

The prospects were not unpromising, because none of the bishops can have been considered to be wholly intransigent except the solitary ultramontane, James Betoun of Glasgow, who had already left Scotland for France in July.[5] Of John Hamilton, the primate, some hopes had been entertained earlier: when he returned to Scotland from France in 1543, along with David Panter, there was 'great esperance that their presence should have been comfortable to the kirk of God. For it was constantly affirmed of some that, without delay, the one and the other would occupy the

---

[1] Cf. p. 67 below. [2] *Cambridge Modern History*, II, 580.
[3] Except, presumably, ministers and schoolmasters.
[4] Laing, II, 92 (Dickinson, I, 338). [5] *Cal. S. P. Scot.* I, p. 455.

pulpit and truly preach Jesus Christ'.[1] These hopes were disappointed, but the archbishop proceeded with a policy of conservative reform and showed that he was not averse from doctrinal modification.[2] After 1560, it may be added, he was cautious in his dealings with Roman agents, and he appears to have been guided at least as much by family interest as by religious convictions: although he was prosecuted for saying mass, it was alleged that he had declared his readiness to give up the mass if it would serve the interests of the head of his house,[3] and in joining Queen Mary's party after her deposition in 1567 he was associating not only with the whole Hamilton family but with many who were unsympathetic to the Roman catholic cause. Robert Crichton, bishop of Dunkeld, was to show more courage than any of his brethren in negotiating with papal agents,[4] and his attachment to the queen's party after 1567 led to his forfeiture and imprisonment. Yet in later years he appears to have modified his attitude: in 1575 'Robert, bishop of Dunkeld' was invited to take part in the consecration of a protestant bishop,[5] in 1584 he was restored to his see with a view to his being associated with the work of the reformed church,[6] and when he died the town council of Edinburgh gave permission for his burial in their church of St Giles, which they would hardly have done had he been regarded as a papist.[7] William Gordon of Aberdeen had been asked by his chapter in 1559 'not to be over familiar with them that are suspect contrarious to the kirk, and of the new law', but to 'avoid the same';[8] in 1562 he refused to receive the papal nuncio then visiting Scotland;[9] and from his action in 1577 of instituting a reader of the reformed church as vicar of Aberdeen it may perhaps be deduced that he accepted the new order in his last days.[10] Patrick Hepburn of Moray had offered to assist the Lords of the Congregation and

[1] Laing, I, 105 (Dickinson, I, 48); cf. Herkless and Hannay, *Archbishops of St Andrews*, V, 8–9.

[2] Pp. 33, 35 above; cf. Spottiswoode, I, 372.

[3] *Cal. S. P. Scot.* II, No. 9.   [4] Pollen, *op. cit.* 135.

[5] Reg. Pres. I, 120 (17 May 1575); R.S.S. VII, 186. The possibility that 'Robert' is a scribal error cannot be excluded.

[6] Reg. Pres. II, 114.

[7] *Extracts from Records of Burgh of Edinburgh*, IV, 405.

[8] Keith, *History of Church and State in Scotland*, I, cxxii.

[9] Pollen, *op. cit.* 155.   [10] *Spalding Club Misc.* II, 45.

vote with them in parliament, but he was alienated by their action in sacking the abbey of Scone, of which he was commendator, and withdrew his offer;[1] yet his adherence to Rome was so much in doubt that he was not considered a suitable person to receive an invitation to the council of Trent,[2] he was a member of the parliament of December 1567 which ratified the reformation and gave the reformed church legal establishment, and in 1569 he agreed to contribute to the repair of the cathedral of Elgin so that the people could convene there 'for hearing of the word of God'.[3]

The bishops present at the parliament of 1560 included St Andrews and Dunkeld and also the aged William Chisholm of Dunblane. The reformers' case was put before St Andrews at some length by spokesmen whom he knew well and who were themselves no fanatics—John Winram, subprior of St Andrews and afterwards superintendent of Fife, and John Douglas, rector of St Andrews university and later Hamilton's successor in the archbishopric—and there was also a serious consultation between the archbishop and the duke of Châtelherault, his half-brother. The conclusion of these talks was reported to be 'without hope', for the archbishop was 'determined in that mind he was of at present to end his life'. He asked for a copy of the reformers' Confession of Faith, but the sceptical 'doubted it be to send it to France before the lords send, rather than any mind to examine its verity or reform his conscience'. Dunkeld showed even less disposition to accept a religious change, for Randolph reported that he remained 'as obstinate as ignorant' and that he declined to listen to Knox, whom he characterised as 'an old condemned heretic'. However, when the Confession was debated in the parliament, the line taken by Hamilton, Crichton and Chisholm was not wholly negative. According to Maitland, 'thus far they did liberally profess, that they would agree to all things that might stand with God's word, and consent to abolish all abuses crept in in the church not agreeable with the scriptures, and asked longer time to deliberate on the book propounded'; according to Randolph, Hamilton said of the Confession that 'as he would not utterly condemn it, so was he loth to

---

[1] Laing, I, 360 (Dickinson, I, 189-90).
[2] Pollen, *op. cit.* 55.   [3] *R.P.C.* I, 677.

give his consent thereto', and Crichton and Chisholm concurred.[1] Whether the primate was wavering or merely trimming when, a few weeks after the parliament, he was reported to have 'given over his mass and received the common prayers',[2] cannot be determined, but during the session of the parliament the attitude of those bishops was at any rate sufficiently hesitant to discourage lesser men from resisting the acceptance of the new Confession.[3]

It seems very likely that several bishops could have been won over. But there were difficulties on the other side as well. It is hard to imagine Knox accepting John Hamilton as a colleague, just as it is hard to imagine that Bonner, had he chosen to conform, would have been acceptable to the ultra-protestants of England, who were aggrieved that 'these bloody bishops and known murderers of God's people' were suffered to live.[4] Acquaintance with the lax morals of some of the bishops, and with their record of opposition to what the reformers conceived to be the truth, suggested that a succession from them should be repudiated on the ground that 'the miracle is now ceased' and that the existing clergy should be disowned: 'in all the rabble of the clergy there is not one lawful minister, if God's word, the practice of the apostles and their own ancient laws shall judge of lawful election.'[5]

Yet, in spite of such a discouraging declaration, there were bishops, as well as many clergy of lower rank, who continued, apparently unchallenged, to perform ministerial and episcopal functions under the new regime. Alexander Gordon, consecrated for the archbishopric of Glasgow in 1551 and, when he failed to gain possession, created titular archbishop of Athens, had been nominated to the bishopric of Galloway in 1559 and was already a firm adherent of the reformed cause before the parliament of August 1560. There is no evidence of any intermission in his administration of his diocese, and the official record in 1562 of his financial reward as 'overseer' of Galloway[6] no doubt represents a situation which had

---

[1] *Cal. S. P. Scot.* I, pp. 461, 462, 465, 467.
[2] *Ibid.* No. 911.
[3] Laing, II, 122 (Dickinson, I, 339); Winyet, *op. cit.* 12.
[4] *Cal. S. P. Scot.* I, No. 554, and *Cal. S. P. For.*, 1559–60, p. 63.
[5] See pp. 104–5 below.
[6] *Thirds of Benefices*, pp. 131, 137, 146, 150.

continued unchanged since 1560.[1] Adam Bothwell, who had been provided and consecrated to the see of Orkney in the autumn of 1559, was in his diocese from the spring of 1560 until the spring of 1561. During that period he suppressed the Latin rite and organised a reformed ministry, and his 'visitation, oversight and labours taken upon the kirks of Orkney and Shetland' received financial recognition similar to that given to the bishop of Galloway.[2] Robert Stewart, brother of the fourth earl of Lennox and uncle of Henry, Lord Darnley, had become 'administrator' of the see of Caithness in 1542, at the age of nineteen, but seems never to have been consecrated. Sharing in his family's exile after their forfeiture in 1545, he spent many years chiefly in England, where he clearly conformed to Henrician and Edwardian Anglicanism, and he was appointed to a prebend of Canterbury. Like Adam Bothwell, he was in his diocese during part of the critical period of 1560-1 and by the end of 1561 was known to be a member of the reforming party.[3]

Bothwell and Stewart were not present at the parliament of 1560, but those who attended and voted on the reforming side included Gordon of Galloway, James Hamilton, bishop of Argyll, and John Campbell, styled 'elect of the Isles'. Hamilton of Argyll was never consecrated, and while he continued occasionally to perform certain functions in his capacity as bishop[4] he took no real part in the work of the reformed church. He held the subdeanery of Glasgow, and possibly preferred the quiet enjoyment of that prebend to the arduous life of a Highland bishop, but from the small part which he played in affairs it may perhaps be inferred that he was infirm either mentally or physically. John Campbell was only one of two or three claimants to the bishopric of the Isles, and although he joined the reformed cause he could do no work for it in the diocese.

Here then were five bishops, two of them duly consecrated, who had joined the reformers, and three of them continued their work under the new regime. About this important fact there has been

---

[1] See in general *Dumfries and Galloway Nat. Hist. and Antiq. Soc. Trans.* 3rd ser. XXIV.

[2] *Thirds of Benefices*, p. 152. See in general 'Bishop Adam Bothwell and the Reformation in Orkney' in *Scot. Church Hist. Soc. Records*, XIII.

[3] *E.H.R.* LX, 357 nn. 2, 3.

[4] E.g. Breadalbane Papers, 17 Aug. 1576.

something like a conspiracy of silence, and a country which later on boasted that it had 'reformed from popery by presbyters' has forgotten the labours of reforming bishops. Orkney, Caithness and Galloway were, as it happened, small and remote dioceses, but the facts suggest that had more bishops conformed as Bothwell, Stewart and Gordon did there would have been no serious difficulty about the imitation in Scotland of the 'decent Anglican process', although voluntarily instead of by compulsion. But it is, of course, equally clear that in the 'succession' there was at that time no interest whatever.[1] The reformers had two consecrated bishops actively engaged on their side, and one or two more—Hepburn of Moray certainly and Gordon of Aberdeen probably—would have agreed, if pressed, to take part in a consecration. No such effort was made, and the succession lapsed.

However, at the time of the parliament of August 1560, when the negotiations with the bishops had plainly been inconclusive, the only statute bearing on the subject of ecclesiastical polity was one which forbade any bishop to exercise jurisdiction in virtue of authority derived from Rome. This did not make a very serious change in the *de facto* position, it went no further than the anti-papal clauses of an English act of supremacy, if, indeed, it went as far,[2] and, while it ought to have been fatal to the archbishop's legatine authority, it did not—so at least it might have been argued—affect the normal episcopal powers. The whole outcome was therefore at this point indecisive, for the majority of the bishops had neither committed themselves to the reformation nor been removed from office to make way for protestant successors. There was, indeed, one see in which the bishop could clearly be disregarded, for James Betoun of Glasgow was now an exile in France, and steps were almost at once taken to provide a substitute: on 28 August Archbishop Betoun's agent reported to his master that 'John Willock is made bishop of Glasgow, ... and placed in your place of Glasgow.'[3]

---

[1] Cf. pp. 104–5 below.

[2] Cf. Lethington's request to Randolph in 1563 for a statute containing all the cases of Praemunire—'meant for the weal of the prelates' (Laing, vi, 532; *Cal. S. P. Scot.* i, p. 678).

[3] Keith, *op. cit.* iii, 10.

But there was as yet no general appointment of substitutes for the recusant or hesitant bishops, and at what date there took place the nomination of the superintendents who were ultimately appointed to supersede them is not wholly clear. Knox assigns to a point immediately before the meeting of the parliament of August 1560 a general nomination of ministers and superintendents,[1] but Randolph's report on 25 August was that order had been taken 'for the ministers' and said nothing about superintendents.[2] There are other indications that Knox's chronology is sometimes untrustworthy,[3] and, while it is not inconceivable that there was a general nomination of superintendents in or about August 1560 and that it proved abortive except for Willock's appointment as 'bishop of Glasgow', it seems much more likely that Knox misplaced an incident which belongs to the spring of 1561.

The parliament of 1560, which had settled neither polity nor endowment, was quite clearly followed by renewed discussion of these subjects and by further work on the 'book of reformation'. Even Knox, who has preserved a version of the Book of Discipline which bears to have been commissioned on 29 April 1560 and completed on 20 May, in the course of his narrative assigns the composition of the book, and even the commission to compile it, to a point after the August parliament,[4] and while this may be merely one of his chronological lapses it may suggest that in his recollection the vital period of discussion and decision had been after, and not before, the parliament. Further, the unanimity with which later writers, from Row and Calderwood onwards, have assigned the compilation of the book to the later months of 1560 cannot be wholly the result of carelessness and the mere repetition of error. The fact which is most clearly beyond dispute is that the Book of Discipline as we know it is a document approved by a convention of nobility and barons in January 1561. But it is equally clear that it had previously been discussed and modified at a meeting of an

---

[1] Laing, II, 87 (Dickinson, I, 334 and n.).
[2] *Ibid.* VI, 119 (*Cal. S. P. Scot.* I, p. 472).
[3] It is in any event odd that Knox assigns his own nomination to Edinburgh to this point, although he had been elected as minister there fully a year before.
[4] Laing, II, 128 (Dickinson, I, 343 and n).

ecclesiastical convention of some kind, presumably the meeting usually regarded as the first general assembly, which began on 20 December 1560. For such discussion and modification we have the testimony of Row,[1] and the book itself discloses that it had been under consideration by an authoritative ecclesiastical organ and had undergone modification at its hands: in the sentence defining the bounds of the superintendent of Lothian there is the phrase 'and thereto is added, by consent of the whole Church, Merse, Lauderdale and Wedale', and we have no knowledge of any meeting in this period which could speak for 'the whole Church' except the assembly of December 1560.

Beyond that it is impossible to go, though textual criticism might go some way towards disentangling the 'book of reformation' of the summer from later accretions.[2] Certainly the book as we have it is an uneven and ill-proportioned document, possibly as a result of the stress and haste of the three weeks between 29 April and 20 May but just as likely as a result of a later period of discussion and modification.[3] It is probable enough that, as Row says, the different 'heads' were allocated to different contributors, but there is little to support his further statement that the compilers subsequently met together to review the work as a whole, and much to suggest rather that the different parts were thrown together without adequate editing. If so, some of the contributors must have been more realistic than others, for at points the book implies a triumphant reformed church, with the gospel truly and openly preached in every kirk and assembly of the realm and with such favourable political conditions that sweeping claims to ecclesiastical property could be successfully asserted, while elsewhere it reveals full consciousness of the imperfections of the time, when

[1] John Row, *History of the Kirk of Scotland* (Wodrow Soc.), 16. This account might be held to suggest that the revision was commissioned by the assembly between 20 and 27 December and approved at the adjourned meeting fixed for 15 January (*B.U.K.* 1, 7).

[2] The wording of the preface in what is believed to be the oldest MS. (Laing, II, 184 [Dickinson, II, 280]) may suggest that the original 'book of reformation' included only the heads concerning doctrine, sacraments, discipline and 'policy of the kirk', that is, the heads now numbered 1, 2, 7, 8 and 9, and that all the remainder was inserted later.

[3] Pp. 64-5 below.

the kirk mustered only a handful of ministers and had no immediate prospect of being adequately staffed. Some of the unevenness might indeed be explained by the special need to provide for the initial stages in setting up the reformed organisation: for example, there is more detail about the admission of ministers than about the manner of their supervision, and there are explicit statements about the method of appointing superintendents but only limited information about their functions. But it is hard to see any logical reason for the inclusion of a vast amount of detail about the university curricula, and the failure, on the other hand, to define matters of central importance like the composition of the 'great council of the church' and its relations with the civil authority, or for the contrast between the care with which the scale of ministers' stipends is laid down and the failure to show, except in the most general terms, how the funds to pay those stipends were to be raised and administered. Details like the appearance twice over of the statement that elders and deacons must be elected annually lest they become too powerful,[1] or the discrepancy between the general statement that there should be 'twelve or ten superintendents' and a scheme which apportioned the whole country among no more than ten superintendents, hardly argue in favour of the book's careful revision.

Such being the nature of the Book of Discipline, it left much undetermined, but it was clear enough on the right of the reformed church to succeed to the major part of the ecclesiastical revenues and the need to redress the balance of effort and resources in favour of the parishes. The compilers laid claim not to the existing ecclesiastical structure, consisting as it did of benefices each with its appropriate revenues, but they did propose that the reformed church should inherit all the spirituality and part of the temporality, and use it for a system based on the needs of the parishes, where there was to be an educated ministry who would in time raise an instructed people. The existing structure was to be swept away, the

---

[1] Laing, II, 226, 234 (Dickinson, II, 305, 310). It is to be noted that while the second of those statements occurs in the section on discipline, which would certainly form part of the original 'book of reformation', the first of them occurs in the section on rents and patrimony, which, it has been suggested, may have been a later insertion (p. 62 above).

existing benefices were to be 'dissolved' and temporality separated from spirituality by the extrication of teinds from other ecclesiastical revenues, so that the funds which derived from parishes would remain within the parishes and the entire spirituality be made available for the stipends of ministers, for education and for poor relief. The temporality of the monastic houses was not mentioned, but it was implied that the spirituality of those foundations, consisting of the teinds of appropriated churches, should, like other parochial revenues, be available for the needs of the reformed church. The spirituality of the bishoprics and cathedrals was to be distributed in the same manner, but their temporality was to be allotted to support the universities, where the ministers would be trained, and to pay the superintendents, whose task it would be to supervise the work of the ministers. There was provision for a complete educational system, with primary and secondary schools in every village and town, and for a system of poor relief. The whole scheme was devised with an eye to the parishes and to the spiritual, intellectual and material welfare of the people in the parishes. But— with the exception of the silence about the monastic temporalities, which were tacitly relinquished to the abbots and commendators— all competing claims, whether of crown, of laymen or of churchmen, were disregarded.

These radical proposals were not such as could command universal acceptance, and it is plain that there was a period of controversy over them, within the ranks of the reforming party, partly because the nobles declined to approve of schemes which threatened their own hold on some of the ecclesiastical wealth and which would have reduced to the status of paupers their numerous kinsmen who held benefices, but perhaps partly also because 'divers men were of divers judgments' on the details of polity. There was freedom and safety to wrangle as long as Francis II of France lived and the return of Mary to Scotland seemed remote or improbable. But when Francis died in December and it was realised that Mary would be thrown back on Scotland, there was a new urgency for a settlement and for unity among the reformers. Here there may have entered an element of haste which helped to make the Book of Discipline the untidy document it is. At any rate, an ecclesiastical convention, representative of 'the whole church', sat from 20 to 27 December and was then adjourned until 15 January, on which date 'a general convention of the whole nobility' was appointed to meet.[1] On 27 January 1560/1 'a great part of the nobility' approved the Book of Discipline, on condition that clergy of all ranks who supported the reformation should enjoy their livings for life, provided that they maintained ministers.[2]

It appears that the next step, consequent on this approval of the Book of Discipline, and not at any earlier date, was the nomination of superintendents. Official documents relating to the appointment of the superintendents of Fife and Lothian make it clear that their nomination had been subsequent to the approval of the Book of Discipline by the lords.[3] Moreover, while Randolph had said nothing of superintendents in August 1560, he reported in a letter written on 5 March 1561 that the superintendents had been nominated;[4] and while the ecclesiastical convention of December 1560, known as the first general assembly, had been silent about superintendents, the second assembly, in May 1561, passed an act in their favour.[5] Finally, whatever may be the truth about the date of the nomination of the superintendents, their effective appointments date from the spring of 1561 or later: Spottiswoode was appointed to Lothian on 9 March, Winram to Fife in April;[6] as John Erskine had so late as December 1560 merely been 'thought apt and able to minister', it is barely conceivable that he can even have been nominated as a superintendent before 1561, and it appears that he was not formally 'elected' as superintendent of Angus until the beginning of 1562;[7] Willock, although he had been made 'bishop' of Glasgow in August 1560, had to go through the usual procedure, and was formally admitted as superintendent in September 1561;[8]

---

[1] Laing, II, 138 (Dickinson, I, 351-2). [2] *Ibid.* 129-30 (Dickinson, I, 344-5).
[3] *Reg. K. S. St A.* I, 72-5; Warrender Papers, vol. A, fo. 93 (in Appendix).
[4] *Cal. S. P. Scot.* I, No. 967; cf. p. 61 above.
[5] *B.U.K.* I, 8 (Calderwood, II, 126). Knox correctly places the 'election' of superintendents after the convention of January 1561 (Laing, II, 143 [Dickinson, I, 355]).
[6] Laing, II, 144 (Dickinson, II, 273); *Reg. K. S. St A.* I, 72-5.
[7] *B.U.K.* I, 4 (Calderwood, II, 46); *Extracts from Records of Burgh of Edinburgh,* III, 129.
[8] *Cal. S. P. Scot.* I, p. 555; Keith, *op. cit.* II, 87.

the appointment of John Carswell to Argyll cannot be dated.

None of the appointments, it will be observed, conflicted with the jurisdiction of the three bishops actively engaged on behalf of the reformed church. One might further hazard the speculation—although it is nothing more—that four of the districts assigned to superintendents were selected because they coincided roughly with the dioceses of the more intransigent bishops—the absentee Betoun of Glasgow and the three who had taken the conservative line in the parliament.[1] The reason for the omission of appointments to the two superintendencies which covered the dioceses of Aberdeen, Moray and Ross may thus have been that there was still uncertainty about the attitude of Bishops Gordon of Aberdeen, Hepburn of Moray and the recently appointed Henry Sinclair of Ross: what foundation there was for hopes of Gordon and Hepburn has already been indicated, and of Sinclair it should be recorded that in 1562, when Queen Mary thought that he might receive a papal brief, he intimated that he could not venture to see the papal nuncio, and made excuses,[2] and that in his capacity as parson of Glasgow he had no scruples about furnishing bread and wine 'to the halie communion' of the reformed church.[3]

While a complete and uniform system of supervision had not yet been set up, the reformed church was now, in 1561, equipped with a regional organisation under which its work could go forward throughout the greater part of the country. But its position in relation to the state and in relation to the ecclesiastical revenues was still undefined. In other words, questions of establishment and endowment had still to be solved.

Francis and Mary had indeed authorised the meeting of a parliament in 1560, but one at which it was to be lawful 'for all those to be present who are in use to be present' and which was not to deal with the religious question but to submit it to the king and queen. The parliament which met in August, however, was attended by a large number of lairds or 'barons', below the rank of lords of parliament,

---

[1] Erskine's district included the diocese of Brechin, which happened to be in effect vacant, for Donald Campbell, although nominated, had not obtained possession. Carswell superseded the ineffective James Hamilton.

[2] Pollen, *op. cit.* pp. 132, 134.   [3] *R.P.C.* I, 492.

who were not 'in use to be present'; it did deal with religion; and, although the queen never formally denied the validity of its legislation, neither did she ever ratify it. Whatever the reforming preachers might say, cautious men, more especially those of a conservative and lawyerly outlook, may well have had doubts whether papal authority could be abrogated by an act of any Scottish parliament, even if adhering fully to constitutional forms; and if so, they must have been still more uncertain whether papal authority could be legally abrogated by a parliament of unusual composition, a parliament which had been forbidden to deal with religion, a parliament whose legislation did not receive the royal assent. It was not merely out of force of habit or because they were antipathetic to the reformation that for another decade or so some notaries continued to insert the pontifical year in their instruments,[1] and it was certainly no lack of sympathy for the reformation which caused the government of James VI to continue the formula that its gifts of church property were to be as valid as if made at Rome with bulls following thereon.[2] But even leaving aside the more nebulous misgivings, it was plain that, as the legislation of 1560 was not ratified by the queen, the only recognition which the reformed church enjoyed in law was that given by a proclamation issued by Mary a few days after her arrival in Scotland, forbidding meantime any 'alteration or innovation of the state of religion . . . which her majesty found public and universally standing at her majesty's arrival in this her realm'.[3] It was for violation of that proclamation, and not for violation of the act of parliament of August 1560 forbidding the Latin rite, that 'mass-mongers' were prosecuted in succeeding years.[4] When parliament met again in 1563, statutory establishment was still not conceded, although official recognition of the reformed church was implied in an act providing that ministers should

---

[1] E.g. Morton Charters, 21 Aug. 1565 (Box 12), 18 Dec. 1567 (Box 36); Erroll Writs, No. 776 (dated 1570). There is an Orkney example of 1565 where the parties were certainly adherents of the reformation and where spaces were left for the number of the indiction and the pontifical year (Craven, *History of the Church in Orkney*, II, 29, cf. 11).

[2] The Register of the Privy Seal shows that this went on until at least 1580.

[3] *R.P.C.* I, 266–7.

[4] E.g. Pitcairn, *op. cit.* I, II, 428*, 435*.

have the manses and glebes.[1] Not until April 1567, in the desperate days between the Darnley murder and the Bothwell marriage, did Mary pass an act rescinding legislation contrary to the reformed religion and taking the reformed church under her protection.[2] After Mary's deposition and her supersession by her infant son under a protestant regent, the legislation of 1560 had to be enacted as of new in the first parliament of the new reign, and only at that point, in 1567, did the reformed church attain legal establishment by authority of crown and parliament. Nor was the precarious situation of the reformed church between 1560 and 1567 a matter only of constitutional theory, though it may have been especially plain to lawyers like John Sinclair, later Lord President, who remarked, as Knox complained, that 'we have nothing of our religion established, neither by law nor parliament';[3] for the general assembly itself implied the truth of Sinclair's assertion when it petitioned in 1565 'that the sincere word of God and Christ's true religion, now at this present received, be established, approved and ratified' and that the mass and the papal jurisdiction be suppressed.[4] Contemporaries, whether in Scotland or in England, were fully aware that establishment became a reality only in 1567.[5]

If the reformed church did not enjoy establishment, neither did it enjoy adequate endowment. Its claims were sweeping enough, not only in the Book of Discipline, but in a resolution of the first general assembly (December 1560) that all who had been in 'the ministry of the pope's kirk' should receive no provision beyond that made for paupers, and in the slightly more modest demand of the second that ministers' stipends should be the first charge on the teinds of each parish. A more realistic attitude had meanwhile prevailed when the lords in January 1561 decided that beneficed men who joined the reformed cause should enjoy their livings for life provided that they contributed to the maintenance of the ministry. Some prelates who conformed did support ministers from their revenues,

---

[1] *A.P.S.* II, 539.   [2] *A.P.S.* II, 548 c. 2.
[3] Laing, II, 385 (Dickinson, II, 81).
[4] *Ibid.* 484–5 (Dickinson, II, 148–9).
[5] Cf. Laing, I, 297 (Dickinson, I, 145), VI, 429–30; *Zurich Letters* (Parker Soc.), I, 198–201; *A.P.S.* III, 71; *Cal. S. P. Scot.* IV, p. 204; *B.U.K.* I, 94–5, 120.

while some clergy who did not accept the reformation suffered temporary confiscation at the hands of protestant magnates, by whom pittances were paid to ministers, but such expedients did not amount to a settlement, and no solution of the financial problem had been attained when Mary returned from France in August 1561. Yet if the queen's recognition of the reformed church meant anything at all, some provision had to be made for the ministers. Towards the end of the year negotiations began between the privy council and the beneficed clergy. On 22 December four of the bishops offered a quarter of their revenues for one year, to be employed as the queen thought fit, but the council, in view of the uncertainty of the amount required for the maintenance of the reformed clergy and for the 'support of the queen's majesty, above her own proper rents, for the common affairs of the country', decided that if necessary a third or more of the fruits of every benefice should be uplifted yearly 'until a general order be taken'. On 15 February 1562 came a decision that the requirements of crown and kirk amounted to a third of the church's wealth, while the right of the 'old possessors' to the remainder was expressly reserved. It was ordained further that the revenues of chaplainries, prebends and friaries within burghs should be wholly devoted to hospitals, schools and 'other godly uses', and that friary buildings as yet undemolished should be preserved by the burghs for educational and other purposes.

The device thus adopted for the temporary settlement of the financial problem was not wholly revolutionary, for the practice of periodically mulcting the prelates, at least, had been established for a generation, and the 'assumption' or uplifting of thirds could be presented as merely an extension, if a drastic one, of a method of ecclesiastical subvention to the crown which had become familiar. When the bishops offered to place a quarter of a year's revenues at the crown's disposal they must have been aware that they would have to contribute on a generous scale, and, although they protested at the final decision in favour of the annual levy of a third, they had some grounds for satisfaction, or at least relief. At the worst, by sacrificing the third they preserved their two-thirds; the payment of thirds for collection by the crown and partly for crown needs did not imply surrender to a new ecclesiastical regime; in the event of a religious reaction the thirds might be at least partially recoverable; and this levy might be tempered, as earlier levies had been, by inefficient collection and by opportunities for evasion and delay. In the eyes of conservatives generally, the device had the advantage of preserving the entire ecclesiastical structure, which the Book of Discipline had proposed to subvert. To protestants the plan seemed likely to commit the crown, now rendered financially dependent on revenues taken from the church, to the maintenance of reform; and the compromise might heal those divisive tendencies in the ranks of the reformers which earlier discussions of finance had revealed. Politicians may have calculated that the danger of an over wealthy and independent reformed church had been averted. The ministers, assuming that their needs had a prior claim on the thirds, might congratulate themselves on an endowment in some ways more satisfactory than that envisaged in the Book of Discipline: thirds were to be uplifted from all ecclesiastical revenues, including the temporalities to which that book had made no claim; collection by crown officials might be more effective than attempts by the kirk to exact teinds and rents from parishioners and tenants; and the problem of devising machinery for the separation of teinds from rents and for recovering the teinds of appropriated churches for parochial uses was circumvented.

On the other hand, it was a grave weakness that nothing was done to determine the proportions in which the fund accruing from the assumption of thirds should be divided, and a struggle between the demands of the crown and the needs of the kirk was foreseen at the outset. Knox's anxiety was that the devil, who already had the two-thirds and part of the third, would ere long have the whole of the thirds. And, although his judgment was hard on the many adherents of the reformed church who were in possession of the two-thirds of their benefices, his forecast proved to be not unfounded. Yet there was something, too, in Maitland of Lethington's allegation that 'the ministers being sustained, the queen will not get at the year's end to buy her a pair of new shoes', because payment on the scale laid down in the Book of Discipline would have quite swallowed up the thirds, and the proposed stipends met the objection that 'many lords have not so much to spend'. But in practice the crown and the kirk were not the only parties concerned, because inroads were made on the amount available for distribution, through the remission of many thirds. While it was only justice to remit thirds when crops had suffered damage from nature or from man, and there could be no complaint about the general remission to the universities or perhaps even about that to the lords of session, a great many remissions were made to persons enjoying the queen's favour and to magnates so powerful that the exaction of their thirds must have been considered impracticable or impolitic. When thirds were not uplifted from rich prelacies like St Andrews priory, the abbeys of Holyrood, Coupar, Dryburgh and Cambuskenneth and the archbishopric of Glasgow, the total fund available for the crown and the kirk suffered heavy loss. These remissions, an evil in themselves, aggravated the difficulties caused by the further action of the crown in appropriating an excessive proportion of the thirds to its own needs.

At first there was fair play, or something like it. An analysis of the account for 1562 shows that if the expenses of administration, the uncollected arrears and the balance remaining unexpended are deducted, some £53,000 in money was available for distribution. Of this the reformed church received almost exactly a half, the crown less than a quarter, and others (by remissions and pensions) rather more than a quarter. If the remissions are disregarded, the reformed church's share can be put at nearly two-thirds. Besides money, there were considerable quantities of cereals and other crops, which were divided in similar proportions, except that remissions were somewhat heavier. In succeeding years, however, the demands of the crown increased. It was an unusual, almost a novel, experience for the Scottish government to have so much ready money at its disposal, and the funds of the 'collectory' of thirds were constantly raided for casual disbursements of every kind. There had been a substantial credit in 1561 and 1562, but in 1565, when the crown's share amounted to £32,000, there was a deficit of £16,000 and the ministers were said to be 'frustrate of their stipends'.[1]

As a result of the failure of the parliament of 1560 to settle polity

[1] See in general *Thirds of Benefices*, Intro.

and endowment, and the adoption subsequently of the compromise represented by the 'assumption of thirds', there were for several years two distinct ecclesiastical structures in Scotland. On one hand were the reformed congregations. Their doctrine and their services alone were officially recognised, and it may be said that they enjoyed a kind of establishment *quoad sacra*. On the other hand, the entire structure of the old regime, from the archbishopric at the top to the chaplainry at the foot, had not been subverted, but remained intact. It was a curious situation, which defies simple definition. The reformed church, though not in the full sense established, was certainly officially recognised; but equally the old structure was still established, in the sense that the law maintained it. Again, the reformed church's right to an undefined proportion of the thirds could hardly be called endowment; but the old structure was still endowed to the extent of two-thirds of its ancient revenues.

The important truth that 'the entire structure of the old regime remained intact' is one which has escaped the notice of the many writers on church history who are not familiar with official records. Anyone who looks, for example, at the Register of the Great Seal or the Register of the Privy Seal will find in their pages few traces of the reformed church as an institution before 1567. While there is plenty about those 'reverend fathers in God', the bishops of Scotland, and even about the archbishop of St Andrews as 'primate and legate', there is nothing about a general assembly, and while there is plenty about diocesan and cathedral dignitaries and about parsons and vicars, references to ministers, exhorters and readers are hard to find. This evidence in itself discloses the essential fact that the benefices remained in being, contrary to the proposals of the Book of Discipline, which had proposed to subvert the structure of the benefices by dissolving the prelacies, separating teinds from temporality and establishing a completely new financial system.

Not only did the old structure remain intact and endowed, with the bishops attending parliament and serving on the council and with all the clergy still granting charters and tacks of the revenues which were still legally theirs; to some extent the old structure continued to operate. Assuming that the legislation of 1560 was valid, the bishops had indeed been deprived of the powers which they derived from papal authority, but beyond that their rights were not expressly curtailed. They continued, if only intermittently, to exercise jurisdiction in matrimonial cases: Archbishop Hamilton issued a dispensation for marriage to the earl of Bothwell and Lady Jane Gordon in February 1565/6, but although this is the best known example of such a dispensation after 1560 it is not the only one, and in May 1563 we find the archbishop's commissioners pronouncing a sentence of divorce.[1] When Queen Mary thought fit, in December 1566, formally to 'restore' Archbishop Hamilton's consistorial jurisdiction,[2] protestants were indignant;[3] but it is not at all clear that the judicial powers of the bishops had ever wholly lapsed. And if the bishops had thus still some claim to consistorial jurisdiction, their functions in connection with the disposal of benefices were almost wholly unchallenged. The bishop's power to give collation had not been taken away by any legislative act, and the function was not assigned to the superintendents of the reformed church until 1567.[4] Between 1560 and 1567, therefore, while the crown showed a certain hesitation about making presentations and usually preferred to dispone benefices by simple gift, other patrons in general adhered to the traditional procedure of presentation followed by episcopal collation, and the bishops themselves continued to make provisions to the benefices which were in their own gift.[5] Official record described a presentee as having been 'lauchfullie providit be the ordinar bischop' and an archbishop as acting 'be his ordinare authority', and the crown, in making an appointment, took care that 'ane maist reverend fader in God, James, archebischop of Glasgow, collator ordinare, . . . in no wayis be prejugit and hurt of his rycht'.[6] Collation by a bishop remained the normal

---

[1] See G. Donaldson, 'The Church Courts', in *Introduction to Scottish Legal History* (Stair Soc.), pp. 366-7.
[2] *R.S.S.* v, 3145.
[3] Laing, II, 539-41 (Dickinson, II, 194-6).
[4] *A.P.S.* III, 23 c. 7.
[5] *R.S.S.* v, Intro. ix-xii and references given there. For other illustrations, see *Calendar of Laing Charters*, No. 727; *Protocol Book of Gilbert Grote* (S.R.S.), fos. 120, 121; *Yester Writs* (S.R.S.), No. 741; Reg. Ho. Charters, Nos. 1896, 1975; Protocol Book of Thomas Johnson (MS. in Reg. Ho.), No. 506; Sir William Fraser, *The Haddington Book*, II, 265-6.
[6] *R.S.S.* v, *loc. cit.*

method of obtaining admission to a benefice and was recognised as conferring an indisputable title.

The survival after 1560 of the ancient ecclesiastical structure is one feature, but only one, of the essential moderation of the Scottish reformation. Ever since the archbishop of Canterbury's orderly instincts were shocked by the proceedings of the Scots in 1559, and he exclaimed, 'God keep us from such a visitation as Knox hath attempted in Scotland, the people to be orderers of things,'[1] the Scottish reformation has been thought of as a sudden and tumultuous upheaval. But it was at once less precipitate and less radical than is often believed. From many points of view the year 1560, the conventional date of the Scottish reformation, is not very significant, and must have been much less definitive in the eyes of contemporaries than it has come to be in the text books. Many changes had already taken place before 1560; contemporaries might have been hard put to it to define exactly what changes, if any, had been legally and constitutionally made in 1560; and after 1560 offices and emoluments remained substantially in the hands of those who had enjoyed them before. In many respects the proceedings of the Scots were much less violent than those of the English. The Marian bishops in England were imprisoned, and ultra-protestants clamoured for their blood; but the Scottish bishops and dignitaries retained their revenues, or at least two-thirds of them, and sat on the council, in apparent amity, alongside supporters of the reformation. There was in Scotland in 1560 no act of supremacy, no act of uniformity, and a dozen years passed before there was any deprivation of clergy who declined to accept the reformation.[2] Not only so, but so many of them did not decline to accept it, and took office as ministers, exhorters and readers under the new regime, that personal continuity in the service of parishes was a very conspicuous feature in Scotland as well as in England. Again, there was in Scotland no dissolution of the monasteries. The abbots continued to draw their revenues as long as they lived; the monks continued to enjoy their portions and their quarters in the precincts after the reformation as before it; and the house remained a corporation for all legal purposes. Indeed, the year 1560 can have meant very little in the history of a Scottish monastic establishment, except that religious observances of the old type ceased, if they had continued so long, and recruitment came to an end.

The reformation was achieved in Scotland with surprisingly little dislocation of persons or institutions, and certainly with less bloodshed than was the English reformation. It is true that Scottish conservatives did put a handful of heretics to death, over a period of thirty years; it is true that Scottish protestants, on their side, did murder a cardinal and hang an archbishop—the latter, however, for purely political reasons; and it is true that there was a statute imposing the death penalty for saying mass, but not more than two, and very probably only one, priest, suffered that extreme punishment. There was in this country which has been described as 'backward'[1] none of that cold-blooded scaffold and faggot work which was so conspicuous in the England of Henry VIII, Mary and Elizabeth Tudor.

While the old structure survived and to some extent continued to operate, there had developed alongside it the new structure of the reformed church. In short, the duality which began to take shape with the emergence of protestant congregations before 1560, so far from coming to an end in that year, had only become more distinct. The new structure, consisting essentially of regional and local units and directed by a general assembly, did bear a rough resemblance to the scheme proposed in the Book of Discipline—in so far as comparison can be made with the somewhat amorphous church order there outlined—but a document which never received the statutory authority which alone could have put it fully into effect, and which Knox inserted in his *History* only to show 'what the worldlings rejected', must not be mistaken for a constitution which was ever in operation. Before it can be concluded that any proposal of the Book of Discipline was put into practice supporting evidence must be adduced from other sources. Each part of the organisation of the reformed church therefore requires examination.

[1] *Cambridge Modern History*, II, 550.

CHAPTER IV

WORD AND SACRAMENTS:
THE PARISH MINISTRY

BY 1560, Scots had for more than a generation been able to watch the course of the reformation in other lands, in Scotland itself they had heard reformation principles expounded by men who had learned them in England or on the Continent, and they had, many of them, come to their own conclusions as to the course which a Scottish reformation would have to take. Little that was novel was likely to emerge in Scotland. As the phase of theological instability among continental reformers was now all but at an end and opinions on both justification and on eucharistic doctrine had crystallised, it followed that theology was hardly in dispute among the Scottish reformers, 'and indeed theology is marvellously little in evidence in connection with the Scottish reformation'.[1] Liturgical principles, too, there had been ample time to work out, and both in that age and later the Scots showed little or no originality in devising their forms of worship, but readily accommodated themselves to the use of service-books composed in other countries. Nor can the Scottish reformation be said to have much significance even in the initiation of ideas on ecclesiastical polity; its interest lies in the adaptation to the peculiar circumstances of Scotland of ideas on polity which had by this time become the common property of all the reformers of western Europe.

The proposals for the reform of ecclesiastical polity with which the Scots were familiar in 1560 had not, in the main, been argued laboriously from scriptural texts; but proceeded rather from certain axioms which were assumed to be self-evident and which from their nature could hardly admit of dispute. The reformers did not in this particular appeal much to theory, still less to any great extent to theology, but they knew what was required of a church generally in the light of the scriptures and specifically in the light of

[1] G. D. Henderson, in *S.H.R.* xxix, 186.

the needs of their own day, and those requirements were their starting point.

The first of those axiomatic requirements was the preaching of 'the Word'. The need for preaching was realised on all sides, and conservative reformers as well as radicals had shared not only in explicit proposals for the increased provision of sermons[1] but also in the demand for more preaching which had been implied in the reiterated denunciation of non-preaching clergy as 'dumb dogs'.[2] The concomitant of the preaching of 'the Word' was the administration of the sacraments, and how firmly the idea had taken root in Scotland that the ceremonies and traditions of the church differed from the institution of Christ is shown by the repeated allusions even of lay writers to the distinction between them.[3] There was unanimity among the Scots, as among the reformers of western Europe generally, that the indispensable marks or notes of the visible church were the preaching of 'the Word' and the administration of the sacraments.[4]

But that was about as far as dogma extended. How those marks or notes were to find expression, how the essential requirements were to be fulfilled, were matters at the discretion of each church, and it was understood that practice could, and would, vary. No church as yet held up its polity as a model to others, and Calvin's advice that one church should not despise another because of a difference in 'external discipline'[5] was generally followed as long as he lived. The first reformers, unlike their successors of both the presbyterian and episcopalian persuasions, did not believe that they had discovered in the scriptures a polity fully defined and divinely appointed for all times and places. This became clear when English presbyterians began to advocate the adoption of what they

[1] Pp. 33–4 above; cf. *Gude and Godlie Ballates*, p. 170, and Lindsay, *Works*, II, 287.

[2] E.g. Robert Richardson, *op. cit.* p. 154; Winyet, *Certane tractatis*, pp. 8, 14; *Wodrow Soc. Misc.* I, 150; Lindsay, *Works*, I, 358. No doubt the phrase originated from the application of Isaiah, LVI, 10.

[3] E.g. Lindsay, *Works*, I, 51, 199, 275; *Gude and Godlie Ballates*, pp. 173, 176–7: cf. Winyet, *op. cit.* p. 5.

[4] E.g. Augsburg Confession, Art. VII; Article XIX of the Church of England; Calvin, *Institutes*, IV, 1, 9 (trans. Beveridge, III, 21).

[5] *Institutes*, IV, X, 32 (Beveridge, III, 225).

conceived to be the one and only permissible polity and were at first met not by a counter-assertion of the divine right of episcopacy, but by the argument that since there was not 'one certain and perfect kind of government prescribed or commanded in the scriptures' therefore a particular form of church order could not be indispensable.[1] The latitude allowed to each church in framing its polity to suit its circumstances is clearly implied in the first Book of Discipline: its sections on polity (unlike those on doctrine and worship) hardly ever refer to what is commanded in the Word of God, and refer to apostolic precedent only to repudiate it; instead, the appeal is to 'expediency'—'we judge it expedient', 'we have thought good', 'a thing most expedient', 'it is most expedient', 'this order we think expedient'. This was a practical, and not a doctrinaire, approach; the situation was one presenting practical problems, and the proposals of the reformers offered practical solutions.

If, in addition to the preaching of 'the Word' and the administration of the sacraments, there was a third 'mark' of the church, it was not the 'historic episcopate', or the 'apostolic succession', or 'parity of pastors' or any other characteristic of the ministry; it was 'discipline'. The cry for discipline is prominent in the writings of the continental reformers who had most influence in Britain and in those of English and Scottish divines of every school of thought, and Calvin's description of discipline as the 'sinews' of the church was repeated not only in the Scottish Book of Common Order but in the writings of the Elizabethan bishop of Salisbury, John Jewel.[2] Again, when the Scots Confession of 1560 elevated 'ecclesiastical discipline uprightly administered as God's word prescribes' to formal parity with word and sacraments as one of the 'notes by which the true kirk is discerned from the false',[3] it was only express-

---

[1] Whitgift, Works, I, 6, 184–5; III, 214; cf. p. 201 below.
[2] Calvin, Opera, XIII, 76; Laing, IV, 203; Jewel, Works, II, 986. Cf. John à Lasco, Opera (ed. Kuyper), II, 170 f.; Bucer, Scripta anglicana, pp. 40–5; Latimer, Sermons, p. 258; Strype, Memorials, II, I, 496, 590, II, II, 20–1, 481; Original Letters (Parker Soc.), I, 123; Pilkington, Works, pp. 211, 380–2; Hooper, Later Writings, p. 51. See also H. F. Woodhouse, The Doctrine of the Church in Anglican Theology, pp. 60–1, 107.
[3] Laing, II, 109–10 (Dickinson, II, 266).

ing an idea which was officially countenanced in England in Edward VI's reign and in the early years of Elizabeth's and which survived among the stoutest supporters of the Anglican establishment for two or three decades.[1] Yet there was no real agreement on the equality of discipline with word and sacraments: to Calvin, who pronounced that 'wherever the word of God is purely preached and heard and the sacraments administered according to the institution of Christ, there is a church of God',[2] discipline was clearly subordinate; and the Scottish Book of Discipline, while it advanced theological reasons for the conjunction of word and sacraments, justified discipline only by practical arguments similar to those advanced in favour of the office of superintendent,[3] and elsewhere it included among things 'utterly necessary' not only the true preaching of the word and the right administration of the sacraments, but also the requirements that there be 'common prayers publicly made, that the children and rude persons be instructed in the chief points of religion, and that offences be corrected and punished'.[4] In view of this evidence, the conclusion is inescapable that, while discipline was desirable, hardly anyone seriously believed it to be as important as word and sacraments.

However general the agreement on the need for discipline, there was room for some diversity in the machinery which was to apply it, and indeed the general flexibility of reformation thought on

[1] The second part of the homily for Whitsunday declared that the church 'hath always three notes or marks whereby it is known—pure and sound doctrine, the sacraments ministered according to Christ's holy institution, and the right use of ecclesiastical discipline'. Cf. *Liturgies of Edward VI*, p. 513; Becon, *Catechism*, p. 42; Cardwell, *Documentary Annals*, I, 232; Sermon by John Copcot in 1584 (Lambeth Palace MSS. vol. 374, fo. 122); *Tracts ascribed to Richard Bancroft* (ed. Peel), p. 95.

[2] *Institutes*, IV, I, 9 (Beveridge, III, 21).

[3] 'Neither can the church of God be brought to purity, neither yet be retained in the same, without the order of ecclesiastical discipline' (Laing, II, 227 [Dickinson, II, 306]); 'without the care of superintendents, neither can the kirks be suddenly erected, neither can they be retained in discipline and unity of doctrine' (*Reg. K. S. St A.* I, 75).

[4] Laing, II, 237–8 (Dickinson, II, 312). It may be observed that the Danish *Ordinatio ecclesiastica*, which the Book of Discipline resembles in other respects, brackets together the preaching of the gospel, the administration of the sacraments and the exposition of the catechism.

polity was especially marked in this particular. The theory generally current among the reformers was that 'wherever the magistrate is godly and Christian' (that is, in countries where the reformed church was, as we should say, established), there was no need of any authority other than the civil power to 'rule and punish the people', but that where the prince was not 'godly', discipline in this sense would be in the hands of a congregational consistory or eldership.[1] The existence of this assumption explains why resort was had to the election of elders not only in the 'privy kirks' which existed in Scotland before 1560, but also in the congregations of Anglicans exiled in Mary Tudor's reign. No one seems to have had any doubt that this was the proper proceeding in congregations which did not enjoy the countenance of the civil power. Even in an established church, however, it was not always easy to determine the relation between the church, desirous of the punishment of evildoers, and a civil power which would punish sin as crime, and the respective shares of church and state in the exercise of discipline presented something of a problem which was still unsolved in 1560. In Elizabethan England, although it was expected that the civil power would 'truly and indifferently minister justice, to the punishment of wickedness and vice', yet the 'primitive godly discipline' of which the Commination service spoke, whereby 'notorious sinners were put to open penance and punished in this world', was not unknown in practice.[2] When even the established Church of England had 'discipline' in this sense, it is hardly surprising that in Scotland the congregational consistory, or kirk session, originating in the 'privy kirks', was retained and fostered after 1560. The Scots did not deny that the magistrate had a duty to correct the vicious,[3] nor

---

[1] See p. 185 below.

[2] Strype, *Annals*, II, I, 134; Grindal, *Remains*, pp. 451–7. For illustrations of the proceedings of secular courts against immorality, see H.M.C., *Report*, IX, 156. A great deal of the matter in E. R. Brinkworth, *The Archdeacon's Court: Liber Actorum*, 1584 (Oxfordshire Record Soc.), is hardly distinguishable from the contents of a Scottish kirk session register.

[3] The first Book of Discipline indeed classified sins into those punishable by the state and those not so punishable, but in 1562 the general assembly petitioned for punishment by the state of fornication, which according to the Book of Discipline properly pertained to the church (Laing, II, 227, 339–40 [Dickinson, II, 49, 306]).

did they contend that the eldership was necessary in the different political circumstances obtaining in England, where—so it was officially acknowledged in a letter sent on behalf of the general assembly—'God of his providence and mercy' had erected the archbishops of Canterbury and York as 'principals in ecclesiastical jurisdiction'.[1]

The first and second marks of the church meant a strong emphasis on the work of the parish, where alone the word would be preached and the sacraments administered. The third mark, if 'discipline' was indeed such a mark, did not so clearly involve the parish, for discipline was to be applied at every level and its effective administration was not necessarily a function of a congregational organisation, but in Scotland the fostering of the kirk session as an instrument of discipline reinforced the emphasis on the parish. A reaction in favour of the secular clergy and the parish church was not, indeed, wholly a novelty, for signs of a movement away from the religious orders can be discerned earlier,[2] but several features in the reformation strengthened this trend. The movement was anti-monastic, because there were objections to the vows of the religious orders and criticism of the system of monastic services (and if the monks' prayers were worthless, the monasteries were mere 'nets to collect the goods of laymen').[3] The reformation was also critical of cathedrals and collegiate churches—monuments, as most of them were, to the neglect of the parishes, because the services in them contributed little towards bringing the gospel to the people, and their dignities and canonries were maintained mainly at the expense of the clergy serving the parishes. Again, while not hostile to the episcopal principle, the reformation was strongly critical of the wealthy and worldly prelates of the existing order.[4] Thus the reformers were antagonistic to all the parts of the ecclesiastical structure which had drained revenues from the parish churches.

In practice, it was congregational organisation which came first

---

[1] S. P. Scot. Eliz. IX, No. 9 (*Cal. S. P. Scot.* II, No. 54). One of the signatories of the letter was John Knox, whose earlier criticisms of the Church of England's lack of effective discipline (Laing, III, 85*-6*, v, 519–20; *Troubles at Frankfort*, pp. 55, 65) did not lead him to denounce its episcopal courts as invalid.

[2] P. 11 above.　　　[3] *Formulare*, II, 72.　　　[4] See chapter v.

in Scotland, because with the 'privy kirks' the new church system had started to develop at its lowest level. The proposals of the Book of Discipline likewise put their emphasis on the parish, to the extent that they are far more explicit about congregational organisation at the bottom than about any supreme organ of government at the top. And even as the reformed church emerged from obscurity to enjoy a measure of official countenance, its organisation was still only at parochial level, for months passed before a general assembly met or superintendents began to operate.

The form which public worship took in a Scottish parish was shaped by the current stress on word and sacraments and by the balance between the two. It was not the intention of the reformers to consign the sacraments to neglect or obscurity, or, in particular, to depose 'the Lord's service' from the central place in public worship on the Lord's day; indeed, they would have contended, with a good deal of justice, that it was their intention to restore, and not to displace, that sacrament—to restore it, that is, as a corporate action of communion in which all could and should join. But the sacrament was not to be separated from 'the Word', and this principle was interpreted to mean not only that a celebration of Holy Communion must be accompanied by a sermon, but also that no minister should be authorised to administer that sacrament unless he was qualified also to preach. However, if the one extreme of emphasis on the sacraments to the extent of relegating preaching to a secondary place was thus avoided, so equally there was avoided such an emphasis on 'the Word' that all else was to be subordinated to the sermon. The 'reading of common prayers', which was no less essential a part of public worship than 'the preaching of the Word' and 'the administration of the sacraments', was provided on occasions when there was no sermon and also as a preliminary part of a service which included a sermon; there was also the ordered reading of the scriptures and, of course, the singing of metrical psalms and canticles.

The ideal, which would have made a celebration of Holy Communion the central service every Sunday morning, proved to be impracticable, mainly because the medieval habit of infrequent Communion could not be eradicated and was irreconcilable with the reformation conception of that sacrament as a congregational, corporate action. The Communion service, far from being weekly, had to be no more than quarterly or half-yearly, though by selecting for its observance Sundays which were not festivals, and especially by avoiding Easter, the normality of the Communion was plainly demonstrated. In this situation, the core of ordinary Sunday morning worship was a service consisting mainly of a sermon followed by a long intercession, concluding with the Lord's Prayer and the Apostles' Creed—a service which represented the first part of the Communion service and which therefore corresponded to the English Ante-Communion, up to and including the Prayer for the Church. This core was preceded by a service consisting of a confession of sins, psalms and lections, a service which corresponded to the Mattins of the Prayer Book. Thus the old English tradition of Ante-Communion preceded by Mattins was exactly paralleled north of the Border. The very words might be the same, because the Book of Common Prayer was at first quite widely used in Scotland, but even when its words were displaced by those of the Book of Common Order the content of the services was still identical.[1]

The structure of the parish ministry was governed by those forms of worship. Ministers were those fully qualified to preach and to administer the sacraments. Exhorters were authorised to preach and could therefore conduct the whole of a normal Sunday morning service. And readers were permitted to read the 'common prayers' and to read homilies (from the English Book of Homilies). The intermediate office of exhorter, which was somewhat anomalous in a church laying equal emphasis on word and sacraments and which may never have been meant as anything more than a temporary expedient, disappeared in the early 1570s, and its disappearance is possibly to be associated with a change which at that point raised the status of readers. From the outset some readers had been nothing more than assistants in parishes which had ministers, and their principal function in Sunday worship was to conduct the preliminary service before the sermon, consisting of confession of

[1] See in general G. Donaldson, *The Making of the Scottish Prayer Book of 1637*, pp. 13–16.

sins, psalms and lessons (the equivalent of Mattins), so that this service came to be known as the 'reader's service'; but other readers, although they had pastoral responsibility for parishes which were without ministers, were at first censured when they ventured to do anything more than read the prayers, lessons and homilies.[1] In 1572, however, readers were authorised to administer the sacrament of baptism and to officiate at marriages,[2] and the duty of catechising children was also laid upon them.[3] Their office thus became curiously like that of the Anglican deacon; and, with the elimination of the exhorter, the Scottish reformed church had now, in its superintendents, ministers and readers, something very similar indeed to the 'threefold ministry' of bishop, priest and deacon.

If the administration of word and sacraments was thus in the hands of a professional ministry, all other functions in the church were committed to laymen. The Book of Discipline prescribed that each congregation was to have its elders for the exercise of discipline and its deacons as finance officers. It was an important distinction from the practice of the later, presbyterian system, that elders and deacons were at first elected annually, as the Book of Discipline had insisted.[4] There was no possibility of mistaking such annually elected elders for an order in the ministry, for they were manifestly lay officers and represent an element of lay control, an element of anti-clericalism. Just how powerful this element was is demonstrated by the remarkable proposal of the Book of Discipline that these purely lay officers should 'admonish' and 'correct' their minister and even (with the superintendent's consent) depose him.[5]

[1] E.g. *Reg. K. S. St A.*, I, 177 n. 179.
[2] *B.U.K.* I, 211 (Calderwood, III, 175). Whether readers regularly baptised it is hard to say. The general assembly in 1576 forbade readers to administer the sacraments unless they were also able to preach (*B.U.K.* I, 372), but this may have been merely a move in the attempt presently made, under presbyterian influence, to abolish the office of reader altogether. On the other hand, there is ample evidence of readers celebrating marriages (e.g. Perth kirk session register [MS. in local custody], 7 July 1578, 23 Mar. 1578/9, 2 Nov. 1601, 31 Jan. 1602).
[3] *Ecclesiastical Records of Aberdeen* (Spalding Club), p. 23.
[4] Laing, II, 234 (Dickinson, II, 310). The evidence for the continuance of the practice of annual election is to be found in the kirk session registers. Cf. p. 222 below.
[5] *Ibid.* 235 (Dickinson, II, 310).

In view of the obviously lay character of the eldership in this period, it would seem indisputable that the equation, sometimes made today, of bishop, priest and deacon with minister, elder and deacon, is much less appropriate than the equation, already suggested, of bishop, priest and deacon with superintendent, minister and reader.

Where the ministers, exhorters and readers were to come from in the first instance was one of the questions on which the Book of Discipline had not been realistic, and where they did in fact come from is a question which has not yet been adequately investigated by historians. Only the merest outline can be given of the process by which the staff of the reformed church was gradually expanded until, after two or three generations, the gospel could at last be 'truly and openly preached in every kirk and assembly of the realm', as the compilers of the Book of Discipline had optimistically urged in 1560.

The proposals made in 1560 to exclude the existing clergy from the ministry of the reformed church proved an idle threat, and in practice that ministry was largely recruited from the ranks of the dignitaries, prebendaries, parish priests, chaplains, canons regular, monks and friars. Over the whole country at least a quarter, and in some areas more than a half, of the parish clergy continued to serve under the new regime, usually ministering in the same church and to the same congregation as before, and when there are added to them the other clergy, secular and regular, beneficed and unbeneficed, who accepted office as ministers, exhorters and readers, it can be said with some confidence that well over 50 per cent of the staff of the reformed church was recruited from men who had been in orders before the reformation.[1] Where the remainder came from it is not easy to determine. It was remarked by a Jesuit observer in 1562 that the ministers were 'laymen of low rank, and are quite unlearned, being tailors, shoemakers, tanners or the like',[2] but he could hardly afford to sneer, because, while a very high proportion of the ex-priests and ex-monks were fit only to be readers, a good many of the men found capable of the full ministry have no known

---

[1] See 'The parish clergy and the reformation', in *Innes Review*, x.
[2] Pollen, *op. cit.* p. 135.

antecedents in ecclesiastical records, and if they had indeed been tailors, shoemakers or tanners they must have been fairly well educated, albeit possibly self-educated, men. Perhaps this Jesuit visitor was inclined to generalise about the humble origins of the ministers because of some well-known instances, like William Harlaw, a tailor, who was thought suitable to become minister of St Cuthbert's at Edinburgh. Paul Methven, again, is said to have been a baker; but after being minister of Jedburgh he served in the Church of England, became a prebendary of Wells, and was the ancestor of the noble family of Methuen—a somewhat remarkable career for a baker.[1] No doubt godliness was a more important consideration than academic attainments, but it must be observed that there were already some professional men who were non-clerical, or at least non-priestly, and examples can be found of their admission to the ministry. For instance, Mr Alexander Allardyce, who became minister of Kirkcudbright, was presumably a Master of Arts; he has not been found among the pre-reformation clergy, but he does appear in 1561 as a 'servitor' of Bishop Alexander Gordon,[2] and it may be that the bishop had employed him in some administrative or secretarial capacity before he decided to admit him to the ministry. Again, Francis Hume, who became reader at Dalry in Galloway, had appeared as a witness to a tack by Bishop Gordon in 1559,[3] and is unlikely to have been a tradesman. A clearer case is that of William Lauder: he was a Master of Arts, and a notary by apostolic authority, but not a priest, and is found authenticating or witnessing various deeds in Orkney, usually in association with Bishop Adam Bothwell, before the bishop made him minister of Yell and Fetlar in Shetland.[4] A man of this type would have an education far superior to that of the majority of the pre-reformation parish priests, and consequently would be more fitted for

[1] Harlaw had served in the Church of England under Edward, and Methuen had received some education from Miles Coverdale, so neither came to the Scottish ministry directly from his trade.
[2] Protocol Book of Nicol Thounis (S.R.S.), No. 46.
[3] Reg. Ho. Calendar of Charters, No. 1773.
[4] E.g. Records of the Earldom of Orkney (S.H.S.), pp. 263, 270, 343–4. Lauder subsequently acted as the bishop's chamberlain for Shetland (Protocol Book of Gilbert Grote [S.R.S.]).

admission to the full ministry of word and sacraments. The teaching profession was another source of reformed clergy: examples are Andrew Simson, master of the grammar school of Perth and minister of Dunbar, Thomas MacGibbon, master of the grammar school of Dundee and minister of Moneydie, and George Cochrane, master of the song school at Ayr and reader at St Quivox.

However variable the quality of the recruits for the reformed ministry may have been, the numbers were found with quite remarkable rapidity. In Perthshire, for instance, there were by 1567-8 at least twenty-one ministers, fifteen exhorters and forty-two readers at work—seventy-eight in all, a figure which, although by no means satisfactory for one hundred parishes, was not hopelessly inadequate. It is at this point—1567-8—that we first have lists of the reformed clergy in the area, yet we are not completely in the dark as to the position at a much earlier point, for in 1561 and 1562, although we do not have the names of the men who were serving, we do know the total sums expended on stipends. Now, the Perthshire total for 1562 was £2,621 6s. 8d., which is only £70 less than that for 1569 (£2,691 16s. 11d.), and it is a reasonable deduction that the staff of the reformed church was already practically the same by 1562 as it was to be six years later.[1] Even for 1561, we find that the figure was £2,036 3s. 4d. This is £600 less than the figure for 1562—nearly 20 per cent less—but even so it would seem that in the first year when the reformed church was organised there may already have been over fifty ministers, exhorters and readers at work in Perthshire. Similar calculations for the diocese of Galloway suggest that in 1561 there were already some thirty ministers, exhorters and readers at work in the forty-five parishes, and in 1563 there were nearly forty.[2] In the diocese of Orkney, there were in 1563 at least seven, possibly nine, ministers and at least fourteen readers, and in 1567 there was a total of about thirty, for thirty-six parishes. Galloway and Orkney were remote areas, and Perthshire

---

[1] It is true that in 1569, owing to financial stringency, many men were not receiving the full stipends to which they were entitled, but in this area the deficiency was usually small, and the inference drawn from the comparative figures is hardly vitiated.

[2] *Dumfries and Galloway Nat. Hist. and Antiq. Soc. Trans.* 3rd ser. xxx, 48–9.

included tracts of wild and mountainous country, but a district like East Lothian does not show a higher ratio of clergy to parishes—only some twenty clergy for twenty-five parishes in 1567—although the clergy there included a significantly higher proportion of ministers (thirteen of them). When we recall the prevalence of pluralism and non-residence in the unreformed church, and when we keep in mind that at any given moment there is bound to be a certain number of vacancies, it is possible to say with some confidence that within a very few years the reformed church had given the parishes of Scotland a more adequate ministry than they had had for generations.

If an examination of various areas were to reveal significant differences in the progress towards the attainment of an adequate ministry, it might be possible to discover what factors determined the pattern. It is obvious that the main credit for the development and extension of the reformed ministry must lie with the superintendents and bishops, who were responsible for the examination and admission of all those ministers, exhorters and readers. There is, however, no reason to believe that Bishops Gordon and Bothwell, in Galloway and Orkney, enjoyed pre-eminent success, or even, as the figures would suggest, that their labours were slightly more fruitful than those of Superintendent Winram in Perthshire—though it may be observed that they had the advantage over him of having much smaller areas to administer. It would seem just as likely that any variation between districts may have arisen from the degree of support given by influential laymen. In areas like Angus, Fife and Ayrshire there must have been many lords and lairds who were prepared to give their influence and support to the reformed ministry from the outset. In Galloway, too, Bishop Gordon's task must have been facilitated by landed families who lost no time in attaching themselves to the reformed cause, for Sir Alexander Stewart of Garlies and Sir John Gordon of Lochinvar were among those who signed the Book of Discipline in January 1561. Even in the heart of Perthshire, again, Colin Campbell of Glenorchy undertook in May 1561 to pay a stipend for a minister at Kenmore,[1] and such action is unlikely to have been unique.

[1] William A. Gillies, *In Famed Breadalbane*, pp. 261–3.

For information about the expansion of the reformed ministry throughout the country it is customary to rely on the *Fasti ecclesiae Scoticanae*, and (provided that recourse is had to the important supplementary material in volume VIII) that work is adequate to show the general picture. There is, however, one important qualification: the principal sources for the study of ecclesiastical personnel in that period—the Accounts of the Collectors of Thirds, the Register of Ministers, Exhorters and Readers and the Register of Assignations and Modifications of Stipends—are records which arose from a financial system which did not extend to the dioceses of Argyll and the Isles. Taken in conjunction with the general paucity of material for West Highland history, this has resulted in an apparent dearth of reformed clergy in large tracts of the country until after 1600. But this apparent absence of effort by the reformed church may be an illusion arising from the exclusion of the west from the organisation which produced the records on which we principally rely for our knowledge of the early reformed clergy elsewhere.[1] It must be abundantly plain that in central Argyll, the area dominated by the Campbell earls, the work of the reformed church had the fullest secular support from the outset: both the fourth earl and his son (who succeeded in 1558) signed the 'First Band' of the reforming lords in 1557, and, by a conjunction fortunate for the reformers, the influence of the earls was associated with the work of John Carswell, to whom they were patrons. Carswell's primary sphere of work was no doubt in central Argyll, but as superintendent of Argyll and, later, bishop of the Isles, he may have organised reformed congregations in many areas.[2] It was understood that he should provide stipends for ministers out of the revenues of the bishopric and the abbey of Iona,[3] and it is of course most creditable to him that he translated the Book of Common Order into Gaelic. The foundations had already been laid when, in 1574, the sixth earl of Argyll was reported to have planted ministers and appointed stipends throughout Lorne, central Argyll and Cowal and to have insisted on the use of Carswell's translation in public worship.[4]

---

[1] Cf. pp. 25–6 above for the general state of the Highlands.
[2] He gave collation to parsonages in Harris and Skye (*R.S.S.* v, 3246).
[3] J. B. Craven, *Records of Argyll and the Isles*, p. 10.   [4] *Cal. S. P. Scot.* v, p. 34.

While the conditions which affected the relative strength of the reformed ministry in different areas were complex, its expansion generally throughout the country was determined mainly by financial circumstances, which in turn depended on politics. The Book of Discipline had proposed the recovery of parochial revenues for parochial purposes: offerings were abolished, but all teinds were to be available for the work of the parishes. The exacting of teinds, it had long been recognised, raised many problems if the farmers were to have fair play, and the Book of Discipline, which insisted in any event that teinds should be 'reasonably taken', had returned to a proposal made a generation earlier by King James V, that 'every man should have his own teinds'.[1] The tacksman, whose function it had been to collect the teinds and pay to the church a fixed annual sum, was condemned as a middleman, and the farmer was to retain his whole crops but to pay to treasurers acting on behalf of the reformed church a composition for his teinds—'that which justly shall be appointed unto him'.[2] No details are given as to how such compositions were to be adjusted or how this system was to operate in practice. It was, however, envisaged that not only compositions for teinds, but also other church revenues raised locally, like the rents of friaries, chaplainries and collegiate churches, were to be pooled in the hands of local treasurers and made available for godly uses, including education and poor relief.[3] But the principal purpose for which those revenues were to be used was, of course, the payment of ministers, exhorters and readers, for whom stipends were appointed on a very generous scale. All these proposals were part of the unrealised 'devout imagination', and did not get beyond paper at the time.

Instead of entering upon the enjoyment of the teinds or compositions therefor, the reformed church had to be content with an undetermined proportion of the fund derived from the thirds of benefices. This fund could at the best provide stipends only on a much lower scale than the Book of Discipline had proposed, little or nothing could be taken from it for other godly uses like education and poor relief, and there was no provision for the increased

---

[1] *State Papers of Henry VIII*, IV, 667.   [2] Laing, II, 222 (Dickinson, II, 303).
[3] *Ibid.* 224–5 (Dickinson, II, 303–4).

finance which would be necessary as the reformed ministry expanded. The position was not, indeed, by any means unsatisfactory at first, for in 1561 and 1562 the thirds were not exhausted by the demands upon them, and there was thus no great financial obstacle to the rapid initial development of the ministry between 1560 and 1563, which the figures already given have indicated. But the prospect for the future was not promising, and the situation deteriorated owing to the mismanagement of the thirds between 1564 and 1567, to the extent that some men found it impossible to continue in the ministry. Even had the numbers of ministers, exhorters and readers who were at work in 1567 been no higher than the numbers in 1562, it would still have been a creditable achievement, and the evidence is that there was actually a slight expansion even in this difficult period, though it was achieved only at the cost of a reduction in the stipends paid.

In 1567, with Mary's deposition and the improvement in the political position of the reformed church, it was provided that the church should have the prior claim on the thirds, which were in future to be gathered in by collectors appointed by the general assembly. Now there were indeed 'church treasurers' receiving revenues on behalf of the church, very much as the Book of Discipline had proposed (though they operated on a regional and not on a parochial basis), but the experiment was a failure. The church's collectors apparently lacked the authority to make their work effective, and the government to which they looked for support had only partial control over the country in a time of tumult and civil war. By 1569 it was complained that the collectors were universally disobeyed; officers and messengers were roughly handled when they attempted to enforce payment; and the contempt with which processes for non-payment were regarded became notorious. Attempts were made to strengthen the machinery by giving powers to superintendents and bishops, but they do not seem to have brought about much improvement. Some districts fared better than others, but there were many instances where a minister was receiving only a half or less of the stipend to which he was entitled.[1] It is not surprising that the modest development of

[1] *Thirds of Benefices*, pp. xxx–xxxiii.

the reformed ministry from about 1563 to 1567 was followed by something like a standstill between 1567 and 1573.

In 1573, as the civil war against Mary's adherents drew to a close, the strong and statesmanlike administration of the earl of Morton brought about a reorganisation of ecclesiastical finance. The chaos inherited from preceding years was reduced to order and the crown resumed the collection of thirds. Particulars were elicited of many revenues previously concealed, and a list of 'new enterit benefices' made its appearance in the collector general's account for 1573.[1] A fresh survey of parishes and ministers was made, and it was arranged that bishops and superintendents, in collaboration with representatives of the council, should assign to each minister or reader a stipend 'taken of the first and readiest duties of the kirks and parishes where they serve'.[2] Such local assignations had been craved in the past, and if they became effective would result in a great simplification. These new financial arrangements were accompanied by an attempt to bring about a more efficient distribution of clergy and some reorganisation of parish divisions. Such an idea was not new, for the assembly of June 1563 had petitioned for the union of churches where two or three were in close proximity.[3] Moreover, it had already been the practice for a minister to take the responsibility for two or three adjacent parishes which were served by readers, but this arrangement now took on a more formal complexion, for the assembly provided that 'till God of his mercy shall thrust out more labourers unto his harvest' one minister should be placed over three or four kirks, with readers to assist him,[4] in very much the same way as a twentieth-century minister may have the oversight of two or three parishes served by 'lay missionaries'. The familiar statement that the Regent Morton combined parishes in order to be able to pocket surplus stipends would appear to be a libel, for he really deserves credit for a great improvement in the payment of stipends. That the complete overhaul of financial administration carried out in 1573–4 was the beginning of a better era for the church cannot be doubted by anyone who compares that slim, ill-written and untidily kept volume, the

---

[1] *S.H.R.* xxxii, 93.   [2] *B.U.K.* i, 277–80; *R.P.C.* ii, 261–4.
[3] *B.U.K.* i, 33 (Calderwood, ii, 227).   [4] *Ibid.* 296 (Calderwood, iii, 309).

'Register of ministers, exhorters and readers and their stipends', which extends from 1567 to 1573, with the orderly series of substantial folios, constituting the 'Register of assignations and modifications of stipends', which begins with the year 1574.[1] Financial reorganisation was only one of many developments which at this time affected the reformed church and strengthened its constitutional position,[2] and the brighter prospects of a 'new deal' were at once reflected in a marked expansion of the numbers of reformed clergy in certain areas.[3]

Ever since 1567, men serving in the reformed church had been entitled to succeed to benefices on their vacancy,[4] and as the years passed benefice after benefice was filled by a minister or a reader. To that extent there was a financial improvement, but the average vicarage was not in itself adequate as a stipend—even less adequate now than it had been before 1560, for the value of money continued to fall. Supplementary income came from revenues formerly belonging to friaries, from chaplainries and from prebends, all of which were sometimes granted to ministers, as well as from the thirds which were still exacted from benefices held by men not serving in the reformed church. Substantial improvement, however, could not come until the teinds appropriated to the religious houses were systematically made available for stipends; as things were, they could be tapped only by way of the thirds,[5] but towards the end of the century there were several instances of the separation of a parsonage from an institution to which it had been appropriated, and its allocation to a minister.[6] By the 1590s, the usual picture has come to be of a minister maintained by a bunch of revenues drawn from diverse sources: he would have a vicarage in his parish,

[1] The volume for 1574 is in the National Library of Scotland (MS. 17.1.4), the succeeding volumes are in the Register House.
[2] Pp. 171, 175–6 below.
[3] The parishes of East Lothian now had twelve ministers and twenty readers, and the total for Galloway rose to about fifty. In Orkney the 1567 figures were practically unchanged.
[4] Pp. 152–3 below.
[5] E.g. in 1587–9 there were eleven gifts of money or victual from the third of Arbroath, towards stipends.
[6] E.g. eight parsonages were disjoined from Kilwinning abbey in 1591 (R.S.S. LXII, 146–7).

he might have the parsonage if it had been extricated from the appropriating institution, he might have a chaplainry or a prebend of a collegiate church, he would have an allotment from the thirds and perhaps a pension from some other source. Thus John Hepburn, who was minister at Brechin, Kilmoir, Cookston and Buttergill, had a stipend derived from the treasurership of Brechin, the parsonage and vicarage of Cookston, the parsonage of Buttergill, the parsonage of Navar, a chaplainry in Finavon, the subdeanery of Brechin, the bishopric of Brechin and the abbey of Arbroath;[1] and Cuthbert Boncle, minister of Spott, had a stipend made up from the parsonage of Spott, the prebend of Belton (in the collegiate church of Dunbar), the archpresbytery of Dunbar and the archbishopric of St Andrews.[2] This was a cumbrous, makeshift arrangement, which must have caused considerable difficulty and much litigation.

In this situation, the rate of growth of the ministry could hardly be spectacular. The conspicuous improvement noted in 1574 was not maintained, there may here and there have actually been some retrogression, and at the best progress continued to be slow. It was something of a confession of failure that when the presbyterians were in the ascendant for the first time in 1581 they planned to reduce the number of parishes in the country from an estimated nine hundred to six hundred—and at the same time proposed, in their doctrinaire way, to deprive the ministers of the assistance of readers.[3] After another fifteen years the general assembly stated that, leaving aside the dioceses of Argyll and the Isles, there were four hundred churches 'destitute of the ministry of the word'.[4] This, if strictly accurate, would mean that the number of ministers cannot yet have exceeded five hundred and that only some two hundred additional ministers had been found in a quarter of a century; the four hundred parishes without the 'ministry of the word' were, of course, served by readers, whose office the presbyterians had not succeeded in abolishing.

---

[1] R.S.S. LVI, 146. This was a less miscellaneous assortment than it seems, for the subdeanery of Brechin was founded on the parsonage and vicarage of Cookston.
[2] *Ibid.* fo. 152.   [3] Calderwood, III, 520, 526.
[4] *B.U.K.* III, 876 (Calderwood, V, 416).

In the course of time, through a series of developments which it is impossible to trace here, the financial situation improved. The church had never ceased to press its claim to the teinds as its proper patrimony, and this claim, never formally denied, received practical acknowledgment in the commissions for plantation of kirks appointed by King James in 1617 and 1621, and, more comprehensively, in the settlement of the church property by Charles I. By Charles's settlement the abbey lands remained substantially with the nobles in whose favour the abbey properties had by that time been 'erected' into temporal lordships—as the first Book of Discipline had tacitly conceded they should remain; but all teinds were at the same time at last made available for the purposes of the reformed church—as the first Book of Discipline had proposed. The arrangements made in Charles's reign, arrangements which permitted every man to have his own teinds, secure against the appropriation of a tenth of his actual produce, but which permitted him to pay a composition in lieu thereof, were nothing else than the device which the first Book of Discipline had envisaged.

The financial improvement in the later years of James VI's reign, and in Charles I's, was accompanied by the completion of the extension of the parish ministry. From about 1620 almost every parish, even in the most remote parts of the country, had its minister. As the ministry expanded, the need for readers to serve parishes had diminished, but readers long continued as assistants to ministers. The kirk sessions developed with the ministry, and it seems safe to accept that their discipline was in operation everywhere by 1620 or so.[1] It would seem, therefore, that the reformers' requirements of the preaching of the word, the administration of the sacraments and the exercise of discipline, under a fully qualified ministry, were attained generally throughout the country in the first two decades of the seventeenth century. On the history of education in this period much work remains to be done, but on the whole the indications are that in this field, too, great progress was made. Certainly the first legislative support for the Book of Discipline's design of a school in every parish came with an act of council in 1616 and an act of parliament in 1633, and it is plain that

[1] See pp. 222, 225 below.

in certain parts of the country—though by no means in all—the number of parish schools was by this time very high.

If money and men had to be found to provide for the preaching of the word and the administration of the sacraments, it was equally necessary to ensure that there should be premises where those functions could be performed. Few features of the reformers' policy have been the subject of such widespread misunderstanding as their attitude to church buildings. In spite of repeated, detailed and expert contradiction, the idea still prevails that Scottish medieval churches were generally destroyed at the reformation—prevails to an extent hard to credit in anyone who has used his eyes in looking around him at the churches which survive today, but harder to credit in anyone with the slightest knowledge of history. It has already been explained that many churches were in a bad state before 1560; it must further be observed that a good many buildings did not fall into ruin until long after 1560—the nave of Holyrood, for example, was entire until after the middle of the eighteenth century, when a new roof proved too much for the old piers; and in Aberdeen and Elgin cathedrals the catastrophe was the fall of the central tower, at Aberdeen in 1688 and at Elgin in 1711. Nor did destruction by the 'auld enemy of England' end with the reformation, for most of the best hewn stone for building the Cromwellian fort at Inverness was taken from the cathedral of Fortrose, the abbey of Kinloss and the priory of Beauly. If we take into account the Scottish abbeys and cathedrals partially ruined before 1560, those not ruined until considerably after 1560, and those still standing today, it becomes at once apparent that the number reduced to ruin in 1560 cannot have been considerable.

The misunderstanding—as distinct from deliberate misrepresentation—of the reformers' actions with regard to the buildings is very largely a mere matter of idiom, hinging on the meaning of the phrase 'cast doun'. The suggestion has been made that 'cast doun' meant only 'the destruction of much of the internal decoration and furniture',[1] but it is just as likely that the phrase was used in the same metaphorical sense as we use 'overthrow', and did not mean physical destruction of the fabric; it was not unlike the 'suppress' of the

[1] Marquis of Bute, *Essays on Home Subjects*, p. 260.

Book of Discipline. Lesley, for instance, says that 'Trinitie College and all the prebendaris houssis thairof' were 'cassin doune',[1] but the truth is that Trinity College church remained entire until the middle of the nineteenth century, when it was 'cassin doune' by the North British Railway Company. Again, according to Pitscottie, the abbey of Dunfermline was 'caist doune';[2] but the nave still stands today and a good deal of the remainder seems to have been standing until the great tower fell in 1753. Another example is the collegiate church of Restalrig; the general assembly ordered it to be 'utterlie castin downe and destroyed',[3] but the walls of the choir—and it has yet to be proved that there ever was a nave—in part endured, and, repaired and reroofed, form a church which is still in use today. The grossest exaggeration about what happened started at the time, for the English bishop, Jewel, wrote on 1 August 1559 that 'all the monasteries are everywhere levelled to the ground'.[4] Perhaps at even that early date people were misled by the words 'cast doun'.[5]

The precise fate of a cathedral depended to some extent on whether or not it was necessary as a parish church. Where there was no centre of population around the cathedral and neither the need nor the resources for the maintenance of the whole building—as happened at Iona and Lismore and to a lesser degree at Dunkeld and Dunblane—or where the population was served by an adequate parish church, as at St Andrews, the cathedral was wholly or partly neglected from the outset. But where the cathedral was necessary for worship and there was a population with resources to maintain it, the cathedral was preserved; the conspicuous examples are Glasgow and Kirkwall. The observance of the distinction is implied in the Book of Discipline,[6] and it can be traced in official record: on the one hand, the general assembly, in 1573, took into consideration the 'sustaining and upholding of cathedral kirks which are parish kirks' and ordained that 'the same must be done as it was

---

[1] Lesley, *History*, p. 275.
[2] Pitscottie, *Historie and Cronicles of Scotland* (Scot. Text. Soc.), II, 168.
[3] *B.U.K.* I, 5 (Calderwood, II, 46).   [4] Jewel, *Works*, IV, 1215.
[5] For the whole subject, see the exhaustive study in Hay Fleming, *Reformation in Scotland*, chapters X and XI. Reference may also be made to John Jamieson, *Bell the cat, or who destroyed the Scottish abbeys?*
[6] Laing, II, 188 (Dickinson, II, 283).

wont to be before';[1] on the other hand, the lead roof of the cathedral of Fortrose was given to Lord Ruthven in 1572 on the ground —an incorrect one, as it happened, for this cathedral had been a secular foundation before the reformation and was used for reformed worship after it—that this cathedral was 'na paroch kirk bot ane monasterie to sustene ydill belleis'.[2] Financial exigencies apparently led to the removal of the lead, or some of it, from Elgin, Aberdeen and Glasgow, as well as Fortrose, but it was not intended that this should be followed by the abandonment of the buildings. Certainly, little time was lost in taking measures to preserve and maintain some of the cathedrals. A sum could even be voted from the hard-pressed thirds for the repair of the cathedral of Brechin in 1569;[3] in the same year the bishop and canons of Moray agreed to contribute towards the repair of Elgin cathedral so that it could be used for reformed worship;[4] and in 1571 the general assembly instructed certain commissioners to deal with the government 'for preservation and upholding' of the cathedral of Glasgow.[5] Very much the same principle applied to abbey churches as applied to cathedrals, for the naves of many abbey churches had been parish churches before the reformation and were preserved as parish churches after it.[6] Even the friaries in burghs, which suffered most in 1559 and 1560, were not by any means all destroyed, for some of their churches were subsequently put to use as parish churches. In short, the attitude of the reformers to the buildings was shaped by purely functional considerations. It had not yet occurred to anyone to preserve cathedrals or abbeys as museum pieces or for the benefit of sightseers, and no doubt there would have been far more deliberate destruction of buildings considered redundant if the reformers had had the means of demolition and a use for the materials of the fabric. As it was, once a building was no longer being maintained, the weather was the principal agent of disintegration, and, especially if there was a centre of population nearby, the walls served as a quarry for building stone. These factors applied elsewhere, and

[1] *B.U.K.* I, 280 (Calderwood, III, 297).   [2] R.S.S. XI, 106.
[3] *Thirds of Benefices*, p. 230.   [4] *R.P.C.* I, 677.
[5] *B.U.K.* I, 189 (Calderwood, III, 41).
[6] E.g. *R.P.C.* II, 431–2 (Jedburgh).

Scotland has no monopoly of ruined abbeys. On the destruction of church furnishings and ornaments and the incidental damage to the fabric, the last word by way of moral judgment was said by Hay Fleming: 'Even at the worst, the burning of images and the smashing of altars were very innocent amusements compared with the burning of heretics.'[1]

The suggestion that the reformers, as a matter of deliberate policy, destroyed parish churches, or had any desire to destroy parish churches, must be met by ridicule. They inherited the results of perhaps a generation of neglect, dilapidation and destruction, and their concern was not the demolition but the repair of churches required for parochial purposes. The first Book of Discipline excepted from the foundations which were to be 'suppressed' those which were 'presently parish churches or schools',[2] and it laid down that 'the churches and places where the people ought publicly to convene be with expedition repaired in doors, windows, thatch'.[3] Similar legislation had indeed been passed by the last of the old provincial councils, in the previous year,[4] but there are indications that something was achieved by the reformed church through persistent pressure. Apparently there had been an act of council on the subject before Mary returned from France, and in 1562 the general assembly petitioned the queen for action.[5] Then, in 1563, not only the assembly, but also the privy council and the parliament, legislated for the repair of churches.[6] Proceedings could be, and were, taken, at the expense of the reformed church, to compel those responsible to undertake the repair of churches, and in 1568 we find a number of persons 'at the horn' for not repairing the kirk of Alford 'conform to the extent and modification made thereanent'.[7] This shows that there were already assessments for this purpose, but parishioners were reluctant to tax themselves and there was not always a deacon or 'kirkmaister' to administer funds when they were raised, wherefore in 1573 the bishops and superintendents

[1] Hay Fleming, op. cit. p. 315.   [2] Laing, II, 188 (Dickinson, II, 283).
[3] Laing, II, 252 (Dickinson, II, 320–1).   [4] P. 23 above.
[5] B.U.K. I, 23 (Calderwood, II, 191).
[6] Ibid. 34 (Calderwood, II, 226); R.P.C. I, 246–7; A.P.S. II, 539 c. 12.
[7] Thirds of Benefices, p. 249; R.S.S. VI, 369.

were empowered to nominate persons in each parish for setting a taxation and receiving it, and there is evidence that such taxations were effectively imposed.[1] There are, indeed, plenty of references to the unsatisfactory condition of churches, after 1560 as before it, if only because parsimony and negligence were not extinguished by the reformation, and it is true that in the upheaval of 1559–60, when church property of every kind was regarded as fair game, some parish churches were robbed of timber, stone and other building material; but it would be flying in the face of all the evidence to suggest that such deliberate damage to the fabric of parish churches as did take place was any part of the official policy of the reformers.

The Scots have by temperament less veneration for antiquities than the English, and were always more ready—often far too ready —to tear down and replace an old building when it seemed outmoded. But even so, in very many parishes, perhaps in most, the pre-reformation church, repaired and altered, remained in use until its replacement became necessary with the great expansion of the population in the late eighteenth century and the nineteenth, and the number still in use in the twentieth century is not inconsiderable. Hardly any new churches at all were built until after the end of the sixteenth century,[2] but the early seventeenth century, the period which saw the completion of the expansion of the parish ministry and the nation-wide extension of kirk session discipline, was also a period of church building, and several Scottish churches date from that time. The later years of James VI and the early years of Charles I likewise saw a renewed solicitude for the cathedrals, nearly all of which received repair and embellishment in that period.[3]

The first generation of the reformers did not see their hopes realised, but, in spite of the abandonment of the first Book of Discipline in the 1560s,[4] and in spite of its supersession within a few years by a second Book of Discipline of a different character,

---

[1] *A.P.S.* III, 76*c. 15; *R.S.S.* VI, 2503, VII, 2007.
[2] But see *Cal. S. P. Scot.* XI, 621.
[3] For a summary, see *Proc. Soc. Antiq. Scot.* LXXXV, 125–31.
[4] See chapter VII.

practically everything that the first book had proposed was achieved in the early seventeenth century, under the episcopalian regime of the later years of James VI and the early years of Charles I. When the entire developments in the parishes are reviewed, it emerges as one of the curiosities of Scottish history that so much of the 'devout imagination' of John Knox was achieved by King Charles I.

CHAPTER V

THE 'GODLY BISHOP'
AND THE SUPERINTENDENT

THE reformers' proposals for organisation at parochial level, primary though they were, were not in themselves enough to ensure that the word would be preached, the sacraments duly administered and discipline exercised. Inadequate supervision of clergy and churches had been one of the weaknesses of the late medieval system, and if there was to be discipline among the clergy it was to be provided by an overhaul of the system of oversight of the parishes.

The reformers had no use for the defective episcopate with which they were so familiar. Bishops who lived in idle luxury or who passed their lives largely in the service of the government were 'dumb dogs' and 'idle bellies',[1] pseudo-bishops falsely claiming to be pastors but caring little for their sheep and neglecting their traditional duties of preaching, visitation and charity. In Scotland in the 1530s it had been said that 'it behoved a bishop to be a preacher, or else he was but a dumb dog, and fed not the flock, but fed his own belly',[2] and in 1547 Scottish reformers were debating the article that 'there are no bishops except they preach even by themselves, without any substitute'.[3] In England, Latimer contrasted the duty of preaching with the love of idleness and pomp: 'Sence lording and loytring have come up, preaching hath come down, contrary to the Apostells times. For they preached and lorded not. And now they lorde and preache not'.[4] And a Scottish reformer likewise contrasted idleness and pomp with the duties generally incumbent on a bishop: 'They whom ye call bishops do

---

[1] Laing, I, 239, 407, 432 (Dickinson, I, 115, 225, 243); III, 247.
[2] *Ibid.* I, 46 (Dickinson, I, 20).
[3] *Ibid.* 194 (Dickinson, I, 87). Bishops had frequently commissioned friars to preach on their behalf (*Formulare*, I, No. 273; Lindsay, *Works*, I, 139, 276, 332; II, 89, 313).
[4] Latimer, *Sermons*, p. 66.

no bishops' works, nor use the office of bishops . . . but live after their own sensual pleasure and take no care of the flock, nor regard they the word of God, but desire to be honoured and called, my Lords.'[1]

The contention was not merely that the wealth of the prelates, their neglect of their spiritual functions and their preoccupation with temporal affairs were abuses which needed reform; more than that, the test to determine whether a man was or was not a bishop lay in his faith and his works. And when such a test was applied, it emerged that the existing bishops were false, and not true, bishops. When Friar Seton remarked that 'within Scotland there was no true bishop, if that bishops should be known by such notes and marks as St Paul requires in bishops',[2] he was expressing ideas which were becoming a commonplace, for the essential thoughts on the distinction between false and true bishops appeared in *The descrypcyon of the images of a verye Chrysten bysshop and of a counterfayte bysshop*, attributed to Luther and published about 1536, and in Bullinger's *De episcoporum institutione et functione*, dedicated to Henry VIII in 1538. To differentiate generally between those who were bishops in name and those who were bishops in deed can hardly have been a novelty,[3] but a fresh pungency and precision now emerged, with Knox, for example, denying the old prelates the very name of bishops: he wrote of 'that cruel tyrant and unmerciful hypocrite, falsely called bishop of Sanctandrois', 'Beaton falsely called bishop of Glasgow' and 'the bishops (papistical, we mean)'.[4] In England, similarly, the Marian prelates were 'pseudobishops', while Ridley, after deprivation, was still 'true bishop of London',[5] and Latimer had provided a lively illustration of the same idea in a passage where he referred to the work of that good protestant Coverdale as coadjutor to the octogenarian and conservative Voysey, who had held the see of Exeter since 1519: 'Who

---

[1] Laing, I, 553 (from Foxe).
[2] *Ibid.* 46 (Dickinson, I, 20).
[3] *Decretum*, pars I, dist. XL, c. 12, headed *non est verus sacerdos omnis qui nominatur sacerdos*, pronounced that there are *multi sacerdotes nomine, pauci opere*.
[4] Laing, I, 307; II, 121–2, 131 (Dickinson, I, 153, 339, 346).
[5] *Original Letters* (Parker Soc.), II, 581; *Zurich Letters* (Parker Soc.), I, 29, 31; Laing, III, 299.

is bishop of Exeter? Forsooth, Master Coverdale. What, do not all men know who is bishop of Exeter? What? He hath been bishop many years. Well, say I, Master Coverdale is bishop of Exeter. Master Coverdale putteth in execution the bishop's office, and he that doth the office of the bishop, he is the bishop indeed'.[1] Plainly, there were, or there ought to be, bishops, but the existing prelates did not qualify. And a 'true' bishop was one who was sound in doctrine and energetic in his duties.

Such opinions had an important bearing on the approach to the whole subject of the ministry and the nature of ordination. In general, the reformers did not accept a personal succession in the sense in which it is understood by episcopalians and by many presbyterians today, and so far from holding such a succession to be a mark of the church, they much more commonly repudiated it as an error.[2] In particular, they were unable to discern in the existing bishops the characteristics they looked for in an apostolic ministry. Several of the Scottish bishops were so conspicuous for their lax morals (to which the recorded legitimations of their children still testify),[3] that the reformers could not regard them as the instruments of an apostolic succession or desire to transmit what had been received at their hands. To put it bluntly, they considered it to be demonstrable that the succession had failed.[4] Not only did such an idea pass from reforming theologians to a layman like Sir David Lindsay, who wrote:

> Ye say to the Appostils that ye succeid,
> Bot ye schaw nocht that into word nor deid;

but a conservative reformer like Ninian Winyet, who in theory strongly defended the necessity of episcopal ordination, came very near to the same admission as Lindsay: 'putand in the place of godly ministeris and trew successouris of the apostolis, dum doggis', and

[1] Latimer, *Sermons*, p. 272.
[2] E.g. Hooper, *Early Writings*, pp. 27, 82, 138, *Later Writings*, pp. 90, 121; Cranmer, *Remains and Letters*, p. 13; Laing, II, 110 (Dickinson, II, 266); Bullinger, *Decades*, IV, 28–30.
[3] Hay Fleming, *op. cit.* pp. 45–58. It hardly palliates the scandal that the same child was sometimes legitimated more than once.
[4] Laing, II, 193 (Dickinson, II, 286).

the pious conservative, Abell, had remarked that 'mony of our prelatis now ar membris nocht of Christ bot of Sathan'.[1] It is somewhat less than fair to accuse the reformers of wilfully breaking the succession, for their view was that it had already lapsed. Further, bishops who were enemies to reform, and perhaps persecutors, were held to be disqualified from conferring authority on ministers of the gospel, and only if they were themselves ready to embrace true doctrine were ordinations by them admissible in a reformed church.[2] When the Scots, in 1560, declared roundly that 'in all the rabble of the clergy there is not one lawful minister, if God's word, the practice of the Apostles and their own ancient laws shall judge of lawful election',[3] they were hardly, if at all, going beyond the general consensus of reforming opinion. The emphasis was not on a personal succession, but on faith and on works, which were the test of the true pastor as well as of the true bishop.

In any event, no reformer would have allowed that bishops constituted an order superior to the presbyterate in the accepted sense. This, it is sometimes necessary to recall, was the dominant view in England as well as in Scotland. It had its roots in medieval thought, it had been encouraged by papal centralisation, which sought to depress the bishops into mere delegates of the pope, and at the reformation it fitted well with the royal supremacy in a country like England, where the bishops could be regarded as the 'under-officers' of the crown in its capacity as supreme head or supreme governor of the church. Acknowledgment of the equality of bishop and priest appeared in official pronouncements in England under Henry VIII, it was maintained by the continental reformers most influential in England, such as Bucer and Bullinger, and it is to be found in the

[1] Lindsay, *Works*, II, 279; Winyet, *op. cit.* p. 8, cf. 47; Abell's Chronicle, fo. 86b.
[2] Cf. 'Reformatio Wittebergensis' (1545), in A. L. Richter, *Die evangelischen Kirchenordnungen des sechzehnten Jahrhunderts*, II, 83: 'Et si episcopis auctoritas ordinationis tribuenda est, necesse est ut suam mentem de doctrina declarent. Nam si erunt et manebunt Evangelii hostes, nec volent ullos ad ordinationem admittere sine obligatione ad impiam doctrinam et ad delendam veritatem, non poterit ab eis ordinatio peti. Sed si veram doctrinam amplecti et tueri vellent et idoneis hominibus examen commendare, praeclare mereri de ecclesia possent. Plurimum enim refert ordinationem recte instaurari'.
[3] Laing, II, 91, 115–16 (Dickinson, I, 337; II, 269).

writings of the Elizabethan bishops Jewel and Pilkington.[1] Archbishop Parker was so far from believing in the divine right of the
episcopal office that he wrote thus to Queen Elizabeth's chief
minister:

I refer the whole matter to her majesty and to your order. . . . I refer
the standing or falling altogether to your own considerations, whether
her majesty and you will have any archbishops or bishops, or how you
will have them ordered.[2]

Holding the views they did on succession and on the identity in
order of bishop and priest, the reformers could not have maintained the necessity of episcopal ordination. This was so in England
as well as in Scotland. The preface to the Anglican ordinal left the
door open for the acceptance into the Church of England of men
not in episcopal orders—a door closed by the 1662 revision; and the
relevant article (XXIII) of the Thirty-Nine refers simply to choice
by the men to whom the church has committed the power of
calling ministers. Controversy has centred on the details and the
precise significance of the few ascertainable instances in which men
lacking episcopal orders held office in the Church of England,
but that there were such instances, and that such instances were
authoritatively defended, is not open to any doubt. Matthew Hut-
ton, afterwards bishop of Durham and archbishop of York, declared that orders conferred at Geneva were more sound than those
conferred by the Roman ordinal, and the oft-quoted licence given
by Archbishop Grindal to the Scot John Morrison described his
ordination by the synod of Lothian as being according to 'the
laudable form and rite of the reformed Church of Scotland'. When,
towards the end of the century, opinion began to harden against the
recognition of non-episcopal orders, Francis Bacon thought it a

[1] Tyndale, *Doctrinal Treatises*, p. 229; Burnet, *History of the Reformation*, ed.
Pocock, IV, 340; Lloyd, *Formularies of Faith*, pp. 105, 281; Charles Sturge,
Cuthbert Tunstal, pp. 222–3; Bucer, *Scripta anglicana*, p. 280; Bullinger, *De
episc. instit. et funct.* fos. 65r, 143v, and *Decades*, IV, 108–9; Becon, *Catechism*,
p. 319; Jewel, *Works*, I, 340, 379, III, 272, 293, 439; Pilkington, *Works*, pp. 493–4;
Whitgift, *Works*, II, 265, III, 535–6; Strype, *Whitgift*, III, 221. Cf. Woodhouse,
op. cit. pp. 79–82.
[2] Parker, *Correspondence*, p. 454.

singular novelty that 'some of our men, ordained in foreign parts, have been pronounced no fit ministers'.[1]

As there was thus no necessity for an episcopal system, the form of ecclesiastical polity in a reformed church might be dictated by circumstances. There was a general agreement that when the reformation had been accepted on a national scale and the reformed church was, as we should say, established, then there would be an episcopal system, but that when the reformed church was 'under the cross' (that is, not recognised by the state and perhaps persecuted) and the organisation was mainly congregational, there would be no rank of clergy superior to the pastor of a congregational charge. Obviously, in the first case the civil power could compel the men in possession of bishoprics to choose between acceptance of the new regime and deprivation in favour of men professing the reformed faith, whereas in the second the reformers could not dispossess the existing prelates and appoint new bishops in their places.

The acceptance of this distinction by the English reformers is illustrated by the manner in which they organised their congregations when they were in exile during Mary Tudor's reign. At Frankfurt, although liturgical questions led to the formation of an 'Anglican' party and a 'puritan' party, men like Cox, Sandys, Grindal and Horne (all afterwards bishops) joined in the election of ministers, elders and deacons. There was some uncertainty as to the suffrage for the election of those officers, and as to the desirability of a single chief pastor, but no one seems to have contemplated episcopal government, and the term 'bishop' was rejected because it was held to imply the oversight of a diocese. The organisation of the more 'puritan' congregation at Geneva did not differ from that

---

[1] *Troubles at Frankfort*, ed. Arber, p. 14; Strype, *Whitgift*, III, 185; Strype, *Grindal*, p. 596; Spedding, *Letters and Life of Bacon*, I, 86–7; Hooker, *Ecclesiastical Polity*, VII, XIV, 11; Spottiswoode, *History*, III, 209; Harold Smith, *Ecclesiastical History of Essex*, pp. 37–8. A. J. Mason, *The Church of England and Episcopacy*, and Edward Denny, *The English Church and the Ministry of the Reformed Churches*, attempt to minimise the significance of the instances of the admission of non-episcopally ordained men, but do not appear fully to make their case. The latest discussion of the whole subject, in Norman Sykes, *Old Priest and New Presbyter*, reviews the evidence with caution and restraint.

at Frankfurt, and no contemporary thought it worthy of remark that Miles Coverdale, although he had been a bishop in England, became an elder at Geneva. Episcopal consecration was plainly not held to convey any inherent superiority.[1] At this stage the English reformed church had been 'under the cross'; when it was once more established and under episcopal government, English churchmen did not brand as invalid the system which had been in use at Frankfurt, Geneva and elsewhere. Archbishop Whitgift admitted that there was much to be said for the validity of the orders conferred on William Whittingham at Geneva on the ground that 'he in time of persecution was ordained minister by those which had authority in the church persecuted' and contrasted his case with that of Walter Travers, who 'in time of peace' (when he could have been ordained by an English bishop) 'gaddeth into other countries' in order to receive presbyterial ordination at Antwerp.[2] The truth seems to be that if the Scots discarded the conception of a succession from the bishops of the unreformed church, in England, despite the operation of the mechanics of consecration, Whitgift no less clearly implied a repudiation of any succession from the prelates of Mary Tudor's reign, because in those years the true Church of England had in his view consisted not of the legal establishment with its bishops but of the congregations at home and abroad which had preserved the reformed faith.[3]

But if there were 'false' bishops, whom the reformers thus declined to recognise, there were also 'true' bishops. Despite all the negative or destructive elements in reformation thought on episcopacy, there was a widespread belief in the value of a 'godly' or reformed bishop or superintendent, possessing no sacramental superiority in order over ordinary ministers but more efficient and more energetic than the prelates of the old regime. Such a conception was at least implied in some of the criticism of the unreformed episcopate. When Knox observed that 'a bishop that receives profit and feeds not the flock, even by his own labours, is both a thief and a murderer',[4] the implication was that a bishop ought to feed the

---

[1] Cf. Sykes, *op. cit.* p. 34.
[2] Strype, *Whitgift*, III, 185; Fuller, *Church History*, IX, VII, 51.
[3] Whitgift, *Works*, I, 391.   [4] Laing, II, 398 (Dickinson, II, 90).

flock, and the same inference can be drawn from the remarks of the English bishop Pilkington: 'To be a bishop is to be an officer, a ruler, a guide, a teacher of God's flock in God's church. . . . Is he an officer that does not his office? Nay, surely, but only in name; for he is a thief in his office, and an usurer, that takes the profit and not the pain.'[1] Knox and Pilkington represent a negative approach; but positive statements are plentiful. When German reformers, as early as 1525, had laid down that 'Bishops shall remain: not anointing-bishops nor ordaining-bishops, but such as preach and teach and expound the pure word of God and preside over the church,'[2] they defined the two chief functions of the 'godly bishop', namely preaching and oversight. The insistence that bishops should preach was of course a commonplace,[3] and in England as well as in Scotland men were sometimes exercised as to the arrangements which would best ensure that bishops would be able to perform this function;[4] John Aylmer, later bishop of London, advocated a reorganisation of the episcopal system, so that there would be in each town of importance a bishop who would be the chief preacher in a comparatively small district.[5] Yet the emphasis on preaching never went so far at this stage as to reduce the bishop's status to that of a minister of a single congregation, and the other chief episcopal function—oversight or superintendence—received due attention in the writings of the continental reformers who were influential in this island. John à Lasco published in his *Forma ac ratio* a sermon to be used at the institution of a superintendent, in which he asserted that the office of superintendent (ἐπισκοπή) is of divine ordinance in the Church of Christ and that one minister should be chosen from among the others for order's sake.[6] According to Martin Bucer, bishops must lay aside all worldly cares and devote themselves to

[1] Pilkington, *Works*, p. 604; cf. p. 494.
[2] Kidd, *Documents of the Continental Reformation*, p. 190.
[3] John Major, *Expositiones* (1529), fo. cxv; *Descrypcyon of . . . a verye Chrysten byshop*, sig. E v *verso*, I *recto*; Laing, I, 239; Lindsay, *Works*, I, 139–41, 276, 332, 343, 358, II, 89, 275, 313.
[4] *Zurich Letters*, I, 50–1; Hooper, *Early Writings*, pp. 19, 511; Cardwell, *Documentary Annals*, I, 23; Laing, IV, 518.
[5] Aylmer, *An Harborowe for Faithfull and Trewe Subjectes*, sig. O iv.
[6] A Lasco, *Opera*, ed. Kuyper, II, 57.

reading and teaching the holy scriptures, public and private prayer, the administration of discipline, the maintenance of schools and the care of the poor; in order to ensure that the churches under their charge have competent pastors, they should visit all parts of their dioceses at least once a year to correct faults; in their work they should be advised and assisted by presbyters and deacons, and the synod of each diocese must meet twice yearly.[1] The opinion of the church at Zurich was expressed by Rudolf Gualter, who described a reformed bishop as a person placed over a certain number of churches and having the management of such things as appertain to the purity of religion and doctrine.[2] Calvin's opinions were equally in accordance with the ideal of the 'godly bishop':

Talem nobis hierarchiam si exhibeant, in qua sic emineant episcopi ut Christo subesse non recusent, ut ab illo tanquam unico capite pendeant et ad ipsum referantur, in qua sic inter se fraternam societatem colant ut non alio modo quam ejus veritate sint colligati: tum vero nullo non anathemate dignos fatear siqui erant qui non eam revereantur summaque obedientia observant.

Elsewhere, although censuring the terms 'archbishop' and 'hierarchy', and distinguishing carefully between rule over portions of the church and domination over the whole, Calvin admitted that 'as the wits and manners of men are now, there can no order stand among the ministers of the word except one be set over the rest'; and he conceded that there might fittingly be not only bishops, keeping order in cities and provinces, but even a primate who should not arrogate to himself authority stolen from his brethren, but who should, for the sake of order (*ordinis causa*) hold first place in the synods and maintain a sacred unity (*sanctam unitatem*).[3] It is plain that throughout the whole period during which the reforming movement was developing in Scotland and even in the years when the organisation of the reformed church there was taking shape, there was a remarkable measure of agreement on the characteristics of a reformed episcopate, and the conception of parity,

[1] Bucer, *Scripta anglicana*, pp. 67–8, 69, 73.   [2] *Zurich Letters*, II, 228.
[3] *Commentaries on the Philippians* (English edn. of 1584), p. 4; *Opera*, XV, 332–3; *De necessitate reformandae ecclesiae*, quoted by McCrie, *Miscellaneous Writings*, p. 175 n.; *Institutes* IV, iv and v (Beveridge, III, 74–107).

at least in the later presbyterian sense of the term, was as yet all but unknown. The Helvetic Confession of 1566, which represented the general agreement of Geneva and Zurich and was officially accepted in Scotland, still distinguished between pastors, who 'both keep the sheepfold of the Lord, and provide for things necessary', and bishops, that is 'superintendents and watchmen'.[1]

There was nothing indeterminate about the principles which were in the minds of the compilers of the first Book of Discipline when they came to deal with the oversight of congregations and their pastors. If, as has been suggested, they were specially concerned to deal fully with the initial stages in setting up the reformed polity, this could go far to explain their treatment of the office of superintendent, for the first steps in establishing superintendents were the matters on which the Book was explicit. It was necessary, for one thing, to define their dioceses. This was done by an admirable rationalisation of boundaries. It may seem odd that the demand for episcopal efficiency did not prompt the Scots to increase the number of dioceses rather than to reduce it by three, especially as Knox had remarked that some of the English dioceses were so large that each might be divided into ten.[2] The apparent inconsistency is explained by a comparison of the size of the English dioceses with that of the Scottish. In Scotland there were thirteen sees and about a thousand parishes; in England, although there were about ten thousand parishes, there were only twenty-six sees (five of them recent creations); and three English dioceses—Lincoln, Norwich and London—each contained a number of parishes comparable to the number in the whole of Scotland. The application of Knox's principle of subdivision to the larger English sees would therefore have produced dioceses similar in size to those of the Scottish superintendents. A scheme of ten dioceses with roughly a hundred parishes in each was attractive to orderly minds.

The second point on which the Book of Discipline had to be explicit was the justification for the office of superintendent at a time when it was hard enough to find ministers. There can be little doubt that the compilers were anticipating criticism—not, of course, from anyone who believed in the parity of ministers, but from those

[1] *Helvetic Confession* [London, 1566], p. 58.   [2] Laing, V, 518.

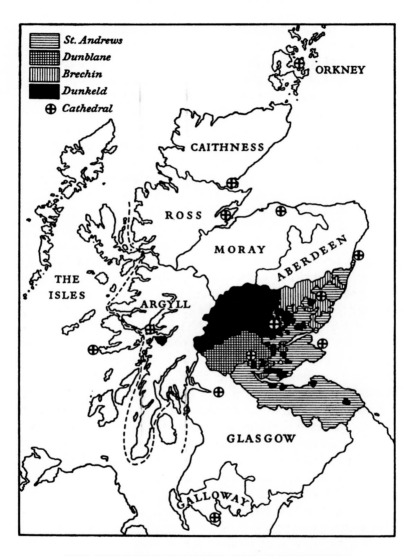

THE SCOTTISH DIOCESES AND CATHEDRALS
IN 1560

BOUNDARIES PROPOSED FOR SUPERINTENDENTS
IN 1560

who would have argued (and argued logically from the reformers' premises) that it was more important at that time to find ministers for parishes than superintendents for dioceses; such a criticism had been levelled against Queen Elizabeth's proceedings in the previous year—'making of lordly bishops before the realm be provided of necessary ministers'—and the man who had made it was now active in Scotland.[1] The compilers were therefore at some pains to explain why they 'thought meet to make difference between preachers' at a time when preachers were so scarce, and why the office of superintendent had a special value in such circumstances— was 'most expedient for this time'—in that superintendents, on their travels, could provide ministrations in parishes not yet supplied with clergy.[2] There is no ambiguity in this passage, and those who have sought to wrest it into an expression of a preference for parity have too often found it convenient to misquote it, even bringing themselves to allege that the Book of Discipline declared the office of superintendent to be only 'an expedient for a time'. The Book of Discipline was much concerned to overcome scruples as to the expediency of superintendents when ministers were few in number, but to have questioned the expediency of the office when ministers were in adequate supply would have been contrary to almost all contemporary thought.

The third thing was to define the method of appointment, both in the immediate future and in later, more settled, times 'after that the church be established and three years be past'. The temporary method—nomination by the lords, followed by a purely formal 'election'—was of course identical with the method of appointing bishops which was in use in England and which was adopted in Scotland in 1572;[3] the later and enduring method—election by the clergy and people of the diocese[4]—was to be a reversion to the primitive model for episcopal elections.

The Book of Discipline is much more explicit about those preliminaries than about the superintendent's powers, and the official

---

[1] *Cal. S. P. Scot.* I, No. 554. The critic was Christopher Goodman.
[2] Laing, II, 198–202 (Dickinson, II, 289–91).　　[3] P. 163 below.
[4] According to Lesley (*op. cit.* p. 270) a proposal had been made in 1558 that bishops should be elected by 'the temporal lords and people of their dioceses'.

it describes is somewhat indistinct. Some of the main points are, indeed, clear: the superintendent was to receive a salary far above that of any parish minister; his office was quite obviously to be one which could not be satisfactorily combined with the service of a parish; he was to examine ministers; he was to visit and inspect ministers and churches, to supervise poor relief and education. On the other hand, judicial functions are referred to merely as 'noting' crimes that may be corrected, there is silence about the composition of the superintendent's court and about the consistorial jurisdiction, nothing is said about appeals from the kirk session to the superintendent and the only point at which the superintendent appears clearly as the link between the parish and the general assembly is in connection with finance. The Book of Discipline's treatment of the office is, however, easily explained: the functions of superintendents were too well known to require elaboration, for the title, and its meaning, were already familiar to contemporaries.

Not only had the term superintendent appeared in Denmark and Germany, but it was in some favour as an equivalent of bishop and of rural dean in England.[1] Its significance lay in its freedom from the associations which the term 'bishop' had with the wealth, idleness and inefficiency of the prelates whom the reformers so vigorously condemned; an English reformer advocated its use on the ground that 'The name of *bishop* hath been so abused, that when it was spoken, the people understood nothing else but a great lord that went in a white rochet, with a wide shaven crown, and that carried an oilbox with him, wherewith he used once in seven years, riding about, to *confirm* children, &c. Now, to bring the people from this abuse . . . the word *superintendent* . . . should in time have taught the people, by the very etymology and proper signification, what thing was meant when they heard that name.'[2] In short, the superintendent was the 'godly' or reformed bishop whose char-

---

[1] A passage in *The Institution of a Christian Man* equates 'bishops or archbishops' with 'superattendants or overseers' (Lloyd, *Formularies of Faith* [1825], p. 109). For the use of the term 'superintendent' in Edward VI's reign, see Hooper, *Later Writings*, pp. xvii, xix. For its use under Elizabeth, see Jewel, *Works*, IV, 906, Strype, *Grindal*, p. 165, Aylmer, *An Harborowe*, loc. cit., and the document (of 1578) printed in Strype, *Annals*, II, II, 695 and in *H.M.C. Salisbury MSS.* II, 195.

[2] Strype, *Memorials*, II, II, 141–2.

acteristics had been described by so many reformers, and when the term was introduced into Scotland it connoted the entire current ideal of a reformed episcopate efficient in preaching and visitation.

In Scotland there had been little indication hitherto of any disposition to abandon the term 'bishop', though it had been remarked that *Episcopus interpretatur superintendens*. It is interpret a waikrife oursear,'[1] but in 1560 the Scots could hardly have used the term 'bishop', for it was uncertain whether the existing bishops would conform or would be deprived if they declined to do so, and it had not yet occurred to anyone that two men could each be styled 'bishop' of the same see. Had the Scots wanted to avoid the connotation of the term 'superintendent' they would surely have found a less familiar alternative, but in any event they drew attention to the identity of the superintendent with the reformed bishop by insisting that the superintendents 'must not be suffered to live as your idle bishops have done heretofore' and by echoing the words in which Scottish protestants, thirteen years earlier, had called for the reform of the episcopate—'they must be preachers themselves'.[2] To a twentieth-century Scot the superintendent is a 'strange monster', as Robert Baillie said the presbytery was to seventeenth-century Englishmen; but to anyone in the sixteenth century, English or Scottish, the meaning of 'superintendent' was perfectly plain.

The superintendent played the leading part in the examination and admission of ministers, exhorters and readers. It would be misleading to speak of *ordination*, because that term represents a concept which was not in the minds of the reformers. It is true that the great majority of the men who became ministers in 1560 and in the next two or three years were already 'in orders'—either Scottish or English—and that there was in practice a personal succession through the numerous clergy who conformed and served under the new regime. It is true, further, that if the imposition of hands was ever completely laid aside it was soon reintroduced.[3] But those

---

[1] Abell's Chronicle, fo. 86*b* ('a wakeful overseer').
[2] Laing, I, 194; II, 204 (Dickinson, I, 87; II, 292).
[3] In 1566 the assembly approved the Helvetic Confession, which provided for *impositio manuum*, and made no exception against this as it did against the observance of festivals (see McMillan, *Worship of the Scottish Reformed Church*, pp. 343–4). Yet the practice was still not universal in the 1590s.

facts meant nothing to the compilers of the Book of Discipline, which cannot be interpreted as meaning anything else than a repudiation of the transmission of orders as usually understood. There is no evidence of the existence in 1560 of a belief that a minister received his authorisation from either a bishop or a group of ministers through a process of succession, and the laying on of hands was 'judged not necessary':[1] 'It is neither the clipping of their crowns, the crossing of their fingers, nor the blowing of the dumb dogs called the Bishops, neither yet the laying on of their hands, that maketh them true Ministers of Christ Jesus.'[2] The whole emphasis, by contrast, was on appointment to a ministerial charge. It is true, again, that many of the men so appointed or (we might almost say) inducted, were already 'in orders', but the Book of Discipline gives no indication that it recognised any ordination, any state of being 'in orders', any clerical character, apart from the holding of a particular charge. That Book is to be interpreted not in the light of either presbyterian or episcopalian practice or theory in this country today, but in the light of principles to which some reformed churches on the Continent still adhere: 'Apart from Baptism and the Lord's Supper, the Reformed Church in Switzerland knows no sacraments and recognises no "sacramentals". . . . Indeed, exception is taken even to the ordination of ministers, on the ground that a Reformed Church only knows an induction by the Church to a particular office, but not an ordination *per se*.'[3] (It may be observed in passing that the repudiation by the Scottish reformers of the imposition of hands and of the whole idea of succession need not dismay those who claim that the Church of Scotland possesses a succession through presbyters which links its ministry to that of the universal church. They may console themselves with the reflection that the Church of Scotland ministry derives from the ministry of the episcopalian establishment of the seventeenth century, in which ordinations were performed by bishops who had themselves received consecration

---

[1] Laing, II, 193 (Dickinson, II, 286).
[2] *Ibid.* 255 (Dickinson, II, 322).
[3] Julius Schweizer, in *Ways of Worship* (ed. Peter Edwall and others, 1951), p. 134.

which linked them to the succession of the Church of England.)[1]

While authorisation did not come from succession, whence it did come is not altogether clear. Some reformers held the doctrine of the priesthood of all male believers so strongly and so literally that they thought merely in terms of setting apart for a special function some member of the Christian community, who thus received his powers by delegation from the body of Christians and not by any sacramental rite from men already in orders. Some went so far as to consider it a matter of indifference by what means church members (who were already in a sense 'in orders') were set apart for the function of the ministry. Thus, Bullinger wrote: 'Neither makes it any great matter whether discreet men chosen of the church, or the whole church itself, do ordain fit ministers; and that either by voices, either by lots, or after some certain necessary and holy manner.'[2] In such a belief we can see one aspect of the significance of the call by the congregation, which would thus be in some sense the source of authority, and it becomes plain why there should be such emphasis on 'election', even if it was nothing more than a mere form. On this view, authority comes up from the congregation, not down from the bishop.[3] It is, of course, true that whatever theory of authorisation is held, ministerial authority derives ultimately from God, but the Book of Discipline makes it clear that although a minister could be commissioned directly by God, such commissioning had still to be followed by 'the nomination of the people, the examination of the learned, and public admission'.[4]

At any rate, whatever the nature of authorisation, there still had to be examination and admission, and it was here and not in any succession that the superintendent or bishop was a necessary officer. Or, to put it differently, whatever the theological implications and

---

[1] This has been challenged on the ground that the episcopalians who were admitted to the establishment in terms of a statute of 1695 took no part in ordinations; but they formed only a very small proportion of the episcopalians who, both after 1638 and after 1690, carried their ministry into the presbyterian establishment.

[2] Bullinger, *Decades*, IV, 134; cf. his *De episc. inst. et funct*. fo. 99v.

[3] It is not difficult to put this interpretation on Article XXIII of the Church of England.   [4] Laing, II, 255 (Dickinson, II, 322).

the nature of the rite of admission, an essential part in the proceedings pertained to the superintendent. 'Ordinary vocation,' the Book of Discipline laid down, 'consisteth in election, examination and admission.' Election, it went on, pertains to the congregation, but should a congregation fail to elect within forty days, the right to appoint devolves on the superintendent and his council (precisely as a bishop possessed the *jus devolutum* on a patron's failure to present). Examination (after election) takes place when the person elected appears in 'the best reformed city or town, that is, the city of the superintendent'. Admission, the Book proceeds, consists in the consent of the people and approbation of the learned minister appointed for examination (deputed, that must mean, by the superintendent, for no one else can have had authority to appoint examiners). Apparently the 'chief minister's' declaration of the candidate's suitability then sufficed, without further action by the superintendent in person.

It may well be that for a time there was some laxity, for there must have been instances between 1559 and 1561, before the position of superintendents or bishops was regularised, of men beginning to exercise their ministry with no other commissioning than that given by a congregation's call.[1] On the other hand, in the same period, the nobles, barons and burgh commissioners are said by Knox to have nominated ministers to a number of the chief towns, with no reference to a congregational call.[2] One of the ministers so nominated was Knox himself, who had months before been 'elected' by his parishioners and was already well established,[3] and it must remain something of a mystery whether in his case and others authorisation came from the nobles, barons and burgh commissioners or from an antecedent or subsequent 'election' by a congregation. At any rate, it would seem from what happened at Peebles that 'election' (even after nomination by a superintendent) had still to be followed by 'admission' at the hands of a superintendent.[4]

---

[1] Cf. Laing, II, 253 (Dickinson, II, 321).   [2] Laing, II, 87 (Dickinson, I, 334).
[3] Laing, I, 388 and n. (Dickinson, I, 211 and n.); *Extracts from the Records of the Burgh of Edinburgh*, III, 63–4.
[4] *Extracts from the Records of the Burgh of Peebles*, 1165–1710, pp. 275, 278.

But the phase of laxity soon passed. The lords, in approving the Book of Discipline in January 1561, recommended that men already acting as preachers who were not found qualified by the superintendents should be demoted to the rank of reader.[1] Steps were presently taken to implement this recommendation and to bring into force what had evidently been the intention of the Book of Discipline: as soon as a superintendent had been instituted in Fife, it was ordained that candidates for the ministry in that area were to have a date and place assigned to them by the superintendent for their examination;[2] the general assembly in June 1562 laid down explicit regulations (to operate retrospectively) for the examination and admission of ministers by superintendents (with the advice of 'the best learned being present'), and in the following December provided that persons who had not been examined and admitted by a superintendent should be inhibited.[3] While the participation of the superintendent in the rite of admission was essential, it was implied that there need not be other ministers to join with him,[4] and the evidence of presentations and collations, which becomes ample after 1567, strongly suggests that the superintendent commonly exercised a sole power to examine and admit. The unique position of the superintendent in the rite of admission possibly explains Knox's denial that he had ordained any ministers;[5] as he was not a superintendent he naturally did not do so. It should be added here that the reformed church claimed that the admission of school and university teachers should, like that of ministers, be in the hands of superintendents,[6] and that the admission of teachers did in practice fall to them after 1567.[7]

The second branch of the superintendent's functions was the supervision of ministers and of the life of the parishes. According to the Book of Discipline, the superintendents were to be energetic in visitation, examining the life, diligence and behaviour of the ministers, the 'order' of the churches, the manners of the people

---

[1] Laing, II, 196 (Dickinson, II, 288).   [2] *Reg. K. S. St A.* I. 75.
[3] *B.U.K.* I, 15–16, 27 (Calderwood, II, 185, 206). See also pp. 150–1 below.
[4] Cf. 'the rest of the ministers, if any be' (Laing, II, 149 [Dickinson, II, 276]).
[5] Winyet, *op. cit.* p. 18.
[6] *B.U.K.* I, 60, 108 (Calderwood, II, 288, 380).
[7] E.g. *R.S.S.* VI, 160, VII, 687.

and the provision for education and the poor.[1] This was a wide commission, and it was not narrowed by the general assembly of June 1562, which laid down generally that ministers must be 'subject to their superintendents in all lawful admonitions', and descended to the particular by mentioning that the superintendent, on his visitations, should inspect the minister's library.[2] While a foreign visitor remarked that the superintendents 'diligently visit the churches'[3], there is a dearth of record evidence about this activity; however, the records of the parish of Canongate suggest that the superintendent came on visitation approximately twice a year[4] and called a general meeting at which the minister, the elders and deacons and the congregation were 'tried' in turn by the device of 'removing' the minister and inviting complaints about him in his absence, then treating the elders and deacons in the same way, and finally inquiring of the minister his opinion of his flock.[5] Such evidence is certainly fatal to the idea that the superintendent's responsibilities were limited to the outlying parts of his diocese. Disobedience to the superintendent, the general assembly had ordained, must lead to 'correction',[6] and 'correction' might involve ultimately suspension or deprivation. The evidence suggests that the superintendent could by his sole authority suspend ministers and readers but that deprivation certainly of ministers and perhaps even of readers required action by the superintendent along with his court.[7] The case of Paul Methven, minister of Jedburgh, who was accused of adultery, was so scandalous that it was brought before the general assembly, but although the assembly ordered inquiry it was remitted to the superintendent of Edinburgh and his court to pass sentence.[8] It was at one stage proposed that the power

---

[1] Laing, II, 204–5 (Dickinson, II, 293).
[2] *B.U.K.* I, 14–15 (Calderwood, II, 184–5).
[3] Pollen, *Papal Negotiations with Queen Mary*, p. 136.
[4] Cf. the reference to Erskine visiting Arbroath twice or thrice a year (p. 127 below).
[5] One instance is given in Ronald S. Wright, *The Kirk in the Canongate*, p. 34, but other instances may be found in *The Buik of the Kirk of the Canagait* under dates 10 July 1565, 11 Dec. 1565, 10 Dec. 1566 (ed. Alma B. Calderwood [S.R.S.], pp. 24, 32, 61).
[6] *B.U.K.* I, 14 (Calderwood, II, 184).
[7] *Reg. K. S. St A.* I, 172–282 *passim*.   [8] *B.U.K.* I, 29 (Calderwood, II, 207–8).

to translate ministers should lie with the superintendent and synod, but it seems that the superintendent could translate by his sole authority.[1]

The important judicial functions of the superintendents arose partly from the fate of the consistorial jurisdiction at the reformation. It has already been mentioned that some of the bishops continued intermittently to exercise their traditional authority in matrimonial cases, and possibly some of their officials and commissaries were still acting, but a large gap remained, and among the candidates for the consistorial jurisdiction were the courts of the reformed church. The kirk session of St Andrews began to act in divorce suits as early as February 1559/60, and in August 1560 the archbishop of St Andrews remarked to his brother of Glasgow, 'the elderis callit of every town takis all the causis of our ecclesiasticall jurisdiction and intromettis with all our office'. At the end of 1560 we find the lords of council requesting the kirk session of St Andrews to give sentence of divorce.[2] With the appointment of superintendents, however, in the spring of 1561, jurisdiction in divorce fell to them: on 19 March the privy council, understanding that John Spottiswoode was superintendent of Lothian and ought to decide on actions of divorce, granted him power to do so 'quhill the next parliament, that further order be taken'; he was to 'adjoyne' to him the ministers, elders and deacons of Haddington, Edinburgh, Linlithgow or Stirling, as necessary.[3] In 1563 the general assembly forbade kirk sessions to decide actions of divorce, and restricted that function to superintendents and those commissioned by them.[4] This phase, when it seemed that the ancient ecclesiastical jurisdiction was going to remain with the new church courts, did not last. There was competition from the court of session, which was approached by petitioners on the ground of the inactivity of the commissaries and possibly also because of some uncertainty about the legality of the courts of the reformed church. The urgent need for a settlement was felt by the general assembly, which in

[1] B.U.K. I, 29, 50, 62 (Calderwood, II, 208, 281, 290).
[2] See *Introduction to Scottish legal history* (Stair Soc.), p. 367.
[3] Warrender Papers, vol. A, fo. 98.
[4] B.U.K. I, 30 (Calderwood, II, 209).

July 1562 petitioned the privy council 'that either they give up universally the judgment of divorce to the kirk and their sessions, or else to establish men of good lives, knowledge and judgment, to take the order thereof', and in June 1563 petitioned 'for constituting judges in every province to hear the complaints of parties alleging adultery to be committed by the husband or the wife'.[1] Action by the state came early in 1564, when the commissary court of Edinburgh was appointed, with jurisdiction in divorce throughout the kingdom, and from this point the superintendents were superseded.[2] It is clear, however, that for a brief period the superintendent's court had shown a strong tendency to inherit the consistorial jurisdiction of the old episcopal courts.[3]

The superintendent's court, as indicated in the council's commission to Spottiswoode in March 1561, consisted of the kirk session of a chief town in his diocese, and it appears further that it was the superintendent's duty to act with any kirk session in any case of special gravity.[4] Obviously, the kirk session of the superintendent's headquarters and principal place of residence was bound to be of special importance, and of the work done by a superintendent and this court we have full illustration in the *Register of the kirk session of St Andrews*, which incorporates the proceedings of the court of the superintendent of Fife. After divorce was removed from the superintendent's jurisdiction, matrimonial cases of lesser gravity—notably adherence—continued to be dealt with by the superintendent, sometimes with, very often without, the advice or consent of a session.[5] Various cases were remitted from time to time by the general assembly to a superintendent and his court or generally to a superintendent, who might then take the advice of the appropriate kirk session.[6] The superintendent played an important part in all disciplinary action, and a somewhat confused act of the general assembly in 1565 seems to support Archbishop Spottiswoode's

---

[1] *B.U.K.* I, 19, 23, 34 (Calderwood, II, 191, 226–7).
[2] Cf. *Reg. K. S. St A.* I, 257.
[3] E.g. *ibid.* 130–1, 140, 150, 155–6, 252–4.
[4] R. S. Wright, *op. cit.* p. 56.   [5] *Reg. K. S. St A.* I, 192–293 *passim*.
[6] *B.U.K.* I, 35, 41 (Calderwood, II, 227); R. S. Wright, *op. cit.* p. 56; 'Inter-diocesan and inter-provincial communication before and after the reformation', in *Scot. Church Hist. Soc. Records*, XII, 77–8.

statement that excommunication could not be pronounced without warrant from a superintendent.[1]

The court or session which was associated with the superintendent's judicial functions was, of course, quite distinct from the diocesan synod, of which we hear comparatively little. The synod is not clearly defined in the Book of Discipline, though it appears to be implied as the body which might censure a superintendent, and its germ may possibly be detected in the clause that once a year an elder and a deacon from each inferior congregation must report to the 'ministry of the superintendent's church'.[2] According to the general assembly of December 1562 the synod was to meet twice yearly and to consist of all the ministers of the diocese, each with an elder or a deacon.[3] The synod may sometimes have had a voice in the translation of ministers, it had an appellate jurisdiction, from the kirk session and from the superintendent's court, and according to a statute of 1567 there could be an appeal to the synod against a superintendent's refusal to give collation.[4] It must be emphasised that the synod at this stage was a superintendent's diocesan synod and not a synod in the later presbyterian sense, for it appears that there was no synod where there was no superintendent.[5]

Generally it may be said that the superintendents performed most of the administrative, disciplinary and judicial functions which in an episcopal system pertain to bishops and in a presbyterian system to the presbytery. They did not, of course, have the sacramental powers, in ordination and confirmation, normally exercised by an order of bishops, and indeed the views on ordination which then prevailed left no room for such bishops as the channel for the transmission of holy orders. Yet not only was there the clearest distinction in function between the minister and the superintendent, but the office of the superintendent or bishop was held to have divine warrant. 'Without the care of superintendents,' it was pronounced

---

[1] *B.U.K.* I, 74–5 (Calderwood, II, 301–2); Spottiswoode, II, 167.

[2] Laing, II, 207, 236 (Dickinson, II, 294, 311).

[3] *B.U.K.* I, 29 (Calderwood, II, 208); cf. Laing, II, 511 (Dickinson, II, 171).

[4] Cf. p. 153 below; *B.U.K.* I, 32–3 (Calderwood, II, 225); *Reg. K. S. St A.* I, 334–5; *A.P.S.* III, 23 c. 7.

[5] *B.U.K.* I, 111. For references to superintendents holding synods, see Richard Bannatyne, *Memorials of transactions in Scotland* (Bannatyne Club), pp. 203, 274.

when Winram was instituted as superintendent of Fife, 'neither can the kirks be suddenly erected, neither can they be retained in discipline and unity of doctrine. . . . Of Christ Jesus and of His apostles we have command and example to appoint men to such charges.'[1] And John Erskine, who was himself a superintendent, declared in 1571 that to take from the bishop or superintendent the power of admitting and overseeing ministers 'is to take away the office of a bishop, that no bishop be in the kirk; which were to alter and abolish the order which God hath appointed in his kirk'.[2] A claim so emphatic for the *jus divinum* of episcopacy is almost without parallel in that period,[3] but it is equally true that no trace can be found in that period of the view that the superiority of superintendents over ministers was contrary to the word of God, or of any belief in parity in the later presbyterian sense. Whether superintendents can be said to have constituted an *order* superior to ministers is a matter which theologians can best determine. It is true that there was only one form of service, used for the admission of either a minister or a superintendent; but (a) John à Lasco's *Forma ac Ratio* provided only one form, although he took a high view of the office of oversight as having divine warrant; (b) even in the Anglican ordinal, although there are two forms, that used for the consecration of a bishop is a mere adaptation of that used for the ordination of a priest, and far the greater part of the two is identical; and (c) the Scottish form was used to make a man a superintendent who was already a minister, and clearly if it raised a layman to the order of the ministry it is a little hard to deny that it likewise raised a minister to a superior order, or, to put it differently, this usage implied that the office of superintendent was as much an order as was the office of minister.

When the superintendent of Angus declared in 1571 that he knew no difference between the office of bishop and that of superintendent[4] he was expressing an idea which must have been a commonplace at the time, especially as the superintendent's resemblance to the bishop, in externals as well as in substance, was much closer than has usually been allowed. He was styled *dominus superintendens*

---

[1] *Reg. K. S. St A.* I, 75.   [2] Calderwood, III, 157–8.
[3] Cf. John à Lasco's views (p. 109 above).   [4] Calderwood, III, 160.

or 'my lord superintendent', and the clerks of the royal chancery designated John Erskine *venerabilis pater*. And if the superintendent's dignity was thus lordly, his emoluments were princely by all Scottish ecclesiastical standards and must have compared not unfavourably with those of a bishop, especially as the income of an episcopal see comprised a great deal more than the personal income of the bishop and as so many of the bishops appointed during the previous generation drew only the residue of the fruits which remained after the 'pensioners' had been satisfied.[1] Moreover, the personal status and prestige of the superintendents were impressive. Spottiswoode, in Lothian, may have been overshadowed by the ministers of the capital, and it is hardly surprising that Knox was mistakenly believed to be 'superintendent of Edinburgh',[2] but he did exercise his functions even in relation to charges within the city[3] and it is clear that little was done at the centre of affairs without his participation. By an arrangement which was unusual, and possibly unique, Spottiswoode, although superintendent, retained his parochial charge at Calder, and his parishioners, complaining that the superintendentship was promotion and a full-time job, denounced him as a pluralist.[4] John Winram, subprior of St Andrews before the reformation, had acted as dean and vicar general in the primatial see before becoming superintendent of Fife. His status was outstanding even in a district where there were able ministers and strong kirk sessions, and the indications are that his prestige and importance increased rather than diminished, in the dozen years after 1561.[5] He continued to reside in his quarters at the priory, he was addressed by the countess of Moray as 'Father', his death was noted as that of 'ane honorable and worshipfull man', and on his tombstone he is designated 'Episcopus Fifanorum'.[6] John Willock, superintendent of the west, had attained such ascendancy among the reformers in 1559 that he was described as 'primate of their religion in the realm' and likely to disdain any controversialist of lower rank

---

[1] Pp. 38–9 above. On the maintenance of superintendents' stipends under adverse financial conditions, see *Thirds of Benefices*, p. xxxv.

[2] *Records of the Burgh of Peebles*, p. 275.   [3] P. 121 above.

[4] *B.U.K.* I, 18, 42 (Calderwood, II, 187, 245).   [5] *Reg. K. S. St A. passim.*

[6] I.e. 'Bishop of the people of Fife'; Hay Fleming, *Reformation in Scotland*, p. 613 and n., 633; H.M.C. *Report* VI, 654–5.

than the archbishop of St Andrews.[1] When he became 'bishop of Glasgow' in 1560, he was at first maintained—so at least it was reported—by an assignation of £1,000 from the revenues of the archbishopric; he kept such state as became a great ecclesiastical dignitary, and on his visitations he received official hospitality like 'other great men'.[2] John Erskine of Dun was a man of landed property, who brought to his office the advantages of superior social status. He had an interest in the temporality of the bishopric of Brechin,[3] and one can only speculate whether he had an expectation that his superintendentship would lead ultimately to the acquisition of the see. It certainly does appear that, while his zeal for the reformed cause was undoubted and his labours on its behalf energetic, he saw to it that his superintendentship was financially profitable: in 1561 he received £765 6s. 8d., and in later years usually from £500 to £700, as superintendent, besides £133 6s. 8d. for a time as commissioner of Aberdeen and £100 at another time for the visitation of Gowrie and Stormont. Like Willock, he received lavish entertainment on his visitations, and when he resided, as he did two or three times a year, in the abbey of Arbroath, he was classed with 'great lords' who consumed the revenues of the house.[4] There is ample evidence of his effective rule over his diocese and of the respect with which his inferiors treated him.[5] The fifth superintendent, John Carswell, was, like Erskine, a well-to-do laird, who acquired an extensive landed estate from his patron, the earl of Argyll,[6] and his castle of Carnassary, commanding one of the wealthiest areas of Argyll and strategically placed where two important routes converge, was an admirable centre from which to exercise the oversight of his diocese. Again like Erskine, while he showed undoubted devotion to the reformed cause, he had a reputation for being grasping, and this, with his powerful physique, made an impression long remembered in Argyll.[7] Before the reformation he had been treasurer of Argyll and chancellor of the

---

[1] *Wodrow Soc. Misc.* I, 267.
[2] Keith, *op. cit.* III, 7 n., 10; *Ayr Burgh Accounts* (S.H.S.), pp. 30, 132.
[3] *R.S.S.* v, 134.   [4] Books of Assumption, I, 333.
[5] *Spalding Club Misc.* IV, 63–72.   [6] *R.M.S.* IV, 1592.
[7] Archibald Brown, *Memorials of Argyleshire* (Greenock, 1889), p. 359; Patrick H. Gillies, *Netherlorn and its Neighbourhood* (London, 1909), pp. 149–53.

chapel royal, and, while he held the 'parsonage' of Kilmartin, it would be somewhat rash to picture him as a humble parish minister.[1]

These five men alone were appointed as superintendents, and although there were repeated proposals, until at least 1569, for additional appointments,[2] no more were made. One obstacle may have lain in the political situation. According to the Book of Discipline, appointment was in the first instance to be through nomination by the government, and it was the lords of council, governing the realm in the queen's absence, who in fact appointed the five.[3] But from August 1561 Queen Mary was ruling in person and could hardly have been permitted, even had she been willing, to nominate superintendents for the reformed church, so that the procedure laid down in the Book of Discipline could not be followed between 1561 and 1567. After 1567, again, the issue was complicated by the question of the future of the bishoprics: if the office of superintendent had ever since 1561 been provisional in the sense that it originated in the uncertain relations between the reformed church and the bishops, it became still more plainly so when the succession to the bishoprics became open to the reformers. But it may be that an even more cogent reason against the appointment of additional superintendents was the need for economy: when the funds at the disposal of the reformed church from the thirds were contracting, it was inexpedient to multiply officials with a salary of £700 or so per annum. In this situation, when the machinery to appoint superintendents could not be operated, and when there were no funds to pay them, resort was had to 'commissioners', who were appointed not by the state but by the general assembly and who received usually only £100 or £200 annually. The five superintendents and the three conforming bishops among them provided the oversight of far the greater part of the country, but the essential functions of supervision were elsewhere performed by such 'commissioners'. While the superintendent held office for life, the commissioner was appointed only for a term, but commissions were so frequently

[1] His collation to the chancellorship is dated 6 Feb. 1558/9. The parsonage of Kilmartin appears to have been a prebend of Argyll.
[2] B.U.K. I, 8, 28, 30, 53–4, 63, 128–9, 146, 148.   [3] P. 137 below.

renewed that there was in practice little difference in tenure. A further distinction was that the commissioners, unlike most of the superintendents, were only part-time overseers, holding parochial charges. But in spite of these distinctions, the term 'superintendent' was very commonly applied to commissioners.[1] The 'visitors' of whom we hear from time to time, appointed to visit particular districts for brief periods,[2] would seem to have been in a different category altogether from either superintendents or commissioners (although they were sometimes called 'commissioners'); they were not salaried officials.

[1] E.g. 'superintendent of Aberdeen' in 1562 (*B.U.K.* I, 29); 'Andrew Hay, superintendent of Glasgow' (Reg. of Deeds, XII, 286); David Lindsay, 'superintendent' of Ayrshire (Protocol book of James Colville, fo. 46).

[2] E.g. Laing, II, 347 (Dickinson, II, 55); VI, 142-4.

CHAPTER VI

THE 'GODLY MAGISTRACY'
AND THE GENERAL ASSEMBLY

THE reformation thus in a very real sense represented a reaction against the frustration and depression of the bishops through the extension of papal authority and the system of papal dispensations, a reaction against the distraction of the bishops from their proper functions through their entanglement in politics and administration. But if the reformation was thus in some sense a reaction in favour of the episcopate, it also represented a reaction in favour of the laity. The thread of anti-clericalism runs all through, partly perhaps by way of lowering the status of the clergy, but more notably by way of elevating that of the laity. It is conspicuous in the developments in worship, for with the use of the vernacular, the composition of metrical psalms, the introduction of a Book of Common Prayer or a Book of Common Order, services became congregational and corporate, services in which everyone could join. With the invitation of the people to communicate at every Eucharist, the restoration of the cup to the laity and the setting up of a table around which the communicants could assemble, the celebration of Holy Communion ceased to be something done by the priest alone, at the altar, and became a congregational, corporate action in which the participation of the people was essential. Somewhat similar conceptions lay behind the stress laid on education, whether directly of the laity themselves or indirectly through the standards now demanded of the ministers, who would in time raise an instructed people, in no danger of falling under the domination of a new priestly caste. In polity, anti-clericalism is to be seen in the idea that discipline over the laity should be exercised not by the clergy but by the laity themselves, acting either as godly princes or as godly magistrates or as members of consistories, that is, elders in a kirk session; it is to be seen, further, again at parochial level, in the idea that congregations should elect their ministers and in the conception, which seems to be implied, that authority ascends from the people and does not descend from the bishop. At the higher levels of the ecclesiastical polity, anti-clericalism meant that although the lower clergy were to be disciplined by an episcopate, yet the episcopate in its turn was to be responsible to a lay authority, with which ultimate control rested. Normally, where the reformed church obtained recognition from the sovereign, authority over the church would lie with the crown, as happened in the Lutheran countries and in England; but exceptionally such authority might lie with the estates of the realm or with lesser magistrates, and that is what happened in Scotland.

To say that the Scottish reformation put ecclesiastical authority into the hands of a secular power may seem as paradoxical as to suggest that the Scottish reformation was a reaction in favour of an episcopate, for later Scottish history was concerned very largely with the church's attempt to repudiate the ecclesiastical supremacy of the civil power. Moreover, to the twentieth-century mind, in Scotland at least, there seems to be something slightly improper about the whole idea of a royal or civil supremacy over the church. But the circumstances and the outlook of the sixteenth century were quite different. Church and nation were then co-terminous: each consisted of the same people, each was coextensive with the whole population, church and state were but different aspects of one and the same society. From this identity it was a logical inference that the magistracy which exercised authority in the state should exercise authority in the church as well. If it was admitted that the crown was head of the state, head of the nation, it was not easy to deny that it was head also of the church which likewise consisted of its subjects. Leaving theory aside, it was only with the help of the crown that papal authority could be abrogated and the papacy superseded, and only with the help of the crown could the existing bishops and other holders of church property and offices be brought either to accept the reformation or to relinquish their benefices to those who would. This was perhaps a somewhat negative function to assign to the magistrate; but it is hard to find any writer of the period who would have restricted the magistrate to this negative activity and denied to him the further, positive duty of maintaining the church reformed, constraining his subjects to submit to its discipline and exercising a general oversight of its life.

It was along such lines that the Anglican settlement was interpreted and justified by the Swiss Bullinger:

> Christes Apostles removed not the faithfull magistrate from the administration of ecclesiasticall matters. . . . The vertuous Queene of England . . . hath done . . . her dewtie and deserved eternall prayse . . . for . . . takyng upon her the case of religion (*religionis causam*), . . . deposing from their estate and office the bishops that were sworne to the pope . . . and preferring to their roomes men sworne to Christ our Lorde and to the queenes majestie. . . . Kynges and magistrates ought to compell their subjectes unto goodnesse. . . . Kinges and magistrates doe lawfully punish, yea and also put to death such as breake the true religion.[1]

An able native defence of Elizabeth's proceedings declared that her authority in church matters meant only that she was 'bound to direct all estates to live in the faith and the obedience of Christian religion, and to see the laws of God and man . . . to be duly observed and the offenders against the same duly punished: and consequently to provide that the church may be governed and taught.'[2] Or, as Bishop Jewel expressed it, 'the prince is put in trust . . . to see that all his subjects, as well priests as laymen, each man in his calling' keep the two tables of the law; 'we say not,' he went on, 'the prince is bound to do the bishop's duty. . . . The prince is bound to see the bishops to do their duties.'[3]

In Scotland, as in all other countries where the movement for reform became strong, there was a claim for the civil power of a divine commission which would render it independent of the papacy, and an insistence that this independent civil authority, responsible to God alone, could reform and govern the church. 'We affirm,' wrote Knox, 'that no power on earth is above the power of the civil ruler; that every soul, be he pope or cardinal, ought to be subject to the higher powers.'[4] It was Satan, he held, who 'hath persuaded princes, rulers and magistrates that the feeding

---

[1] *Bullae papisticae refutatio*, fos. 45v, 47r, 55r, 58f (English translation, 1582).

[2] *Queen Elizabeth's Defence of her Proceedings*, ed. W. E. Collins (1958), p. 46.

[3] Jewel, *Works*, IV, 976; cf. Aylmer, *An Harborowe for Faithfull and Trewe Subjectes*, sig. I 4v, Fuller, *Church History*, IX, I, 6, and Article XXXVII of the Church of England.   [4] Laing, IV, 324.

of Christ's flock pertaineth nothing to their charge, but that it is rejected upon the bishops and estate ecclesiastical',[1] and he adduced a number of incidents in Old Testament history to prove 'that the reformation of religion in all points, together with the punishment of false teachers, doth appertain to the power of the civil magistrate'.[2] But if Knox's studies in the Old Testament provided a scriptural justification for an appeal to the civil power, the idea of making such an appeal was not peculiar to theologians, for it was the basic assumption behind most of Sir David Lindsay's pleas for 'reformation'. In his *Complaynt* he prays the king to make the clergy do their duty and in *The Tragedie of the Cardinall* he counsels

> everyilk christinit kyng
> Within his realme mak reformatioun.[3]

The lay theologian Balnaves, in his *Treatise on Justification*, exhorted 'the king' to suppress idolatry and restore true religion.[4]

In practice, the Scottish government did at times show a certain willingness to respond to the call to make reformation, and a series of incidents in Scotland suggests that it was no idle theory to argue that the reluctance of the clergy to accept effective measures of reform necessitated intervention by the crown. James I had gone no further than exhortation,[5] but James IV requested from the Cistercian chapter general a visitation of the houses of that order,[6] James V took similar action,[7] in 1541 there was an act of parliament for reforming of kirks and kirkmen and in 1559 Mary of Guise requested Archbishop Hamilton to summon the third of his reforming councils.[8] But the civil power or 'authority' to which the Scottish reformers looked for support was not necessarily the crown. *The Three Estates* makes the telling point of the numerical preponderance of the two secular estates:

> Wee set nocht by quhider ye consent or nocht:
> Ye ar bot ane estait and we ar twa
> *Et ubi major pars ibi tota*[9]

[1] Laing, IV, 485, cf. 443, 445.   [2] *Ibid.* 490.   [3] Lindsay, *Works*, I, 51, 143.
[4] Laing, III, 526 f.   [5] P. 3 above.
[6] Easson, *Medieval Religious Houses: Scotland*, p. 25.   [7] Pp. 1, 3, 32 above.
[8] Cf. Lesley, *History*, 269: 'at the desyre of sum temporall lordis and barronis sho caused all the hoill prelattis and principallis of the clargie convene'.
[9] Lindsay, *Works*, II, 269.

—an idea which was surely in men's minds when the vernacular Bible was authorised by parliament without the consent of the clerical estate. If 'the prince' failed in his duty, other constitutional organs would take his place.[1] The nobles, who, in virtue of their official position as counsellors, had the right to be consulted by the prince,[2] were told by Knox not to suppose that because they were inferior, and not chief, magistrates they had no responsibility,[3] for 'the reformation of religion and of public enormities doth appertain to more than to the clergy or chief rulers called kings'.[4] With less emphasis, but still with sufficient clarity, Knox spoke of a larger body than the greater nobility: the community at large must not 'esteem the reformation and care of religion less to appertain to you, because ye are no kings, rulers, judges, nobles nor in authority'.[5] Addressing Queen Mary, he justified his own intervention in the politics of the kingdom on the ground that he was 'a subject born within the same',[6] but in a less unguarded moment he was careful to explain that he assigned power to 'a body of a commonwealth' and not to isolated individuals.[7] With every constitutional organ, then, and at every level in society, there was the same appeal to the laity to act in ecclesiastical affairs. Nor was it the case, as has been argued, that the Scottish reformers intended that the civil power, after purging the church, should then divest itself of ecclesiastical authority. In Knox's words, it was an error for magistrates to suppose that 'the feeding of Christ's flock pertaineth nothing to their charge',[8] and the Confession of Faith of 1560 stated that 'to kings, princes, rulers and magistrates we affirm that chiefly and most principally the conservation and purgation of religion appertains; so that not only they are appointed for civil policy, but also for maintenance of the true religion and for suppressing of idolatry and superstition'.[9] It is undeniable that 'the feeding of Christ's flock',

---

[1] Cf. Laing, I, 411; II, 455–6 (Dickinson, I, 227; II, 131).
[2] Cf. *ibid.* I, 404, 406, 444–9 (Dickinson, I, 222, 224, 251–5).
[3] *Ibid.* IV, 494.   [4] *Ibid.* I, 272 (Dickinson, I, 135).
[5] *Ibid.* IV, 526, cf. I, 411 (Dickinson, I, 227).   [6] *Ibid.* II, 388 (Dickinson, II, 83).
[7] *Ibid.* 442–3 (Dickinson, II, 122).   [8] P. 133 above.
[9] Laing, II, 118 (Dickinson, II, 271, where a note explains how the erroneous reading 'reformation and purgation' arose); cf. *A.P.S.* II, 534, III, 22; and Calderwood, II, 35.

'the conservation of religion' and the 'maintenance of true religion' implied the recognition of extensive authority over the church reformed. There is nothing in the Confession of Faith, any more than in the Thirty-Nine Articles, to suggest that a church should be independent of the civil magistrate, and nothing at all inconsistent with the ecclesiastical supremacy of a 'godly prince'.

There was no incompatibility between the theories of the Scottish reformers or of the continental followers of Calvin and the ecclesiastical supremacy of the prince as it existed in England. It was only an historical accident that in most countries where Calvinism prevailed the reformers found themselves in opposition to the government, with the result that the ecclesiastical authority which they were prepared to concede to a godly prince remained a pious aspiration. The opinions of Anglicans on the subject of the magistrate's authority can in fact be closely paralleled in the writings of continental Calvinists on the one side,[1] while, on the other, Scottish reformers would have had no difficulty in identifying the ecclesiastical functions ascribed to Queen Elizabeth by her apologists[2] with the 'conservation and purgation of religion' which they themselves held to be a function of the prince. And when English churchmen in 1559 exhorted their queen to be 'diligent to suppress all papistry, vice and heresy, and to cause the light of God's Word speedily to shine through all her dominions',[3] their thought was identical with that embodied in the contemporary appeals by the Scottish protestants to Mary of Guise.

It is in the persistent appeal of the reformers to the magistracy, and not in any claim to ecclesiastical independence, that the origin of the general assembly is to be found. The first meeting of the

[1] E.g. Hooper, *Later Writings*, p. 54

I believe that to the magistrate it doth appertain . . . *to take away and to overthrow all idolatry and false serving of God, to destroy the kingdom of Antichrist* and all false doctrine, to promote the glory of God and *to advance the kingdom of Christ, to cause the word of the Gospel everywhere to be preached.*

[2] P. 132 above.   [3] Strype, *Annals*, I, I, 164.

Confessio Belgica (1561), in Kidd, *op. cit.* 685

Non seulement, leur office est . . . *pour ôter et ruiner toute idolâtrie et faux service de Dieu; pour détruire le royaume de l'Antichrist et avancer le royaume de Jésus Christ, faire prêcher la Parole de l'Evangile partout. . . .*

assembly is conventionally assigned to December 1560, but its genesis is to be found in the developments of the preceding three years. In the league known as the 'First Band', signed in December 1557, a group of noble and landed gentlemen who had committed themselves to the reformed cause pledged themselves to 'labour . . . to have faithful ministers . . . to minister Christ's evangel and sacraments to his people' and undertook to 'maintain them, nourish them and defend them'.[1] Thereafter 'the lords and barons professing Christ Jesus convened frequently in council', arranged for the use of the Book of Common Prayer in churches and for preaching 'privately in quiet houses', and carried out their undertaking to maintain ministers.[2] They awaited the consent of 'the Prince' for 'public preaching', and appealed to the regent for the authorising of the scriptures in the vernacular, 'Common Prayers', interpretation of the scriptures, Baptism and Holy Communion in the vulgar tongue, and reform of the lives of the clergy.[3] Then, when the regent failed in what they conceived to be her duty, it was time, according to Knox's theories,[4] for the inferior magistrates to do theirs, and the 'nobility, barons and burghs convened to advise upon the affairs of the commonwealth' suspended Mary of Guise from the administration.[5] Although this action was taken in the name of the absent king and queen and on the grounds of essentially political grievances, the suspension was a transfer of authority from an ungodly regent to godly inferior magistrates. These inferior magistrates constituted themselves or some of their number a 'great council of the realm', under the presidency of Châtelherault, the heir presumptive, and carried on the administration as a kind of provisional government.

The Book of Discipline was a report on worship, polity and endowment made at the request of this provisional government, and it is a report to that government. It does not differ in essence, though it differs in scale, from the earlier supplications to the queen regent, and like them it is directed to the civil power, which alone could have put its recommendations into effect. Clear definition is not,

---

[1] Laing, I, 273–4 (Dickinson, I, 136–7).
[2] *Ibid.* 275–6 (Dickinson, I, 137–8). [3] *Ibid.* 302 f. (Dickinson, I, 149 f.).
[4] P. 134 above. [5] Laing, I, 444–9 (Dickinson, I, 251–5).

indeed, to be found in the book, possibly because much was assumed, possibly because the situation was unstable and the future not assured: it is wonderfully vague about the 'council of the church'[1] which was in certain matters to advise the magistrate or give its consent to the magistrate's proceedings; but the distribution of ministers seems to be left to the wisdom of 'their honours', the lords, who were also initially to nominate the superintendents, while the salaries of superintendents were to be adjusted by 'the prince and council of the realm'[2]—a phrase which quite casually, but very strikingly, implies the kind of establishment for which the reformers were looking.

In the period between the treaty of Edinburgh in July 1560 and the return of Queen Mary from France in August 1561 the reformers were in control of the civil administration and it was 'inferior magistrates' in one guise or another who guided the affairs of the reformed church: according to Knox, the 'commissioners of burghs, and some of the nobility and barons' at some uncertain date arranged the appointment of ministers and superintendents;[3] the lords of the privy council issued the licences for the election of Spottiswoode as superintendent of Lothian and of Winram as superintendent of Fife, in March 1561;[4] and the same lords issued a mandate to Spottiswoode to exercise his office as superintendent[5]— a proceeding surely quite as Erastian as Edward VI's appointment of bishops by letters patent and one which makes it a little difficult to deny that the superintendents derived their authority from the civil power. The superintendents, once they were appointed, acted 'in the name of God and of the secret council, our present and lawful magistrates'.[6] It is plain that just as Knox and his colleagues turned to inferior magistrates to effect the reform of the church, so they turned to them as governors of the church reformed.

Political conditions in Scotland had not been favourable to the realisation of the church-state relationship which the reformers

---

[1] See p. 140 below.
[2] Laing, II, 194–5, 198, 205 (Dickinson, II, 287, 289, 293).
[3] P. 61 above.　　[4] P. 65 above.
[5] Warrender MSS., vol. A, fos. 93, 98. See Appendix.
[6] *Ibid.* fo. 98v. See Appendix.

regarded as ideal, and their church found itself in opposition to the state as represented by the crown. But in the activities of the inferior magistrates in 1560 and 1561 we see the germ of a 'new state' which might have arisen to match the 'new church'. Indeed, while Francis lived and there seemed little likelihood that Mary would return to Scotland, there was a possibility that Mary might be superseded and replaced as sovereign by a 'godly prince' in the person perhaps of the Lord James, her half-brother, perhaps of the earl of Arran (son of Châtelherault, next in the royal succession after his father, and, some thought, a suitable husband for the 'godly princess' who ruled in England). It may even be that lack of agreement on an alternative to Mary was the chief obstacle to her deposition. But expectations of a 'godly prince' were disappointed in December 1560, when Francis died and the Scottish reformers had to face the probability that Mary would return and the sovereign of the Scottish state would not be the governor of the Scottish church. The death of Francis on 5 December, said Knox, 'made great alteration',[1] and a substitute had to be found for the crown supremacy which the Scots were clearly not going to have. As already mentioned, a convention was appointed for 15 January;[2] but in the month of December itself, when hopes of a 'godly prince' had been so suddenly extinguished, there took place what is counted the first meeting of a general assembly (beginning on 20 December). This first assembly was something of an *ad hoc* body, essentially ecclesiastical (in that it consisted mainly of commissioners of 'particular kirks'), though hardly clerical (for the laymen far outnumbered the ministers); but it was complementary to the civil convention summoned for the following month and was indeed 'continued' or adjourned until 15 January, when commissioners of churches were to be present at the convention.[3]

If the first appearance of the general assembly had been related to the apprehensions aroused by the death of Francis, the reformers' foresight was justified when Queen Mary returned to Scotland in August 1561. There are, indeed, indications that Mary was less intransigent on ecclesiastical issues than is often supposed. There

[1] Laing, II, 136 (Dickinson, I, 350).
[2] *Ibid.* 138 (Dickinson, I, 351). Cf. p. 65 above.   [3] *B.U.K.* I, 7.

was something of a Gallican, or anti-Tridentine, element in her French family background. One of her cardinal-uncles was described by the pope as 'damned and a heretic, or, to speak plainly, one of the Protestants', and he went some way towards justifying the papal censure by commending the English Prayer Book as well as by defending episcopacy against the papacy.[1] Mary's policy in Scotland was often disappointing enough to more zealous papalists, and her passive attitude towards the reformed church led to a good deal of criticism, not least from the pope himself. When it suited her own private ends, she could make lavish enough concessions to the reformers, she could enter into a protestant marriage, she could hint at her readiness to accept the English Prayer Book.[2] The young queen of 1561 was not already cast for the part of the Roman catholic martyr of 1587. Mary's sympathisers are apt to forget that she ultimately lost the Scottish throne not because she was a devout Roman catholic, but because she entered into a scandalous, indeed adulterous, marriage with the man universally suspected to have murdered her previous husband—a union blessed by a bishop of the reformed church and condemned by the pope. It would be no difficult exercise to present Mary's fidelity to Rome in her later years as nothing more than a last resort when all else had failed. But if, in the 1560s, Mary was by no means committed to a papalist policy, it was none the less true that a queen who went to mass was at least outwith the reformed church and could not be its supreme head on earth; she could not even be supreme governor of the realm in all spiritual or ecclesiastical things or causes. The general assembly had therefore to continue and indeed to develop.

The general assembly as normally constituted in the 1560s was not merely a 'council of the church' such as the Book of Discipline had mentioned, nor was it, as it is today, a body of ministers and elders representative of the regional or local units of the church. It is, indeed, far from clear that a general assembly in anything like the form in which it actually emerged had been envisaged in the Book of Discipline, although there are references in that document to some kind of ecclesiastical assembly for the entire country—'the

[1] Evenett, *The Cardinal of Lorraine and the Council of Trent*, pp. 206, 250, 417.
[2] *Cal. S. P. Scot.* I, 603; II, 466, 472–3, 475.

whole council of the church' and 'the great council of the church'[1]
—and if their 'honours' (that is, the lords') were to act 'with the consent of the kirk' some kind of representative church council seems
to be implied.[2] The early history of the general assembly has never
been analysed, the original records are not now extant,[3] and the
material which preserves the proceedings of the sixteenth-century
assemblies, consisting as it does of abridgments and selected extracts,[4] seldom discloses the composition of the meetings. Even so,
it is certain that in some at least of the early assemblies it is possible
to discern the same three estates which at that time formed the
Scottish parliament.

The first element was the nobility and baronage. In December
1563, for example, there were present peers and officers of state;[5]
and a minister, in a petition which he presented, addressed the
gathering as 'the maist honorable privie counsell there assembled
with the rest of the nobilitie, the superintendents, ministers, commissioners of provinces and kirks.'[6] In June 1564 'a great part of the
nobility, of those that are called protestants, convened', and a year
later 'the earls of Argyll and Glencairn assisted the church, with a
great company of lords, barons and others'.[7] In June 1566, June
1567, December 1567 and some later assemblies, some of the
nobility were again present, and when a special effort was made to

---

[1] Laing, II, 208, 226 (Dickinson, II, 295, 305).

[2] 'The council of the kirk' and 'the council of the whole kirk' in connection
with the admission of ministers seem to be the superintendent's council. The same
probably applies to 'the whole kirk' which was to translate ministers, for it seems
unlikely that translation was to be a function of a national body, and we know
that in practice it was the superintendent who translated ministers. See Laing, II,
190, 194 (Dickinson, II, 284, 286).

[3] They were destroyed by fire in 1834.

[4] An old selection of acts, known as 'The Book of the Universal Kirk' (edited
by Alexander Peterkin in 1839), was conflated with material in Calderwood's
History and other works to form the *Acts and Proceedings of the General Assemblies*
(Bannatyne and Maitland Clubs, 1839–45). It should be noted that abridgements
made in the seventeenth century are unreliable for descriptions of the composition
of assemblies, because the writers would tend to interpret the evidence in the
light of the practice of their own day.

[5] *B.U.K.* I, 38 (Calderwood, II, 241).

[6] *Cal. S.P. Scot.* II, No. 44. It was 'the lords of the secret council, with the whole
brethren of the assembly' who chose the moderator (*B.U.K.* I, 38).

[7] Laing, II, 421, 484 (Dickinson, II, 106, 148).

muster the nobility in July 1567, by sending missives to named individuals, it was very successful.[1] A statement made in the next decade that one of the elements in the assembly was 'the notable nobles and barons professing the true religion'[2] is borne out by these facts. But, while any 'godly' nobleman seems to have been welcome to attend simply as an individual, not as a representative of anything or anybody, the position of the lesser baronage, below the rank of lords of parliament, is not so clear. As all who held land directly of the king owed suit in the king's court, the lesser barons had a right, and indeed a duty, to attend parliaments and general councils, and statutes of 1426 and 1428 had first endeavoured to enforce their personal presence and then made arrangements for representatives to be elected at the head court of each sheriffdom. But attendance either in person or by representatives had been long in abeyance when, in 1560, 'the barons and freeholders of the realm', pleading their numbers and resources, their concern for 'true religion and common weal of the realm' and ancient statutes in their favour, successfully craved admittance to the 'reformation parliament'. This was exceptional, and it was only after an act of 1587 provided for representation, through the election of commissioners for shires, that the lesser baronage became a permanent element in the Scottish parliament. For meetings of the general assembly, however, superintendents were instructed to warn 'shires', as well as burghs and parish churches, to send commissioners, and references to the presence of 'commissioners of shires' as well as 'commissioners of towns'[3] would seem to suggest that the assembly may have anticipated the parliament by a generation in making provision for the representation, by commissioners, of the lesser landholders.[4]

If nobles and barons thus constituted one element in the assembly,

---

[1] B.U.K. I, 93. And see signatures on p. 110 (Calderwood, II, 382–3).
[2] S.H.S. Misc. VIII, 105.
[3] B.U.K. I, 36–7 (Calderwood, II, 226), 52, 57, 82.
[4] The 'warning' by the superintendents must have been directed to the sheriff of the shire as it was to the provost of the burgh, but the following Sheriff Court Books have been examined, without result, for references to the election of commissioners to general assemblies: Fife, 1563/4–1564/5; Perth, 1563–4, 1566–7, 1567; West Lothian, 1562–6.

it is equally clear that a second element consisted of burgh commissioners, appointed not by any ecclesiastical organ but by the town councils. Even the essentially clerical convention of December 1560 included some 'commissioners of towns', and the accounts of the proceedings of several later assemblies refer to 'commissioners of towns' as well as those of shires and kirks. Further, even when the accounts of an assembly's proceedings may speak only of superintendents, ministers and commissioners of kirks, as in June 1562 and June 1563, burgh records disclose that town councils had sent commissioners.[1] That the burgesses were regarded as a distinctive element or 'estate' in an assembly was shown when articles were submitted to the queen, on behalf of the general assembly, by four lairds 'and James Barron for the burghs'.[2]

The ministers who were present to form the clerical element were sometimes far outnumbered by the groups of laymen already mentioned. A minister's place, it was considered, was in his parish, and ministers were not lightly to 'leave their flock for coming to the assembly'.[3] Those who did come were present either because there was business which concerned them individually or because they were instructed to attend by their superintendents[4] or—exceptionally—because town councils had chosen them as burghal representatives.[5] It might be too much to say that we should think of the superintendents coming up to the assembly, each with a number of ministers whom he had invited to attend, but there are indications that something like this was the practice. Ministers certainly had no prescriptive right to attend the assembly, nor were those who came elected by their brethren.

Some light is thrown on what the assembly was by noting what it was not, for some instructive contrasts can be made. It was not such a general assembly as was later to be proposed by the second Book of Discipline, for that was to consist of ministers and elders chosen

---

[1] E.g. *Extracts from Records of Burgh of Edinburgh*, III, 138, 161.
[2] Laing, II, 486 (Dickinson, II, 150).
[3] *B.U.K.* I, 14 (Calderwood, II, 184).
[4] *Ibid.* 14, 124 (Calderwood, II, 421); cf. *S.H.S. Misc.* VIII, 105 (where 'episcopi', wrongly rendered 'bishops', clearly embraces superintendents, conforming bishops and commissioners).
[5] This course was followed in Aberdeen in July 1567 (Keith, *op. cit.* III, 175–6).

by synods. Nor can it be identified with the national synod or general council adopted by the reformed churches in France, for that consisted of ministers accompanied by one or two elders or deacons who had been elected by the local consistories. There is an equally clear contrast between the Scottish general assembly of the 1560s and the Scottish synods of the same period, for the latter were to be composed of the ministers of the area, each with an elder or a deacon; the synods were essentially ecclesiastical bodies in a sense that the general assembly was not, although, at a time when elders were only annually elected lay officers, even the synods can hardly be called clerical bodies.

The assembly may have been in practice nothing more than a development from the 'great council of the realm', consisting of the protestant lords and their associates, which acted as the provisional government in 1559–61. 'The commissioners of burghs, and some of the nobility and barons', it will be recalled, had appointed superintendents and ministers, and, when such a body associated the reformed clergy with it, the general assembly had arrived. Slightly differently regarded, the assembly was a council of the realm strengthened by the addition of some clerical members—the privy council with superintendents, ministers and commissioners, as it was said to be in 1563.[1] Initially, supreme authority over the reformed church had been vested in the council—a 'godly' council; but with Mary's return the council would become the council of an 'ungodly' queen and might contain other 'ungodly' elements, so that it could no longer have that authority, and another organ of church government had to be devised. In short, the assembly was plainly the 'godly magistracy', or perhaps the 'godly estates', the substitute for the 'godly prince' whom the Scots did not have. Far from being the organ of 'the church', in independence of 'the state', the assembly represents the 'new state' in partnership with the 'new church', it represents the control of the estates over the church, or the control of the Christian community over the church.

---

[1] P. 140 above. The tradition which identifies the first meeting-place of the assembly with the Magdalene Chapel associates it with a building which had recently been used for meetings of the lords of council and session (*Extracts from Records of Burgh of Edinburgh*, III, 1).

And when it is considered alongside the system of lay elders, annually elected, in the congregations, we have a polity which could with some justice be characterised as an anti-clerical democracy.

As long as Mary ruled, the 'new church' or the 'new church-state', represented by the assembly, found itself in an uneasy relationship with the 'old state', represented by the crown. The tension between them was to be seen in questions of endowment, particularly the division of the thirds between the queen and the ministers, and in questions of establishment, notably the toleration and protection of the mass, though possibly the most significant point at issue was the position of the general assembly, whose right to meet, though challenged, was successfully maintained. But if the general assembly was regarded, by some at least, as nothing more than a temporary expedient, pending the accession of a 'godly prince', Mary's deposition, in 1567, led necessarily to a reconsideration of the relations between the reformed church and the crown, now 'godly' in the person of the infant James VI and his protestant regents. Indications are not lacking of a readiness on the part of the ministers to permit the king now to assume those ecclesiastical responsibilities to which, according to reformation thought, he was entitled. The general assembly, at the opening of the new reign, agreed that future sovereigns should promise to 'maintain and defend and by all lawful means set forward the true religion'[1]— phraseology which could be held to imply extensive ecclesiastical authority. Again, when a book which gave the king the title of 'supreme head of the church' was discussed in the general assembly of July 1568 there seems to have been no certainty whether such a title was allowable or not.[2] And an oath of supremacy, exacted from the bishops in 1572 and from all clergy appointed thereafter, acknowledging the king as 'supreme governor of this realm, as well in things temporal as in the conservation and purgation of religion',[3] seems to have aroused no opposition or criticism. Thus the theoretical acceptance of the royal supremacy seems to be clear enough. But it may well be that the theory would not have stood the strain if a

---

[1] *B.U.K.* I, 108–9 (Calderwood, II, 381).
[2] *Ibid.* 125–6 (Calderwood, II, 423).
[3] *Ibid.* 220 (Calderwood, III, 184).

sovereign, however 'godly', had used his authority against what churchmen conceived to be the true interests of the church, and the tension which was to arise when the government attempted to 'intrude' bishops in 1571 provoked language which anticipated the presbyterian doctrine of the 'two kingdoms'.[1]

In any event, if there was a profound change in theory when James VI replaced his mother, it was not at first apparent that there need be or could be much change in practice. The 'godly prince' was an infant, the regents were of varying quality and had a precarious tenure not only of office but of life itself, the king's Roman catholic mother still lived and there was an active Marian faction against whom military operations went on until 1573. When prospects in Scotland were thus far from assured and the massacre of St Bartholomew provided a lesson on the fate of a reformed church under a hostile crown, it was no time to relinquish any safeguards for the reformed religion. The situation was not sufficiently stable to encourage, or even to permit, the abandonment of the general assembly. Not only so, but in spite of an act of July 1568, which may have been aimed at reconstructing the assembly as a primarily ecclesiastical convention (including indeed shire commissioners, but chosen by the synods, and burgh commissioners chosen by the 'council and kirk'),[2] the 'nobility' and 'barons' continued to be an element in its membership. If the survival of such a 'mixed' assembly in the reign of a 'godly prince' was something of an anomaly, the fact was plainly demonstrated in 1572, when bishops had to acknowledge the king as supreme governor of the realm in the conservation and purgation of religion, but were at the same time declared to be subject to the general assembly *in spiritualibus*. Here, it may be, was ambiguity which demanded elucidation.

At this stage provision was made for the effective representation of the reformed church in parliament,[3] and if parliament thus came to contain the same elements as the assembly, the latter became more anomalous than ever. After 1573, when the protestant regime was at last stabilised, the question was seriously canvassed whether the general assembly had outlived its usefulness. The Regent

---

[1] Pp. 161–2 below.   [2] *B.U.K.* I, 124 (Calderwood, II, 421).
[3] See pp. 163, 171 below.

Morton obviously intended to deal with this question as part of his comprehensive settlement of polity and endowment.[1] In January 1573/4 he wrote:

> It is very requisite that in this time of repose which God has granted us after our long troubles we be careful for the good order and provision of the polity of the kirk in things ambiguous and unresolved or not heretofore well observed and executed; that the same . . . may be considered, settled and established. . . . We have thought very expedient that now, against the time of the next general assembly . . . , to be in the beginning of March next, a certain of the nobility, estates and barons . . . may also be present; by whose advice . . . such things may be . . . concluded as may tend to God's glory and the settling of the polity of the true reformed kirk.[2]

When the assembly met in March, it sent a petition to the regent which suggests that the assembly, in its traditional form of a gathering of the three estates, was in practice showing some signs of 'withering away' under the changed political circumstances,[3] and Morton's reply shows how ready he was to welcome such a development or even to proceed to the forcible suppression of the assembly if it should fail to die a natural death.[4] There was opposition to his proposals, at first on the apologetic ground that a future sovereign might again be hostile to the reformation and that the assembly must be preserved as a safeguard.[5] What might have been the fate of the assembly had no novel ideas on the relations of church and state been introduced, and had a claim not been advanced by Andrew Melville to ecclesiastical independence even under a 'godly prince', it would be unprofitable to speculate. But it certainly does appear that there was some hesitation about putting forward a demand that the assembly should continue irrespective of the sovereign's religion and his attitude to the reformed church, and this hesitation supports the contention that the assembly had originally been designed only as a temporary expedient under the rule of a hostile sovereign.

The system set up in the 1560s cannot be called presbyterian, and

---

[1] See pp. 171, 175–6 below.   [2] *Wodrow Soc. Misc.* I, 289.
[3] *B.U.K.* I, 292. Calderwood (III, 305) assigns this to March 1574/5.
[4] Calderwood, III, 306–7.   [5] *S.H.S. Misc.* VIII, 105.

if it must be explained at all in later terminology, it might best
be described as congregationalism tempered by episcopacy and
Erastianism. Superficially viewed, it seems to have contained some
of the elements characteristic of the later presbyterian polity, for
there was a general assembly, there were synods, there were kirk
sessions of elders and deacons, but the resemblance did not go far,
because each of those organs was different in some significant
respects from the later presbyterian organ of the same name—the
general assembly was representative of the magistracy or the estates,
the synods were dependent on the superintendents, the elders and
deacons were merely annually elected lay officers, and superintendents received their commissions from the civil power and not from
any ecclesiastical organ. The individual overseer—whether bishop,
superintendent or commissioner—was an indispensable feature of
the system, the oversight of ministers was in the hands of individuals and not of committees, and there was no hierarchy of courts. The
existence of kirk sessions, which in the sixteenth century were often
called 'presbyteries', would be a poor reason for giving the name
'presbyterian' to the entire system. Such local consistories are com-
patible with an episcopal, a congregational or a presbyterian constitution, and in any event the character of a national polity is to be
found not in the organisation of particular churches but in the
method of federation or subordination by which individual congregations are joined together to form a whole. The body characteristic of the presbyterian system, with its hierarchy of courts, is
the presbytery or *classis*, and this did not appear in Scotland until
some twenty years after the reformation. To call the 1560 system
'presbyterian without the presbytery' involves a contradiction in
terms. Nor is there any contemporary evidence that this polity was
meant to be temporary or to develop into anything else. It did in
fact develop, as will appear in the next chapter, into a system with a
slightly more episcopalian flavour, and, so modified, it was the
polity which in substance endured down to 1690 except during two
or three brief presbyterian interludes.

If attempts to interpret this first constitution of the Scottish reformed church in terms of the presbyterian system familiar in later
times must therefore be made only with great caution, attempts to

see in it a system essentially Genevan or essentially similar to the system developed by the reformed churches in France can be made only by an appeal to fiction rather than to fact. There is not a single feature in the Scottish polity which had parallels only in France or Switzerland; not only so, but the French *Discipline*, with its firm emphasis on parity of pastors and churches and its hierarchy of courts, was founded on principles at variance with those embodied in the Scottish polity. It seems undeniable that the Scots consciously and deliberately rejected the French precedent, and there were elements in their system which suggest imitation rather of the polity of some of the Lutheran churches, especially that of Denmark.[1]

[1] Janet G. MacGregor, *The Scottish Presbyterian Polity*; G. Donaldson, ' "The example of Denmark" in the Scottish Reformation', in *S.H.R.* xxvii.

CHAPTER VII

'CONFORMITY WITH ENGLAND', 1567-73

THE three preceding chapters have described a new ecclesiastical structure—the polity of the reformed church. But an earlier chapter explained that alongside this polity, which was now the machinery by which spiritual functions were performed but which lacked endowment, there still survived the old ecclesiastical structure, which retained the bulk of the endowments but was no longer the machinery by which spiritual functions were performed. A good deal of subsequent history arose from this question: could some means be devised whereby the new structure and the old could be merged, so that the divorce between endowments and spiritual functions would come to an end? To put it so perhaps suggests that the development which took place was more deliberate, more conscious, than it can be proved to have been. It can, however, be said with safety that the persistence of the old organisation of the benefices was to suggest an alternative to the Book of Discipline, which had proposed to subvert the ancient structure. Or, to put it differently, in the old structure there remained in being a mould which was to help to shape the development of the reformed polity.

The thirds were only a temporary expedient, which left as an open question the ultimate disposal of the church property. In particular, it was not determined whether, as the existing holders of benefices died, the benefices would be 'dissolved' according to the proposals of the Book of Discipline or would remain in being and be disponed to other holders; and, if the latter course should be followed, who were the new holders of the benefices to be and how were they to be appointed? In practice, although the Book of Discipline had proposed that lay patronage should be abandoned, the old machinery of presentation and episcopal collation continued to operate;[1] but there was no longer any defined relation

[1] Pp. 73–4 above.

between this machinery and provision for the performance of spiritual functions.

The patron who was of quite central importance was the queen, not so much because of the crown's ancient rights of presenting to benefices in its 'proper' patronage and to benefices in episcopal patronage *sede vacante*, as because of its successful assertion now of comprehensive powers over the disposal of the 'prelacies'. The royal powers had already grown before 1560,[1] and after 1560 there took place a 'silent revolution whereby the crown, assuming papal, and more than papal, powers, took into its own hands the disposal of the ecclesiastical property'.[2] From 1561 the crown disposed without restriction of abbeys and priories, granting them either to lay commendators or to persons who would themselves nominate commendators. In the disposal of the lesser benefices which were in its patronage, the crown in general abandoned the traditional presentation, and resorted to a simple gift.[3] Thus even parochial benefices, benefices traditionally involving the cure of souls, were being distributed, mainly to lay titulars, without any ecclesiastical control over appointment. Crown action in this particular showed hardly any indication that the existence of the reformed church was so much as acknowledged. From the outset there were indeed some beneficed clergy who conformed and served in the reformed church, so that a certain proportion of the ministers of the reformed church happened to be in possession of benefices. But it is abundantly clear that, in the absence of any compulsion on the queen or other patrons to present men able and willing to serve in the ministry, such men were not in general being appointed to benefices.

This trend towards secularisation did not go without challenge from the general assembly. In 1562 it petitioned that 'persons to be nominat to kirks' were not to be admitted without the 'nomination of the people and due examination and admission of the superintendent', and that this provision should be retrospective to 1558;[4] if 'kirks' was perhaps an ambiguous term, which might refer only to pastoral charges in the reformed church, there was no ambiguity

[1] Pp. 37–9 above.
[2] *R.S.S.* v, Intro. ii f. where this development is discussed.
[3] P. 73 above.   [4] *B.U.K.* I, 16 (Calderwood, II, 186).

in the following year, when it was requested that 'when any bene-fice shall vaike, qualified persons may be presented to the superin-tendent of the province'.[1] Such a request, it will be observed, im-plied a departure from the Book of Discipline's proposals for the subversion of the old ecclesiastical structure and for a reallocation of its endowments; the assembly now accepted the existence of the benefices and the rights of patrons, but was pressing for the appoint-ment to the existing benefices of men approved by the reformed church, through the examination of patrons' nominees by the superintendents. But the assembly's requests were not acceptable to the crown, and it remained the law that, while superintendents could admit to pastoral charges, they had no authority to give col-lation to benefices. There was, indeed, something of an *impasse*: there was no machinery whereby the nominee of the patron could be approved by the reformed church, with the result that, while the patron could have his nominee put into possession of the fruits of a benefice, he could not have him invested with the spiritual responsi-bilities properly pertaining to the office.

To find a way out of the *impasse* became a matter of urgency as the financial provision for the reformed church out of the thirds became increasingly unsatisfactory.[2] The contrast between the poverty of the ministers and the enrichment of courtiers and other laymen through their appointment to benefices could lead to this line of reasoning: if, as benefices fell vacant, ministers were appoint-ed to them, then to that extent the reformed church would gain access to ecclesiastical revenues. The reformers now saw that their financial difficulties could be at least partially solved not by revert-ing to the demands of the Book of Discipline but by the imitation of Anglican practice and the taking over of the existing structure of the church; the general assembly therefore reiterated its claim to the succession to the benefices.[3]

The assembly's demands went unheeded until the last months of 1566, when Mary's estrangement from Darnley and her growing partiality for Bothwell evidently made it desirable to conciliate the ministers. In December 1566 a special assignation from the thirds—

---

[1] *B.U.K.* I, 34 (Calderwood, II, 227).   [2] P. 71 above.
[3] *B.U.K.* I, 59, 70 (Calderwood, II, 288, 298).

£10,000 in money, along with a substantial quantity of victual—was allotted for stipends, and in February 1567[1] there began a series of gifts to burghs of the ecclesiastical properties within their bounds.[2] Still earlier, as the beginning of this new phase of royal policy, there had come the first official acknowledgment of the general assembly's claim to the benefices, in an act of council of October 1566, proposing that all benefices worth less than three hundred merks annually should go to ministers.[3] This meant that all the parochial benefices, and a good many more, would fall to the reformed church as they became vacant, and to that extent the two structures would merge. The act was not consistently observed in the remaining months of Mary's reign, but there were instances of its application.[4]

After thus adopting a policy which aimed at the ultimate identification of the reformed church with the old ecclesiastical structure, and finding this policy so far accepted by the government, the general assembly went a step further, and in December 1566 adopted a resolution seeking the co-operation and support of the existing clergy generally: all bishops, abbots, priors and others receiving teinds were to appear at the next assembly 'to give their assistance and counsel . . . in such things as appertain to Christian religion and preaching of the true word'.[5] This resolution shows how far opinion had now moved from the demands of the Book of Discipline and from the earlier repudiation of the clergy of the old regime. It was now contended that the possession of a benefice, at least if its revenues included teinds, imposed on its possessor a function in the church. The old structure, instead of being subverted, was now to be utilised.

The revolution of 1567, which replaced Mary by her infant son under a protestant regent, entirely changed the political situation and the prospects of the reformed church, for full support could now be expected from the state. But in spite of political change, the policy now pursued by the kirk, and put into effect by parliament in December 1567, was the logical sequel to the trend of the immediately preceding years. The succession to benefices generally,

[1] R.P.C. I, 494.   [2] R.S.S. v, xiv n.   [3] R.P.C. I, 487–8.
[4] R.S.S. loc. cit.   [5] B.U.K. I, 92.

as they should fall vacant, was now secured to the reformed ministry, for it became the law that the patron must direct his presentation to the superintendent or commissioner, who thus acquired statutory power to examine presentees and admit them if found qualified; should the superintendent refuse to admit, the patron could appeal to the diocesan synod and then to the general assembly.[1] It was proposed, further, to dispossess unqualified holders of benefices: articles presented to the parliament proposed that no persons not professing the reformed religion should enjoy benefices, and that all benefices disponed otherwise than according to the Book of Discipline (that is, after examination by a superintendent) should be declared vacant.[2] These articles, however, did not become law, and instead acts were passed confirming existing rights: gifts of benefices which had passed the great seal or the privy seal between the parliament of 1560 and the king's coronation were to continue to be full and perfect titles.[3] As 'unqualified' holders were thus to remain in possession, the collection of thirds had to continue, though now with an organisation responsible to the reformed church.[4] Moreover, while there was no dispossession of the 'unqualified', efforts were to be made to reduce their numbers by persuasion and modest financial pressure. One of the articles presented in December 1567 was 'that sik as ar fund qualifiit be the judgement of the kirk sall exerce thair aune office in thair awin kirk. And utheris not qualifiit sall pay the thrid of thair benefice for sustentatioun of the ministeris during thair tymes'.[5] No statute embodied this principle, but in 1568 the general assembly ordained superintendents and commissioners to require 'such as enjoy benefices and have gifts enabling them to the ministry to be present at the next assembly to accept thereof according to their ability',[6] and it in fact became the practice that 'quhair the new providit persoun sen oure soverane lordis coronatioun being admittit to the ministerie servis and makis residence at his awin kirk, the haill frutis of his benefice is assignit to him', while thirds continued to be exacted from 'the auld possessouris, papistis and utheris, for the susten-

---

[1] *A.P.S.* III, 23 c. 7.   [2] *Ibid.* 37 cc. 2, 5.   [3] *Ibid.* 31 c. 26, 33 c. 36.
[4] P. 91 above.   [5] *A.P.S.* III, 37 c. 7.
[6] *B.U.K.* I, 126 (Calderwood, II, 423).

tatioun of the ministrie quhill thay thame selffis sould cum in possessioun of the patrimony of the kirk'.[1]

From 1567 presentations were therefore directed to superintendents or commissioners, instructing them to examine the nominee and admit him if found qualified to serve in the reformed ministry, or, in case of his insufficiency, to report the same so that a better qualified person might be presented.[2] The *jus devolutum*, which the act of 1567 had assigned vaguely to 'the kirk', was in practice exercised by the superintendents.[3] How, if at all, the patron's presentation and the superintendent's collation were reconciled with any right of congregations to choose their ministers is by no means clear. One of the earliest presentations made under the new procedure does indeed instruct the superintendent to give collation 'if he finds him [the presentee] sufficiently qualified, and having the benevolence and election of the parishioners';[4] this would suggest that a congregation might be invited to give its assent to the patron's choice, but even this phraseology did not become part of the common form of a presentation, and the indications are that the wishes of the parishioners, if not wholly ignored, could be influential only by being made known informally to the patron. At any rate, the policy of utilising the ecclesiastical structure in the interests of the reformed church was now both law and practice, and even although it was not fully implemented,[5] the assimilation or merging of the two ecclesiastical structures which had maintained separate identities since 1560 went on steadily.

Besides parochial benefices and cathedral and diocesan dignities, other benefices were now made available to the reformed clergy. 'Common kirks', formerly devoted to the funds of the chapters of cathedrals and collegiate churches, went to ministers,[6] while pre-

---

[1] *R.P.C.* II, 495; cf. *B.U.K.* II, 479.

[2] The series of crown presentations is to be found in *R.S.S.* For other examples of presentation and collation in the period 1567–72 see the following MS. Protocol Books (Reg. Ho.): Duncan Gray, fos. 25, 41, 83; James Nicolson, fo. 104; James Colvill, fo. 46; the printed *Protocol Book of Herbert Anderson*, No. 81; Reg. Ho. Charters, Nos. 2153, 2205, 2207–8; Warrender Papers, vol. A, fo. 381.

[3] E.g. *R.S.S.* VI, 582.   [4] *Ibid.* 82.

[5] Cf. *B.U.K.* I, 127 (Calderwood, II, 425).

[6] E.g. *R.S.S.* VI, 107; and cf. *B.U.K.* I, 129. Since 1561 the revenues of common kirks had gone into the same fund as the thirds.

bends of collegiate churches and chaplainries very commonly went to students for their maintenance at college, in terms of a statute of 1567 laying down that patrons of benefices in collegiate churches, of altarages and of chaplainries, might grant such a benefice to a bursar for his period of study, 'and efter the patroun remuife that bursar furth of the said college, to present ane uther, and swa furth fra ane to ane uther'.[1]

Although the act of 1567 determining the succession to the benefices had been general in its terms, it was not as yet applied to the 'prelacies'. Abbots and priors would be anomalous in a reformed church, while bishops could hardly be appointed until their method of appointment and their place in ecclesiastical administration were defined, and in face of such obvious difficulties the ultimate fate of the greater benefices must still have been considered an open question after 1567, as it had been since 1560.

During Mary's active reign, that is, since 1561, the fate of the prelacies had not been radically different from that of the lesser benefices. To abbeys and priories she appointed lay commendators, but in the bishoprics her policy had vacillated between gifts *pleno jure*, usually to lay titulars, and nomination to Rome for papal provision. In Dunblane, William Chisholm (II), who had been provided by the pope as coadjutor in 1561, quietly succeeded on his predecessor's death in 1564; Brechin went to John Sinclair, president of the college of justice, by papal provision, in 1565, and, on his death in the following year, to Alexander Campbell, a youth of sixteen, by crown gift followed by nomination to the pope; Ross, on the death of Henry Sinclair, was granted to Lord Darnley in 1565,[2] and in 1566 John Lesley succeeded, presumably by papal provision. Concurrently, heavy inroads were made on the episcopal revenues by grants of pensions; two, totalling £600 annually, were given from Ross, and one of five hundred merks from Brechin.[3] Such proceedings suggested that either the episcopate would be maintained as an

---

[1] *A.P.S.* III, 25 c. 13. On 15 Jan. 1570/1 the patrons of an altar in Dundee parish church disponed it to a 'scolar', narrating an act of parliament of 15 Dec. 1567 *de puerorum institutione qui preterea sunt scolis profecti* (Dundee Protocol Books, Thomas Ireland, II, 98). There are numerous examples in *R.S.S.* VI. Cf. *Early Records of University of St Andrews* (S.H.S.), pp. 297 f.
[2] *R.S.S.* V, 2066.   [3] *Ibid.* 1865, 1918, 1921.

instrument of a possible papalist reaction or that crown nominees with no ecclesiastical standing would ultimately form a purely titular episcopate and the episcopal revenues would be secularised. There was, however, a third possibility—the use of the bishoprics for the purposes of the reformed church. Such a course hardly seems one that would have commended itself to the zealous Roman catholic whom some would have us believe Mary Stewart to have been, but she did follow it in one instance: in 1565 John Carswell, superintendent of Argyll, was appointed to the bishopric of the Isles, on the withdrawal in his favour of a candidate who had been nominated by the queen in a supplication to Rome; there was still another claimant to the see, and Carswell's appointment was confirmed in March 1567,[1] significantly at a time when the queen seems to have been seeking a *rapprochement* with the reformed church. The treatment of this bishopric would appear to be what should have been the normal development under a sovereign sympathetic to the reformed church; and it may be noteworthy that in the Register of the Privy Seal there are three examples of experimental styles for the disposal of bishoprics, apparently belonging to October 1566 and April 1567—within the period, that is, when Mary was trying to conciliate the kirk.[2] The general assembly, which as late as June 1565 was still demanding in effect that bishoprics, like other prelacies, should be 'dissolved' and not given to any one man,[3] changed its view with the general abandonment of the Book of Discipline and the general acceptance of the existing benefices, until in December 1566 the summons to all beneficed men to assist the kirk extended to the bishops.[4] No objection seems to have been raised to Mary's action in appointing Carswell to the bishopric of the Isles, nor was the recipient criticised until so late as July 1569, after he had fallen from grace because he had supported Mary after her marriage

[1] The first gift to Carswell, 12 Jan. 1564/5, narrated that Patrick McClane, elect (having the queen's supplication in his favour), had transferred his right to Carswell (*R.S.S.* v, 1885). For Carswell's confirmation, see *R.S.S.* v, 3373. On 21 May 1567 Lachlan Makclane renounced his rights in Carswell's favour (*R.P.C.* I, 511).

[2] *R.S.S.* v, 3099, 3100, 3553.

[3] *B.U.K.* I, 59–60 (Calderwood, II, 288).

[4] *Ibid.* 91–2; p. 152 above.

to Bothwell, and even then the criticism was only to the effect that he had not consulted the assembly in advance.[1]

While the fate of the bishoprics was thus, in Mary's reign, surrounded by difficulties and uncertainty, the bishops who had conformed in 1560 had continued their work in their dioceses. Some earlier historians, who were aware of the facts, did their best to play down the significance of this development,[2] and their successors have usually either been unaware of the facts or have chosen to disregard them. Initially, and indeed during the two or three years when their all-important pioneering work for the reformed church was done, those bishops were not (so far as the evidence shows) acting under any commission from the general assembly. In June 1562, Gordon of Galloway took the curious step of requesting appointment as a superintendent, possibly with a view to regularising his position, though such an appointment would have meant that he would receive a superintendent's salary, in return for exercising his functions over an area larger than his diocese; his request was not granted, but the assembly, which evidently considered that he should be content with his episcopal revenues (including the third which was allowed to him), gave him a commission to carry out a superintendent's duties.[3] In June 1563 the assembly commissioned all three bishops to 'plant kirks'.[4] Such a commission, at this date, is very strange, for most of the kirks in those dioceses were already 'planted', but—assuming that it is correctly reported—it may have been designed to remove any uncertainty as to the legality or

[1] *B.U.K.* I, 144 (Calderwood, II, 490–1).
[2] Calderwood, *De regimine ecclesiae Scoticanae epistola*, p. 3: 'Primum genus paucorum fuit episcoporum qui ejerato papismo se ad causam reformationis adjungebant. His concessum ut fruerentur reditibus, ea lege, ut pastores in suis dioecesibus alerent'. Alexander Petrie, *History of the Catholick Church*, II, 365: 'Whereas of all the bishops three only did embrace or professe the reformed religion, to wit, of Galloway, Orknay and Caitnes, none of them had any power in the Church but by virtue of commission that was given them by the Assembly, upon account that they had the Church-revenues in the places; and they might have supplied the place of superintendents'. Calderwood discloses only a small and insignificant part of the truth, while Petrie's statement that the conforming bishops had no power except through commission from the general assembly is contrary to fact (cf. pp. 58–9 above).
[3] *B.U.K.* I, 15, 28 (Calderwood, II, 184–5, 207).
[4] *Ibid.* 32 (Calderwood, II, 224).

propriety of the action the bishops had taken during the preceding two or three years;[1] on the other hand, it may represent an attempt by the assembly to extend its authority in a new sphere. The assembly may have been anxious to make a formal assertion of its supremacy because it was aware of its weakness in relation to men who had a legal and financial standing which it could not contest; the assembly knew that it could not dispossess a bishop, and, while his 'third' could be 'allowed', it was not so easy in practice to deprive him of it if he ceased to earn it. Both Gordon of Galloway and Bothwell of Orkney became senators of the college of justice, and from 1564, although the assembly continued to recognise them as commissioners, they gave less attention to their episcopal functions: the attractions of life in Edinburgh were considerable; they may, like some of the superintendents, have felt unequal to the heavy labours of their office (especially as the general assembly was more ready with criticism than with encouragement); and they may have been disheartened by the very depressing conditions which the reformed church encountered in 1565 and 1566. Gordon was suspended by the assembly in 1568 on the grounds of negligence, and again in 1569 because he had attached himself to Queen Mary's party. Bothwell was suspended in 1567, mainly because he had officiated at the marriage of Queen Mary to Hepburn, earl of Bothwell, and, although restored by the next general assembly, did not resume his episcopal duties, because he was meantime compelled to relinquish the revenues of his see to Lord Robert Stewart, in exchange for the latter's abbey of Holyrood. The bishop of Caithness appears to have been more single-minded than his colleagues, and his labours proved more acceptable than theirs to the critical brethren of the assembly.[2]

After 1567, the succession to the bishoprics was open to the reformed church. The Book of Discipline's proposals had already been abandoned so far as the lesser benefices were concerned, and no serious effort seems to have been made to revert to its proposals in respect of the greater benefices. One of the articles discussed in

[1] Cf. B.U.K. I, 27 (Calderwood, II, 206). This act, in December 1562, suggested that bishops should be examined and approved by superintendents.

[2] See references on pp. 58–9.

December 1567 was indeed that abbacies should be dissolved, the temporality being disposed of by parliament and the teinds going to the kirk.[1] It was the failure to have this proposal passed as a statute that Moray referred to when he wrote:

Ye know at the parliament we were most willing that the kirk sould have been put in full possessioun of the proper patrimonie; and towards the thrids we exped in our travell, and inlaikit only a consent to the dissolution of the prelacies; quherunto althogh we were earnestly bent, yet the estates delayit, and wold not aggrie therunto.[2]

But there is not a trace of any intention to extend 'dissolution' to the bishoprics, and that the government, at least, never considered any course other than their retention as entities is illustrated time and again by references to 'the lauchfull promotioun and provisioun of ane pasture and minister' to the bishopric of Dunblane, or 'the lauchfull provisioun of ane pastor, prelate or bischop to the said bischoprik' and phrases like 'ay and quhill ane archbischop and pastor be lauchfullie and deulie presentit, admittit and providit' to St Andrews or 'quhasoevir be providit heireftir' to the bishopric of Ross.[3] Bishops of a kind there were going to be. The church, on its side, which had already accepted the general principle of the appointment of qualified men to benefices, seems to have proceeded logically to the argument that bishoprics, like other benefices, should be in the hands of 'qualified' men: the functions of an episcopate were being performed, and it was common sense to use the bishoprics to maintain the men performing them; in 1570, therefore, the general assembly said plainly that the possession of a see involved a function in the church and that bishoprics should be in the hands of clerics and not of laymen.[4] Since Carswell's appointment to the Isles, five bishoprics—Orkney, Caithness, Argyll, the Isles and Galloway—had been in the hands of reformers, and it is hardly conceivable that there can have been any disagreement on the principle that the other bishoprics should be filled, and filled by clergy of the reformed church; the only matter for discussion and possibly negotiation was the provision of machinery whereby

---

[1] *A.P.S.* III, 37 c. 6. [2] *B.U.K.* I, 151 (Calderwood, II, 499).
[3] *R.S.S.* VI, 590, 729, 1001, 1004. [4] *B.U.K.* I, 162.

episcopal appointments could be made agreeably to crown and church. Until that should be done there was an *impasse*, as there had been earlier in the matter of the lesser benefices.

But although the general course of future development can hardly have been in any doubt, the time was one of tumult and civil war, when the government was not likely to risk alienating support by depriving bishops or even by appointing successors to bishops who had been forfeited because they had taken Queen Mary's side against the king and the regents. An appointment to Glasgow, from which the archbishop had been absent since 1560, would hardly be controversial, and as early as 26 January 1570/1 a style for a provision to that archbishopric was actually drawn up.[1] But—through what seems an excess of caution—even this was not proceeded with, and the whole question might have remained dormant until the extinction of Queen Mary's party and the return of political stability had it not suddenly become acute when the primate was hanged in April 1571.

In the following August the government proceeded to appoint John Douglas, rector of St Andrews university, to the vacant archbishopric, of which he had a gift on 6 August.[2] *Joannes archiepiscopus Sanctiandree* was present at the parliament which began its meetings on 28 August,[3] but owing to the failure of the government to consult ecclesiastical opinion before appointing him he found himself in an unhappy position:

> The superintendent of Fife inhibited the rector of St. Andrews to vote as one of the kirk, till he should be admitted by the kirk, under the pain of excommunication: Morton commanded him to vote (as bishop of St. Andrews) under the pain of treason.[4]

In an attempt to satisfy its critics, the government on 8 September appointed commissioners for the examination of Douglas and also

---

[1] *R.S.S.* VI, 1107.

[2] *Ibid.* 1228; Reg. Pres. I, 55. According to Richard Bannatyne, *Memorials of Transactions in Scotland* (Bannatyne Club), p. 178, he was 'made bishop' on 18 Aug. and Calderwood (III, 135) says he was 'presented' to the bishopric on 18 Aug.

[3] *A.P.S.* III, 65.

[4] Bannatyne, *op. cit.* p. 183; Calderwood, III, 138.

of John Porterfield, who had been 'lately nominated and provided' to the archbishopric of Glasgow—'considering', so the commissions ran, 'how necessar it is baith for the advancement of the religioun and kirk of God as for the commoun weill of the realme that personis providit to beschoprikis, be ressoun thay ar to have the charge and owersicht of the inferiour ministeris, be of honest conversatioun [etc.], to the effect that in default of dew examinatioun na avowit inyme to the trewth of God, nor ignorantis, be sufferit to enjoy the patrimony of the kirk'.[1] Superintendents Winram and Spottiswoode, Andrew Hay, commissioner of Glasgow, John Row, commissioner of Galloway, John, Lord Ochiltree, and Thomas Kennedy of Bargany were to examine each archbishop; if they found him qualified, they were to issue testimonials thereon, and failing that they were to notify the king and the regent 'that farther order may be taken towards the said archibeschoprik'.[2] This was not nearly enough, for no provision was made for any 'admission' or authorisation in an ecclesiastical sense, and if the concession looked like mere window-dressing the impression must have been heightened by the fact that on the same day (8 September) James Paton was promoted to Dunkeld by a simple gift.[3] An acrimonious dispute resulted. The unfortunate Archbishop Douglas found that his title was in practice defective, because the collectors of thirds would not permit him to uplift some of his revenues, on the ground that his appointment had not been accompanied by 'consent, assent or admission' of the church.[4]

A full and reasoned statement of the case against the government's high-handed action was presented to the regent by Superintendent Erskine, in a letter written on 10 November. Erskine began by repeating the old contention of the general assemblies that as all benefices deriving revenue from teinds involve a spiritual office, therefore they must be held by men whose qualifications have been approved by the church. The church, he went on, has committed to bishops or superintendents the power of admitting inferior ministers, and he adduced evidence from the scriptures to prove that it was the function of bishops and superintendents to examine

[1] Reg. Pres. I, 61.   [2] Ibid. 61.   [3] Ibid. 61v.
[4] Bannatyne, op. cit. p. 197; Calderwood, III, 156.

candidates for office, to admit them, and to supervise their work. But, while the need for bishops was thus acknowledged, the appointment of such spiritual office-bearers must be controlled by the church, and the most the crown can be permitted to do is to play the part of a patron whose nominees can be either accepted or rejected. Therefore, although the superintendent's office and the bishop's are identical, yet the superintendent, who has been appointed by the church, must hold his ground against such bishops as have now been intruded by the state.[1]

The regent responded by inviting the superintendents to meet on 16 November at Leith (then the seat of the government while Mary's supporters held Edinburgh castle), and he attempted to put pressure on the church, and at the same time retaliate on behalf of Archbishop Douglas, by forbidding any payments to be made to the collectors of thirds. But when Erskine made it plain, in a further letter, that this would not induce his co-operation, the prohibition was withdrawn, and the regent, on 15 November, sent Erskine this reasoned plea for consultation:

Our meaning it was, and is still, to procure the reforming of things disordered in all sorts, as far as may be, retaining the privilege of the king, crown and patronage. The default of the whole stands in this, that the polity of the kirk of Scotland is not perfect, nor any solid conference among godly men, that are well willed and of judgment, how the same may be helped. . . . It will be found that some have been authors and procurers of things that no good polity in the kirk can allow: whereanent we thought to have conferred specially with yourself, and to have yielded to you in things reasonable, and crave satisfaction of other things alike reasonable at your hands.[2]

In response to this conciliatory appeal, Erskine asked the superintendents and 'some of the commissioners of the kirk' to meet at Leith. After further discussion between some superintendents and ministers on one side and the regent and his council on the other,[3] an extraordinary general assembly met at Leith on 12 January 1571/2 and appointed commissioners to treat with representatives

[1] Calderwood, III, 156–62.
[2] Bannatyne, *op. cit.* pp. 203–6; Calderwood, III, 163–5.
[3] Bannatyne, *op. cit.* pp. 208, 213; Calderwood, III, 165.

of the government.[1] The achievement of their deliberations was to provide machinery which gave the church a voice in the selection of bishops—machinery which had been awaited since 1567—and to make arrangements which superseded the unilateral action taken by the government in the previous September.

The bishoprics were to remain in being, and the boundaries of the dioceses were not to be altered, but were to continue unchanged 'at least until the king's majesty's majority or consent of parliament'. As bishoprics fell vacant, persons qualified and of at least thirty years of age were to be nominated within a year and a day, and nomination lay with the civil power, as it had done before the reformation. After nomination there was to follow election by chapters, consisting of ministers. Nomination by the civil power, followed by a purely formal 'election', had of course been the method of appointment of the superintendents, in 1561, but the Scots did not now, in 1572, follow either that precedent or English example so slavishly that the possibility of the rejection of the government's nominee was disregarded, for a formula for rejection was expressly provided. Following election came a ceremony of 'inauguration'. Once again, as in 1560, canonical consecration could no doubt have been obtained had it been desired, but it was presumably thought that a more appropriate and respectable spiritual lineage would be furnished by linking the new bishops with the reformed episcopate of superintendents and commissioners and with the reformed ministry generally. For the 'inauguration' of John Douglas as archbishop of St Andrews, a mandate was directed to 'the reverend father in God, Robert, bishop of Caithness, the superintendents of Angus, Fife, Lothian or any other lawful bishops and superintendents within this realm, or any two of them . . . commanding them to consecrate the said Master John Douglas'.[2] When the ceremony took place, the sermon was preached by John Winram, dean and vicar-general of the diocese of St Andrews and superintendent of Fife; Robert Stewart, bishop of Caithness, joined with Spottiswoode, superintendent of Lothian, and David Lindsay, minister of Leith and commissioner of Ayrshire, in laying hands on the new archbishop. In subsequent conse-

[1] *B.U.K.* I, 204–5 (Calderwood, III, 170 ff.).　　[2] Reg. Pres. I, 76.

crations there was a similar use of superintendents, commissioners and conforming bishops, to whom in due course were added bishops who had themselves been consecrated according to the new formulae. The rite of admission of a bishop was almost the same as that previously used for superintendents, but imposition of hands took the place of mere 'taking by the hand', and, while the style for the mandate to consecrate specified a minimum of two conse-crators, some of the mandates actually issued specify three,[1] and two of the accounts of consecrations which have been preserved show that three consecrators took part.[2] It may be that, whatever the source of authority of the ministry set up in 1561, the intention was, now that that ministry was securely established, to preserve a succession within it. But some rite of admission there had to be, if the bishops were to be empowered to exercise spiritual functions, and the necessity, at the same time, to confer on the bishops indis-putable titles to their sees would itself go a long way to explain why the rite of admission so closely resembled the traditional episcopal consecration.

Care was taken to make no innovation in ecclesiastical adminis-tration. The new bishops were to exercise no greater jurisdiction than did the superintendents 'until the same be agreed upon', and they were to be subject to the kirk and the general assembly *in spiritualibus* as they were to the king *in temporalibus*, or, as the as-sembly phrased it, 'subject to the discipline of the general assembly as superintendents have been heretofore in all sorts, as members thereof'. In the ordination of ministers, a bishop was to have the ad-vice of the best learned of his chapter, to the number of six at least, any member of the chapter having a right to be present and to vote, and a bishop was not to grant admission to a benefice without the consent of three well qualified ministers—provisions which inci-dentally imply that a distinction between ordination and induction, unknown in 1560, had now emerged.[3]

[1] E.g. *R.S.S.* vi, 1474.
[2] Calderwood, iii, 206–7; *Spalding Club Misc.* ii, 46–7.
[3] *B.U.K.* i, 209, 294 (Calderwood, iii, 172, 308). When Archbishop Douglas, at his inauguration, was asked if he would be obedient to the kirk, and usurp no power over it, he answered that he would claim no greater power than the council and general assembly should prescribe (Calderwood, iii, 207).

The whole scheme deserves far more credit for statesmanship than it has usually been given. The rights of the crown, which had been accustomed for two generations and more to nominate the bishops, had to be reconciled with the claims of the church; the formulae of appointment had to comply with tradition and precedent to the extent that they would confer secure titles on the new bishops, but must at the same time be in accordance with reformation principles on ecclesiastical polity. All this was achieved. There were, indeed, some points obviously open to objection: election was not to be, as the Book of Discipline had proposed, by the clergy and laity of the diocese, but by the chapters alone; although the examination of the qualifications of a bishop, involving *inter alia* a trial sermon, was no mere formality,[1] the machinery provided for appointment turned out in practice to be no effective safeguard against somewhat improper promotions, because while one or two of the bishops were distinguished, and several of them respectable, others resembled rather the adventurers who had been making their way into episcopal office before the reformation; and the retention of the old irrational diocesan boundaries, even as an *interim*, was a disappointment to men whose principles were all directed towards greater efficiency in the system of oversight. But all these were matters of detail, and none of the essentials of the settlement were at variance with the principles of the reformers. Indeed, it is difficult to detect any grounds on which serious objection could have been raised, and it is not surprising to find that the evidence as to the state of opinion indicates general acquiescence. The resentment caused by the initial action of the government in September 1571 clearly gave way to general approval of the agreed scheme of January 1572.

The gathering at Leith which had appointed the commission to agree on plans for episcopal appointments had been termed a 'convention' because it was outwith the ordinary course of meetings of general assemblies, on the analogy of the 'convention' of the civil constitution, which differed from a parliament in that it was summoned with less formality and for more limited business. However, not only did the 'convention' itself claim the 'strength, force and

[1] Cf. James Melville, *Diary* (Wodrow Soc.), p. 32; Calderwood, III, 341-2.

effect' of a general assembly, but the assembly of August 1572 referred to it as a general assembly, a minister who preached before it accounted it a general assembly, and the historian Row numbered it in the series of general assemblies.[1] If the membership appears to have been small—something over sixty, with ministers in a majority[2]—it must be remembered that we have few contemporary standards by which to judge it and also that the country was still in an unsettled state, which made travelling hazardous.[3] But no one has ever suggested that the convention was in any way 'packed', and it may be taken to have been generally representative of opinion. An account of the impression which its proceedings made on a dispassionate observer is worth quoting at length:

> Sum doubt standinge betwix the Regent and mynisters of the kirke touching the order of admission of Bisshops and others entringe to spirituall promotion for that no certaine law toward the police of the kirke was established sen the papestrey was abolished, in a quiet conference kepte at Leeth in the later end of January, the mater is agreed. And so far as may be the order of the kirke of England followed. This order is assented unto be certaine commissioners appointed from the Counsell and the assembly of the kirke. The Regent hes allowed it, and promittit to have it enacted by parliament as a law. It is alreddy entered in execution, and one Mr. Jhon Douglas, ane agit learned man, rectour of the universitie, nominated in favour of the Erle of Morton to the Archebishoprik of Sainctandros, is admited by the same order. The same order cometh in practize voluntary, and it is thought ther shall not be grete lett to have it allowed by parliament.[4]

The next normal meeting of a general assembly had been appointed for March 1572, at St Andrews, but as that assembly was not a plenary one,[5] the conclusions reached at Leith were not ratified until the meeting of the next ordinary assembly, in August 1572. That assembly raised no objection in principle to the new constitution and accepted even the titles of archbishop, archdeacon, dean and so forth (although these were obnoxious to some ministers)

---

[1] *B.U.K.* I, 204, 246 (Calderwood, III, 168, 220); David Fergusson, *Tracts* (Bannatyne Club), p. 61; Row, *History*, p. 45.

[2] *B.U.K.* I, 203–4.   [3] Bannatyne, *op. cit.* p. 217.

[4] S. P. Scot. Eliz. XXII, No. 24 (*Cal. S. P. Scot.* IV, pp. 133–4).

[5] Bannatyne, *op. cit.* p. 217; cf. Calderwood, III, 168.

with a proviso that in agreeing to them they must not be held to sanction popery. It may well be that there was a certain uneasiness lest the comprehensive acceptance of the styles and titles of the pre-reformation and Anglican episcopate might involve more than mere changes of form, yet those who thought that those titles savoured of papistry were hypercritical, because all along there had been ministers of the reformed church who bore such titles as 'archdeacon', 'chantor' and the rest, denoting their possession of certain benefices. However, the recommendation of this assembly was the reasonable one that, while the retention of the old styles had obvious advantages from a legal point of view, their use for ecclesiastical purposes would be better avoided: 'archbishops', they suggested, should be known as 'bishops', but only 'in those things concerning the function of the kirk'.[1]

The approval thus given generally by the assembly is in accordance with the opinions of those individual ministers whose views are on record. Of the three superintendents who were still active—Carswell died in this year, and Willock had gone off to England—Erskine had been a principal architect of the scheme now adopted, and Winram and Spottiswoode took part in the 'inauguration' of Archbishop Douglas. There is therefore no reason to doubt the truth of Spottiswoode's son's assertion that his father had expressed a preference for 'the old polity' over the presbyterian system which displaced it.[2] The unhesitating approval of Douglas's third 'consecrator', David Lindsay, is illustrated by his reference to 'the buik devysit in Lieth, quhairin the order of the election of byschops with mony other gud articles is continit'.[3] John Row, minister at Perth and commissioner of Galloway, is said by his son, the historian, to have been favourable to episcopacy at this time,[4] and David Fergusson, minister of Dunfermline, preached a sermon before the convention of Leith which sufficiently demonstrates his sympathy with its objects.[5] Against such evidence of approval by individuals, reinforcing as it does the approval given by the general assembly, no instance can be set of any expression of disapproval.

The search for a condemnation of episcopacy in the writings of

---

[1] *B.U.K.* I, 246 (Calderwood, III, 221).   [2] Spottiswoode, *History*, II, 337.
[3] *Cal. S. P. Scot.* IV, No. 519.   [4] Row, *History*, p. 415.   [5] Fergusson, *op. cit.*

John Knox has been assiduous, but so far fruitless, and its abandonment is long overdue. Knox was a man of his time, sharing the views of his contemporaries and not anticipating the presbyterians —or, for that matter, the episcopalians—of the next generation. Nor is it true to say that he had no occasion to define his attitude to episcopacy, for he spoke his mind freely enough about what he considered to be the defects of the Church of England, and even condemned its system of discipline and the size of its dioceses, without denouncing the office of a diocesan bishop. His refusal of an English bishopric, when he was offered one in Edward VI's reign, had arisen not from any disapproval of the office of bishop but from 'the foresight of trouble to come',[1] that is, his foreboding that the happy days of Edward would not last; and his prudence possibly saved him from the fate of Ridley, Latimer and Hooper.[2] Worldly wisdom was equally apparent when Knox declined to become a superintendent in Scotland: in giving as his reason that he 'thought his estate honourable enough', he must have meant that as minister of the capital he had an exceptional status,[3] a stipend comparable with that of a superintendent and paid with greater regularity than were most stipends in those years, and a position of unique influence in church and state—all without the arduous duties of which the superintendents so often complained. His professed preference for energetic pastoral work in a humble sphere, and his boast of being 'a painful preacher of the blessed evangel' instead of 'a great bishop',[4] can hardly be taken at face value.

In 1571, Knox shared in the general indignation at the government's action in appointing bishops without consulting the church, and for months his attitude was coloured by this and by his hostility to the choice of John Douglas for St Andrews. A letter written by

[1] Peter Lorimer, *John Knox and the Church of England*, p. 191.
[2] It may be that Knox, knowing that the offer would involve the spoliation of the bishopric in the interests of the Protector Northumberland, recoiled from acceptance on that ground (F. O. White, *Lives of the Elizabethan Bishops*, p. 153; Charles Sturge, *Cuthbert Tunstal*, pp. 293–4).
[3] In the Register of Stipends (1567), Knox's name appears in splendid isolation, not with those of other ministers.
[4] McCrie, *Knox* (1874), pp. 354–5, 438; *Cal. S. P. Scot.* IV, No. 452; Laing, VI, 122; *Thirds of Benefices*, pp. xxxv, 297.

him on 3 August 1571, exhorting the general assembly not to suffer 'unworthy men to be thrust in into the ministry of the kirk, under what pretence so ever it be',[1] may allude to Douglas's appointment, which was announced only three days later. It certainly seems to have been unfortunate that, although the formulae agreed on in January 1572 were subsequently used to make appointments to the archbishoprics *de novo*,[2] without reference to the proceedings of the previous September, and although a new candidate was found for Glasgow, yet for St Andrews the name of the aged and infirm—though eminently respectable—John Douglas was again put forward. The chapter itself agreed to his election only after some controversy.[3] Knox, with his essentially evangelical and pastoral outlook, was strongly opposed to the extension of university influence in the church, as he explained forcefully in August 1572,[4] and he may well have objected for that reason to the choice of the rector of a university for the vacant primacy; but if he exclaimed, as he is reported to have done, 'Alas! for pitie, to lay upone an auld weak man's back that quhilk twentie of the best gifts could nocht bear. It will wrak him and disgrace him',[5] his criticism was directed not at the archbishop, or yet at the government, but at the general assembly, which insisted that Douglas should continue to hold his university appointments along with the archbishopric.[6] This was, in any event, only a criticism of detail, not of principle, but, when Knox's anger was aroused by the suggestion that he had hoped for the archbishopric for himself, he is said to have proceeded to the more general protest that the 'kirke of Scotland suld not be subject to that ordore which then was used, considering the lordis of Scotland had subscryvit, and also confirmed in parliament, the ordore alreadie and long agoe appointed, in the buike of discipline.'[7] By this remark, if it is correctly reported, Knox can only have meant that the 'dissolution of the prelacies' in a financial sense,[8] a

---

[1] *B.U.K.* I, 199 (Calderwood, III, 134).
[2] Reg. Pres. I, 71, 75. [3] Bannatyne, *op. cit.* p. 223.
[4] *B.U.K.* I, 247 (Calderwood, III, 222). [5] James Melville, *Diary*, p. 31.
[6] Bannatyne, *op. cit.* p. 228; *B.U.K.* I, 241 (Calderwood, III, 210–11).
[7] Bannatyne, *op. cit.* pp. 256–7.
[8] John Erskine, in his letter of November 1571, had emphasised that this still remained the ideal.

reorganisation of diocesan boundaries and election of bishops by clergy and people, were to be preferred to the arrangements now adopted—as no doubt they were—but old age had made him forgetful if he imagined that the Book of Discipline had been confirmed in parliament. All in all, he had good enough grounds for 'opposing himself directly and zealously', as we are told he did, to Douglas's appointment. However, this initial phase of irascible and vindictive senility passed, and when Knox recovered his tranquillity he not only withdrew any criticism of the new arrangements but gave them emphatic approval. In a letter to the general assembly of August 1572 he showed his recognition that the principle applied earlier to the lesser benefices was now being applied to the bishoprics; he therefore urged that 'all bishoprics vacant may be presented, and qualified persons nominated thereunto, within a year after the vaiking thereof, according to the order taken in Leith'; that grants of ecclesiastical revenues must have the approval of a superintendent, a commissioner or one of the bishops 'lawfully elected according to the order taken at Leith'; and that there should be safeguards to secure the efficiency and the sound financial administration of 'all bishops admitted by the order of the kirk now received'. He gave point to his acceptance of the new 'order' by criticising the gift of the bishopric of Ross to Lord Methven, which he held to be a contravention of that order,[1] though his failure to observe that the gift was merely of the temporality during vacancy,[2] according to immemorial custom, may again be indicative of failing powers. Especially when it is noted that all the statements about hostility on Knox's part to the new arrangements come to us indirectly, through either Richard Bannatyne or James Melville, while the solitary definition of his attitude which comes from his own hand is a favourable one, it emerges that it is impossible to draw any distinction between Knox's views and those of his contemporaries whose approval has already been cited. The great reformer's farewell advice to the Church of Scotland was that it should have bishops.

The conclusion must be that, while the government's initial action had produced a divergence between church and state, that

[1] *B.U.K.* I, 247–9 (Calderwood, III, 765–7).   [2] *R.S.S.* VI, 1358.

divergence had been solved by concessions from the government's side, and it is clearly erroneous to assign to this juncture the outbreak of the great controversy between episcopal government and its opponents. Contemporaries of course realised, as posterity has largely failed to do, that the settlement of 1572 had nothing at all to do with church government, but was concerned solely with endowment. Its object was to provide machinery whereby the reformed church could have access to the revenues of benefices from which it had previously been in the main excluded. The bishoprics, as benefices, were not to be 'dissolved' or broken up into temporality and spirituality, and they were to be held by clergy of the reformed church—this was the logical sequel to antecedent developments, and an extension of the principle which had been put into practice with the lesser benefices since 1566. But, apart from the bishoprics, the monastic property as well was dealt with by the convention of Leith. It was provided that no future appointments should be made until temporality and spirituality had been distinguished and arrangements made, with the advice of a bishop or superintendent, for the support of the ministers of the annexed churches from the teinds of those churches; the remaining revenues and the title were to go to persons who were to be examined by the ordinary (bishop or superintendent) before admission and who, besides being qualified to represent ecclesiastical interests in parliament, might properly become senators of the college of justice or be employed by the king in other state business. The same principle of separating spirituality and temporality was to be applied to the deaneries and provostries of collegiate churches, while it was reaffirmed that the prebends of those foundations were in general to go to students.[1] Thus several important steps had been taken towards the further merging of the two ecclesiastical structures.

The church had certainly entered on the negotiations with the government in the expectation of financial advantage,[2] and it had gained such an advantage, to the extent that the secularisation of the bishoprics, of which there had been a very real danger in Mary's reign, was averted, and that certain other classes of benefices were

---

[1] *B.U.K.* I, 210 ff. (Calderwood, III, 173 ff.). Cf. p. 155 above.
[2] Fergusson, *op. cit.*

now added to the heritage of the reformed clergy. What proportion of the episcopal revenues in practice remained with the church, and what proportion was diverted to lay hands, is a matter which has never been studied in detail. Erskine of Dun had guaranteed that, provided that the admission of bishops was controlled by the kirk, no objection would be raised to the diversion to the crown of some of the episcopal revenues, and his candid remark that 'the kirk contendeth not for worldly profit' had invited the government to help itself, but the proceedings which followed must be viewed in the light of precedent. The custom of accompanying episcopal promotions with substantial reservations of fruits to crown nominees was no novelty in Scotland[1] and had been common likewise in contemporary England, where this and every other device were used so successfully that no Scottish government ever milked the bishoprics more effectively than did Elizabeth Tudor.[2] The 'tulchan' bishop, though he received his quaint name in Scotland in the 1570s, was neither a new phenomenon nor one peculiar to Scotland. Yet the financial activities of the so-called 'tulchans' have never been scrutinised, and until this is done it must remain uncertain whether they had a worse record than their pre-reformation predecessors or their English contemporaries. It can be said with some confidence that there is no evidence beyond gossip that they made simoniacal pactions, and that the reservations of pensions on their appointments were on a scale very modest compared with those made in earlier days; on the other hand, after appointment these bishops did dilapidate their benefices by granting feus, tacks and pensions on a lavish scale.[3] Had not hostility to the episcopate emerged on quite different grounds, it seems unlikely that much would have been heard of 'tulchanism'.

Between 1572 and 1577 the procedure approved at Leith was

---

[1] Pp. 38–9 above.

[2] See in general F. O. White, *Lives of the Elizabethan Bishops, passim*; Fuller, *Church History*, V, IV, 55, IX, I, 21, II, 32, IV, 4; Christopher Hill, *Economic Problems of the Church*, pp. 15–17; Sturge, *Tunstal*, pp. 110, 293–4; Smyth, *Cranmer*, pp. 274 f.; Whitgift, *Works*, III, xiii–xv; H.M.C. *Salisbury MSS*. III, 153; Jewel, *Works*, II, 1011; Bancroft, *A Survay of the Pretended Holy Discipline*, pp. 234–5.

[3] The evidence is in the Register of the Privy Seal and the Register of Presentations to Benefices. Cf. *A.P.S.* III, 355.

used for appointments to Glasgow, Dunblane, Dunkeld and Ross, which fell vacant by the forfeiture of papalists or Marians, and to Moray, Aberdeen, the Isles, St Andrews and Galloway as they became vacant by death. In Orkney, where it was impossible to reverse the secularisation of the episcopal revenues,[1] the archdeacon was appointed as a commissioner, and in Argyll, where the ineffective James Hamilton was still bishop, there were apparently 'visitors' under him to do the active work in the diocese.[2] The commissioners who acted while sees were without bishops were still from time to time styled 'superintendents',[3] but the provisional nature of their appointments was fully understood, for a commissioner knew that he ought to offer to demit office when a bishop was appointed,[4] and the situation was clearly illustrated when an act of parliament in 1578 gave certain powers to 'the bishops, and commissioners of dioceses where no bishops are provided'.[5] Besides commissioners of dioceses, however, there were commissioners for smaller areas, to supplement the work of the bishops.

The bishops fitted easily enough into the existing structure of ecclesiastical administration, which was conducted, as it had been ever since 1560, on the assumption that an individual should exercise oversight of ministers and congregations. The bishops were in every respect save finance in the same position as superintendents had been in, and the government of the church was unchanged. The anxiety of the general assembly was not, as some writers have imagined, that the bishops might usurp ecclesiastical functions; it was that they might not be sufficiently energetic in the work which it was their duty to perform. Two assemblies expressed a wish that bishops might be appointed to all vacant sees; the bishop of Dunkeld was censured for bearing the name and not exercising the office of a bishop; and time and again bishops were criticised, just as superintendents were, for not showing enough zeal in the performance of their duty.[6]

---

[1] Cf. p. 158 above. [2] Breadalbane Papers, 17 Aug. 1576.
[3] E.g. *R.P.C.* II, 659. [4] *B.U.K.* I, 297 (Calderwood, III, 304).
[5] *A.P.S.* III, 98.
[6] E.g. *B.U.K.* I, 255, 269–70, 280, 287–8, 300, 306, 314–15 (Calderwood, III, 272, 287–8, 297, 303–4, 330, 335, 341–2).

Certain minor difficulties arose in establishing a *modus vivendi* between the bishops and the superintendents. The principle adopted by the general assembly in March 1571/2, and on the whole adhered to and put into practice in succeeding years, was that superintendents should continue their work as before in areas which were within their districts but not under the jurisdiction of bishops, and should act as assistants, or rather suffragan bishops, in the parts of their districts which fell within the bounds of dioceses where bishops had been appointed. Thus Winram, Erskine and Spottiswoode were 'ordained' to use their 'own jurisdiction as of before in the provinces not yet subject to the archbishopric of St Andrews' and were 'requested' to concur with the archbishop when required, in visitation and otherwise.[1] It may have been in an effort to clarify the situation that John Douglas styled himself 'archbishop of St Andrews and superintendent of Fife',[2] while the portions of his diocese beyond Fife had as their superintendents Spottiswoode, Winram and Erskine. A slightly different approach to the problem, but yielding the same result, is to be seen when the assembly of August 1572 found 'the diocese of St Andrews, wheresoever it lyeth, to pertain to the bishop of St Andrews, and to no other superintendent', but at the same time acceded to the archbishop's request for the assistance of Erskine and Spottiswoode.[3] The superintendents seem to have been reluctant to act as suffragans,[4] perhaps because some bishops were tactless and perhaps because some superintendents were aggrieved at not being appointed to bishoprics, and the assembly may have been trying to mollify the superintendents when it made regulations that a bishop should not give collation to any benefice within the bounds of a superintendent without the superintendent's consent, and suggested that bishops should refrain from visiting within the superintendents' districts.[5] Yet it would be a mistake to read the superintendents' offer to resign, in 1574,[6] as proof that there was tension between them and the bishops, for such an offer was nothing new. From the outset, their office seems to

---

[1] *B.U.K.* I, 242 (Calderwood, III, 209).   [2] H.M.C. *Report*, VI, 636.
[3] *B.U.K.* I, 243–4 (Calderwood, III, 219).
[4] *Ibid.* 264 (Calderwood, III, 273–4).
[5] *Ibid.* 294 (Calderwood, III, 308).   [6] *Ibid.* 296–7 (Calderwood, III, 304).

have been a singularly thankless one. The heavy labours involved were not always remunerated on the generous scale proposed by the Book of Discipline, and, while Erskine (as already explained) fared very well, and the superintendents generally fared better in years of financial stringency than ministers did,[1] there were several complaints of ill-payment.[2] Further, the general assembly had been far from gracious in its attitude: in December 1563, when four of the superintendents were criticised for inefficiency, Spottiswoode and Willock asked to be relieved of their duties, and later Winram and Erskine asked to be allowed to demit office.[3] One wonders whether after their experience of what the conscientious performance of a bishop's duties involved they may have reflected that their criticism of 'idle bellies' had been ill considered. But, apart from Willock, who retired from his labours to the peace of his Leicestershire parsonage, there was no escape but death, and in 1574, as earlier, the assembly declined to accept the superintendents' resignations, reiterating the need for suffragans in the larger dioceses. An interesting experiment was made in Angus, where the experienced superintendent, John Erskine, was instructed to treat the young bishop of Brechin (Alexander Campbell, appointed by Mary) as an apprentice and train him in the work of a bishop-superintendent.[4]

While so very much had been done, from 1566 to 1572, to bring the benefices, great and small, within reach of the reformers, and so to merge the two structures, existing holders of benefices who could not, or would not, perform functions in the reformed church had not been dealt with except in so far as some had been forfeited on political grounds. The earl of Morton, who became regent in November 1572, saw clearly that the reason why the Scottish reformed church had not achieved a 'settled polity' was 'partly through want of the allowance of the authority at the first reformation, and partly because the benefices of cure were of long time suffered to be possessed by persons repugnant to the [reformed] religion'.[5] The 'allowance of the authority' had been enjoyed since

---

[1] See *Thirds of Benefices*, p. xxxv.   [2] *B.U.K.* I, 53, 135, 297, 302.
[3] Laing, VI, 386–7; *B.U.K.* I, 77, 92 (Calderwood, I, 322, 394).
[4] *B.U.K.* I, 303, 305, 317–18 (Calderwood, III, 332, 334).
[5] *Wodrow Soc. Misc.* pp. 289–90.

Mary's deposition in 1567, but it was not until the new government's position was consolidated as the civil war against Mary's adherents drew to a close that the dispossession of benefice-holders repugnant to the reformed religion became possible. A statute of January 1572/3 provided that all holders of benefices must subscribe the Confession of Faith or suffer deprivation.[1] A number of deprivations took place in terms of this act,[2] and the proceeding is an indication that, when the reformed church had at last attained full establishment, coercion was applied to bring about in Scotland the situation which had been brought about in England by the acts of uniformity and supremacy after Elizabeth's accession.

The deprivation of men who refused to accept the Confession of Faith did not, however, remove those who, although they accepted it, yet declined to serve in the reformed ministry. It had been understood that persons appointed since 1567 were under obligation to make residence and to serve,[3] and in March 1572/3 the general assembly passed a resolution which certainly confirmed, probably extended, this obligation: 'all ministeris and uther beneficit persons that hes receivit benefices since the reformation' were to 'make residence at the kirks quher their benefices lyes and use thair office according to the tenor of their admission'.[4] Proceedings were sometimes taken against non-residents: for example, George Sinclair, chancellor of Caithness, was pursued by the collectors of thirds for the two-thirds of his revenues because he did not reside at the kirk of Rogart, which was annexed to the chancellory, and he excused himself on the ground that the said kirk was in the 'high parts' of Sutherland, in the country of the Murrays, who were at feud with the Sinclair family, with the result that the chancellor, for fear of his life, dared not reside at Rogart.[5] The principle that men appointed since 1567, or perhaps since 1560, should serve in the reformed

---

[1] *B.U.K.* I, 212 (Calderwood, III, 175–6); *A.P.S.* III, 72.

[2] Some twenty deprivations are recorded in the Register of the Privy Seal in 1573 and 1574, and a few in later years.

[3] Pp. 153–4 above.

[4] *B.U.K.* I, 258 (Calderwood, III, 278). In 1576 the assembly asked why there should be any distinction in this respect between 'them provided of auld' and 'them provided since the king's coronation' (*B.U.K.* I, 370).

[5] Mey Papers, No. 158.

church was on the whole maintained, but 'non-residence' continued to be a problem for many years.[1]

'Conformity with England', or something very like it, had been brought about, but not by the artificial or abrupt introduction of a new constitution. The suggestion made earlier, that the different courses taken by the two churches of England and Scotland in 1560 arose from the difference in political conditions in the two countries, is supported by the fact that after 1567, when political conditions in Scotland began to approximate to those of England, the ecclesiastical polity of Scotland also began to show marked signs of approximating to that of England. Yet, while the settlement of the Scottish ecclesiastical polity in 1572–3 was the natural and logical outcome of an evolution which can be traced from 1566 or even earlier, a deliberate attempt was made at this point to arrive at 'conformity with England'[2] in an external and formal sense. An examination of the formulae now adopted in Scotland for the nomination of a bishop, the licence to elect, confirmation of the election and restitution of temporality, suggests that English styles had been taken over with only small modifications and that 'so far as may be the order of the Church of England is followed'.[3] Certainly nothing but deliberate imitation can account for the close resemblance between the Scottish and English oaths of supremacy and the similarity between the Scottish statute enforcing acceptance of the Confession of Faith (drawn up in January 1571/2) and the English statute which, nine months before, had imposed subscription to certain articles of religion on beneficed persons who had not been ordained according to the reformed ordinal.[4] In the background to the preparation of the Scottish settlement of 1572–3 there were elements which must have disposed men to borrow from England. The earl of Morton, who had attained chief place among the lords of the king's party in Scotland, had been in England in February and March 1571 and in the following Novem-

---

[1] E.g. Account of Collector General for 1586, fos. 53, 64, 76, 85, 100.
[2] The phrase is a contemporary one (James Melville, *Diary*, p. 45).
[3] P. 166 above. See Appendix B.
[4] 13 Eliz. cap. xii. See Appendix B(3). The oaths of supremacy are printed in parallel in Dickinson and Donaldson, *Source Book of Scottish History*, III, 12–13.

ber his party earnestly besought Queen Elizabeth to 'take upon her the maintenance and protection of the true religion preached and established by law in both the realms'.[1] Not only so, but the fate of the Scottish bishoprics had evidently been the subject of some Anglo-Scottish discussions, for Queen Elizabeth herself made suggestions for the disposal of the two archbishoprics; although, as she advised secularisation—the use of St Andrews to reward the earl of Morton and of Glasgow to reward the Lennoxes[2]—the Scottish government, more tender for the sanctity of church property, did not take her advice. And even apart from such general discussions, there is an indication of a direct link between the genesis of the Scottish settlement and Anglican theories of ecclesiastical polity: on 14 December 1571, when the preliminary discussions about the bishoprics were taking place between the regent and the church representatives,[3] the clerk of the privy council wrote to John Knox, mentioning the preparation of an agreement about the disposal of benefices and recalling from his hands a copy of the *Reformatio legum ecclesiasticarum* which the clerk had recently brought from England.[4] This work, which had been published early in 1571 and had been referred to in debates in the English parliament in April of that year, reflected the reformation ideals and contains an able description of the 'godly bishop':

> Episcopi . . . debent inferiores ordines cleri universumque populum Dei regere ac pascere non sane ut dominentur eorum fidei sed ut seipsos vere servos servorum Dei exhibeant; sciantque authoritatem et jurisdictionem ecclesiasticam non alia de causa sibi praecipue creditam esse, nisi ut suo ministerio et assiduitate homines quamplurimi Christo jungantur.[5]

This seems distinctly to echo Calvin's description of the hierarchy which he would have considered acceptable;[6] and, if this was Anglican episcopacy, there was nothing in it objectionable to any Scottish reformer.

---

[1] *Warrender Papers* (S.H.S.), I, 105.
[2] James Melville, *Memoirs* (Bannatyne Club), p. 236; H.M.C. *Mar and Kellie*, p. 27.
[3] P. 162 above.   [4] Laing, VI, 610.
[5] *Reformatio legum ecclesiasticarum*, ed. Cardwell, pp. 103-4.   [6] P. 110 above.

Formal imitation of England, significant enough in itself, reflected a more solid conformity which extended throughout almost the whole range of ecclesiastical affairs. In Scotland as in England there was now a 'godly prince' as supreme governor, reformed doctrines were defined by law and their acceptance enforced by statute, ecclesiastical administration was in the hands of bishops appointed by the crown, and the work of the reformed church was carried on within the framework of the old ecclesiastical structure. In both countries the obligations of the inferior clergy were the same—to acknowledge the sovereign's supremacy, to subscribe a statement of the reformed faith and to take an oath of obedience to their ordinary;[1] and there is no evidence that Scottish ministers scrupled to accept such obligations. Nor is there much trace of doctrinal divergence, for in both countries a moderate Calvinism prevailed; there is nothing to suggest that Scots considered the Thirty-Nine Articles in any way unacceptable, and indeed the use of the phrase 'articles of religion'[2] to describe the doctrinal standards which Scottish ministers had to subscribe may be a hint that the articles of the Church of England were regarded as a confession suitable for the Church of Scotland.

Even in liturgical matters the differences were not profound.[3] All our information about the opinions of the Elizabethan bishops and those of the Scottish reformers points to very substantial agreement along what would now be considered extremely 'low' lines, and there can be little doubt that, given identical political conditions, Scottish and English worship would have been indistinguishable. As it was, a resolute queen in England maintained the Prayer Book and imposed certain minimum requirements which her bishops, often much against their judgment, tried to enforce. Had there been a similar authority in Scotland in 1560, Knox would have acquiesced as the English bishops did, for like them he conceded that there could be submission to the prince in things indifferent; he

---

[1] This was the invariable requirement before admission to a benefice, as the presentations in *R.S.S.* show.

[2] This is the phrase invariably used in the deprivations recorded in *R.S.S.*

[3] For a full discussion of this subject, see *The Making of the Scottish Prayer Book of 1637*, pp. 7–22.

would certainly not have led a puritan secession, for he condemned those who took that course in England. But in Scotland, in a different political situation, radical tendencies were unchecked, and they issued in the official displacement of the Book of Common Prayer by the Book of Common Order, the use of which was prescribed by the general assembly in 1562 and 1564. Yet even so the two churches were not following wholly divergent paths. The Book of Common Order was itself no mere directory, for 'the *reading* of common prayers' was an essential part of public worship in Scotland, and the Lord's Prayer, the Apostles' Creed, the Doxology, the Ten Commandments and metrical versions of the Magnificat and the Nunc Dimittis were all provided in the 'Psalm Book', as the Scots called the volume which contained the Book of Common Order and the metrical psalms. In England the kneeling posture at the reception of Communion was officially upheld (though it was by no means universal in practice), whereas Scottish communicants, although they knelt to pray, sat when they received, but more important than this difference was the fact that in both countries celebrant and people assembled round a table set lengthwise in the church, so that there was no possibility of mistaking the service for the mass. Again, although the Scottish reformers officially disregarded the Christian year and holy days, the observance of Lent as a season of abstinence from meat was enforced by law and it remained a season when marriages were seldom celebrated, the Kalendar was recognised by the church to the extent that it was printed in successive editions of the Book of Common Order, and holy days are frequently mentioned by name in kirk session records.[1] Somewhat similarly, although the intention was that baptism and marriage should be celebrated only publicly, in face of the congregation, exceptions were made when 'the midwyff deponit on hir conscience the bairne war waik' and when the persons contracting matrimony had special reasons to desire privacy.[2] It may

---

[1] E.g. Perth kirk session records (MS.), 12 Feb. 1581/2 ('First Sonday of Lent' and 'The Rud Day'); 26 Feb. 1581/2 ('xx dayis efter paice' [i.e. Pasch or Easter]); 12 Nov. 1582 ('Andersmes' or St Andrew's Day); 8 Jan. 1582/3 ('Fasterance Evin' or Shrove Tuesday).

[2] *Ibid.* 25 Oct. 1584, 15 May 1587.

be added that godparents regularly appeared at baptisms in Scotland as in England. In short, when we keep in mind the important matter of agreement on the structure of the Sunday morning service,[1] it emerges that the principal differences between the two churches were that there were vestiarian requirements in England, but not in Scotland, and that the Book of Common Prayer was officially maintained in England; but even these official differences were partially effaced by the facts that for years it proved impossible to enforce the wearing of the surplice in England and that for years the Book of Common Prayer remained in unofficial use in Scotland.

That the 'conformity with England' at which men aimed in 1572 extended to worship, as well as to polity and theology, is by no means certain, and it is not until 1584 that we hear of a proposal for 'a uniform order in common prayer' in circumstances which suggest that something more than adherence to the Book of Common Order was in view.[2] But we are told in a significant phrase that the Regent Morton not only 'bore forward his bishops' but also 'pressed to his injunctions and conformity with England',[3] and if there were 'injunctions' relating to liturgical matters it is plain that there was a considerable basis on which liturgical conformity, or at least approximation, could have been developed.

It is true that national conceit had already begun to distort Scottish judgment on matters ecclesiastical, for Knox had written in May 1566:

As touching the doctrine taught by our ministers, and as touching the administration of sacraments used in our churches, we are bold to affirm that there is no realm this day upon the face of the earth that hath them in greater purity; yea (we must speak the truth whomsoever we offend), there is none (no realm, we mean) that hath them in the like purity. For all others (how sincere that ever the doctrine be, that by some is taught), retain in their churches and the ministers thereof some footsteps of Antichrist, and some dregs of papistry; but we (all praise to God alone) have nothing within our churches that ever flowed from that Man of Sin.[4]

[1] P. 83 above.　　[2] *The Making of the Scottish Prayer Book of 1637*, p. 23.
[3] Calderwood, III, 394; cf. James Melville, *Diary*, p. 45.
[4] Laing, II, 263 (Dickinson, II, 3).

Yet a dispassionate survey of the whole field of ecclesiastical affairs discloses that there is little enough evidence at this stage to support the notion, so dear to later generations of Scots, that their country had received a special revelation.

CHAPTER VIII

THE RISE OF THE PRESBYTERIAN MOVEMENT

THE sequence of events down to 1573 may be interpreted as a logical development. There had indeed been a departure from the financial proposals of the Book of Discipline, for the benefices had not been dissolved and their revenues had not been redistributed, but that departure had been made in accordance with suggestions repeatedly put forward by the general assembly itself. On the other hand, there had been no departure from the principles of the reformation so far as they were concerned with the parochial ministry and the system of oversight, and these principles had been adhered to in a settlement which reconciled the needs of ecclesiastical administration with respect for the claims of the crown, which retained the ancient structure in a way which avoided needless dislocation and which—whether logically or not—preserved the authority of the general assembly alongside recognition of the crown as supreme governor.

The developments which had taken place had not in themselves produced a 'settled polity', nor had they solved all problems of endowment. They had, at the best, provided machinery by which a settled polity could have been attained and many problems of endowment solved, but time would have been necessary for the machinery to operate and produce the designed results. Besides, some contemporaries, at least, probably did not regard the arrangements made in 1572 as necessarily permanent, and all could see that the last word had not been said on a number of details, especially the financing of the parish ministry. Yet, with the end of the civil war in 1573 and the beginning of 'this time of repose which God has granted us after our long troubles',[1] the prospects were prospects of stability. The likelihood now was that at no very distant date the two structures, old and new, would merge completely

[1] *Wodrow Soc. Misc.* I, 289.

and that the reformed church would be in full possession of the ancient polity with all its benefices and offices. It is hard to see how any development originating in Scotland itself could have interrupted, far less reversed, the trend towards 'conformity with England', and it certainly would have been inconceivable at the time that within a few years a Scottish cleric would be censured for giving the English bishops the right hand of fellowship and that within a generation a Scottish general assembly would condemn the government of the Church of England as antichristian.[1] That all these prospects proved illusory was the consequence of the emergence, in the first place on the continent, of ideas at variance with those of the reformers, ideas which, when they reached Scotland, dislocated the evolution of the polity of the Scottish church.

The new principles on polity, those of classical presbyterianism, were in part a development from those of the first reformers, with which, indeed, they are sometimes confused. From the negative and destructive elements in reformation thought on episcopacy to the repudiation of the office of bishop was not a very long step. Language previously employed to justify the replacement of idle bishops by efficient bishops was resorted to in refutation of superiority of any kind, and in England was actually turned against men, now bishops, who had themselves used it against their predecessors,[2] while the reformers' emphasis on preaching as a function of a bishop tended to efface the distinction between the bishop and the presbyter and to encourage the definition of a bishop as nothing more than the minister of a congregation.[3] What was novel was the contention that, as superiority in jurisdiction, as well as in order, could no longer be conceded, there was now no room for a permanent overseer, however 'godly', and an episcopate of even the most limited type fell under condem-

---

[1] James Melville, *Diary*, p. 141; Calderwood, VI, 3.

[2] Harleian MS. 7581 contains a puritan petition which uses the opinions of Archbishop Cranmer and Bishops Latimer and Aylmer; Martin Marprelate quoted Aylmer in his *Epitome* (ed. Petheram, pp. 36–7); cf. *Seconde Parte of a Register*, I, 80.

[3] *The Discrypcyon of . . . a verye Chrysten Bysshop* (1536) had proclaimed that 'spirituall bysshops . . . are all the preachers of the worde of god in cyties, townes and vyllages' (sig. M vii verso, cf. N vi and vii).

nation. If it was admitted that a minister might be commissioned as a 'visitor', his office must be only temporary and he must, unlike most bishops and superintendents, retain a congregational charge.

This new emphasis on parity, by excluding the individual overseer, would itself have necessitated a new stress on courts and councils, and it did in practice lead to the advocacy of an entirely new organ, the presbytery or *classis*, to take over the functions previously exercised by bishops or superintendents. But the same stress on courts and councils emerged from other features in the presbyterian programme. To the presbyterians, 'discipline' had new meanings—a wider one in that it was used to denote the entire presbyterian polity, indeed the entire presbyterian programme,[1] but also a narrower one, for now only one organ for the correction of evildoers was recognised, namely the congregational consistory or eldership. If the eldership was the only valid means of discipline, not only were the rights of episcopal courts to exercise disciplinary functions denied, but an end was put to the distinction which the reformers had made between non-established churches, with their elderships, and established churches, where the punishment of the wicked was a function of the magistracy. The conflict between the older view and the new claims for the eldership appeared in the disputation between Withers and Erastus at Heidelberg in 1568, and it was an important feature in the controversy between puritans and conformers in England. Erastus maintained the reformation standpoint against the novel view which denied that 'the difference of having a Christian magistrate and having none' had any effect on the need for the eldership. At a later stage, Archbishop Whitgift, defending the English establishment against the presbyterian Cartwright, admitted that there might be 'sessions' in time of persecution, but urged that 'God hath provided the civil magistrate and other governors to punish and correct vice and other disorders in

---

[1] 'Discipline' had indeed been used in a wide sense in Calvin's *Institutes* (IV, X, 32, Beveridge, III, 225), in the French *Discipline* and the Scottish Book of Discipline; but as late as 1572 English puritans defined 'ecclesiastical discipline' as 'admonition and correction of faults' (*Puritan Manifestoes*, p. 9), while in 1574 Walter Travers defined it as 'the polity of the Church of Christ ordained and appointed of God' (*Full and Plaine Declaration*, p. 6).

the church,' and concluded that the 'seignory' was 'inconvenient in the time of Christian princes'.[1]

In Scotland, where the kirk sessions, originating under a sovereign hostile to the reformation, had continued unchallenged under a 'godly prince', there was no need to fight a battle on the narrow ground of the rights of the eldership; but the issue between the rival views of Withers and Erastus had wider ramifications, important in Scotland as elsewhere. The presbyterian view, in opposition to the 'Erastianism' of the reformers, was that church and state do not form one society, but two societies, which are to be kept carefully distinct. The reformers had of course criticised the old prelates for holding offices in the state,[2] but in no other particular is it possible to detect any correspondence between their views and those of the presbyterians. According to the latter, there were 'two kingdoms', and the sovereign of the state was only a member of the church, over which he was not permitted to exercise any authority. Thus the reformers' 'godly prince' disappeared along with their 'godly bishop'. Not only was the magistrate thus to be excluded from ecclesiastical authority, but all laymen, properly so-called, were likewise to be excluded from a voice in church affairs. The elder was no longer to be an annually elected lay officer; he was to be appointed for life, which meant that he ceased to be a layman as generally understood, that he received indelible *character* and that his office could be mistaken for an order in the ministry—a concept carried to its logical conclusion by those who contended that ministers and elders were alike ordained as presbyters and that the distinction between them was one between preaching presbyters and ruling presbyters. But although the status of the elders was thus in theory raised, their powers were curbed, for the authority over ministers assigned to the lay elders of 1560 was withheld from the quasi-clerical elders of later times: 'The spirit of the prophets is subject to the prophets' was an excellent text with which to bridle pre-

[1] Erastus, *Explicatio gravissimae questionis*, esp. thesis lxxiv; Whitgift, *Works*, I, 389–90, III, 166, 175–8, 209, 217–19; *Zurich Letters*, II, 251; Udall, *Demonstration of Discipline*, p. 5; Hooker, *Ecclesiastical Polity*, Preface, II, 4.

[2] E.g. Tyndale, *Exposition*, pp. 247, 273; Cranmer, *Remains and Letters*, pp. 38, 56 n.; Latimer, *Sermons*, pp. 67, 176; Coverdale, *Remains*, p. 244; Laing, V, 519; Aylmer, *An Harborowe*, sig. D iv verso, F iii recto.

sumptuous kirk sessions.[1] The presbyterian proposals therefore implied not only that, as the magistrate had no ecclesiastical authority, therefore the general assembly must retain its place even under a godly prince; it implied, further, that the assembly must lose its character as a version of the three estates of the realm, that it must shed its genuinely lay members and that it must become a mere gathering of ministers and elders representing the lesser courts of the presbyterian hierarchy. In one phrase, what was aimed at was not a democracy, but a clerical oligarchy.

Presbyterian thought as a whole had a quality, doctrinaire and intransigent, which had never characterised the discussions of church order among the first reformers. With a claim of scriptural, apostolic and dominical sanction for one system exclusively, polity was elevated to the rank of a dogma, expediency was disregarded and the right of each church to frame its polity in its own way could no longer be conceded. It was appropriate, therefore, that the presbyterian movement was an international movement, active in England and Scotland concurrently and advised, if not directed, from the Geneva of Theodore Beza.

The cry for 'parity' was heard in England before it was heard in Scotland, and on the continent before it was heard in England. And conflict between presbyterian principles and the principles on polity hitherto accepted appeared in Switzerland before it appeared in this island. At Geneva, Beza moved from a grudging acknowledgment of episcopacy[2] to a condemnation of the episcopal system as it existed in England and then to a denunciation of even the very modest variety of episcopacy existing in Scotland, and he also committed himself to the advocacy of the exclusive rights of the eldership in the exercise of discipline. The development of his views led to a breach with the church at Zurich which was first evident in 1568, when Bullinger and Gualter, at Zurich, sent letters of sympathy to Erastus, while Beza wrote a treatise condemning him.[3] In the next decade, while Geneva inspired the English and Scottish presbyterians, Gualter, dissociating himself from the party in

[1] J. L. Ainslie, *Ministerial Order in the Reformed Churches*, p. 135.
[2] E.g. in his *Confession of Faith* (1560), English edn (1565), fo. 108v.
[3] Figgis, *Divine Right of Kings*, pp. 294–6, 304–5.

England which sought the introduction of presbyterian government, condemned their violence and defended episcopacy. He opposed the notion that there was a form of government applicable in all circumstances, and continued to favour the right of princes to prescribe polity to their churches.[1] He illustrated his growing dislike of Geneva by the remark, 'The Genevians do still endeavour to thrust their discipline upon all churches,' and by a wish that Beza would conduct himself *modestius et humilius*.[2] Bullinger adopted the same attitude, accusing the presbyterians of thirst for power and of greed.[3] The breach which thus came about in the *entente* between Geneva and Zurich illustrates the novelty of the presbyterian programme, even on the continent.[4]

Beza's views were conveyed to this island in a series of letters, beginning in 1566, in which he condemned the English church order, and those letters were publicised partly by their inclusion in the 1573 and 1575 editions of Beza's *Epistolae* and partly by the reprinting of two of them in English puritan publications.[5] In 1572, when Beza learned of the emergence of a formal episcopate in the Scottish reformed church, he wrote to Knox, warning him not to be persuaded to subject the Scottish church to bishops—'just as bishops engendered the papacy, so the pseudo-bishops (the dregs of the papacy) will introduce worldliness; those who desire a sound church must beware of this plague'. Knox ignored the warning, but the letter became famous as Beza's seventy-ninth epistle and was long remembered by presbyterians.[6] This letter to Knox was not the last of Beza's epistolary interventions in Scottish affairs,[7] but, whatever may have been the influence of Beza's writings, his

---

[1] *Zurich Letters*, II, 225–35, 249–54; H.M.C. *Salisbury MSS.* II, No. 192 (W. Murdin, *State Papers*, p. 276).

[2] *Zurich Letters*, II, 237–9; Strype, *Annals*, II, I, 470.

[3] *Zurich Letters*, II, 240–3, 244–8.

[4] Cf. Sykes, *Old Priest and New Presbyter*, pp. 52–5.

[5] Letter to Grindal, June 1566 (*Puritan Manifestoes*, pp. 43–55; Beza, *Epistolae*, VIII; Strype, *Grindal*, pp. 167–8); letter to Bullinger, 3 Sep. 1566 (*Zurich Letters*, II, No. liii; Strype, *Annals*, I, II, App. xxix); letter to 'certain brethren of the Church of England', 24 Oct. 1567 (Beza, *Epistolae*, XII; *Troubles at Frankfort* [ed. Arber], p. 239; Strype, *Grindal*, p. 507).

[6] Laing, VI, 613–15; Row, *History*, p. 52; Beza, *Epistolae*, LXXIX; Strype, *Whitgift*, II, 164; Calderwood, VI, 12.   [7] P. 191 below.

views were presently being expounded in Britain by men who had themselves become his disciples at Geneva, and their work had far-reaching results.

Thomas Cartwright, while still at Cambridge, had come under Genevan influence, and after his expulsion from Cambridge because of his condemnation of episcopacy he visited Geneva, where he lectured at the academy for some months from June 1571, and in January 1571/2 Beza obtained permission for him to attend meetings of the Geneva consistory in order to study its working, so that he would be able to report on it in England and defend consistorial discipline against its critics.[1] It is possible that the Englishman accompanied Beza when he went to La Rochelle to act as moderator of a synod which revised the French *discipline*, and so had an opportunity of seeing the French reformed polity at work.[2] Cartwright's return to England, in 1572, coincided with, if it did not inspire, the second *Admonition to parliament*, which outlined the complete system of consistories, conferences and provincial and national synods, laid down that 'ministers must be equal, and the order must be that some must be governed by all, and not all by some, in the church government', and identified the bishop with the pastor of a congregation.[3] Two years later, presbyterian principles were elaborated by Walter Travers in his *Ecclesiasticae disciplinae explicatio*, which was at once translated into English by Cartwright. The previous existence in England of a vigorous puritan movement, in opposition to the establishment on liturgical and vestiarian issues, has tended to obscure the fact that a new party, with new principles, emerged under the leadership of Cartwright and Travers. The leading puritans of the first decade of Elizabeth's reign did not become prominent in the presbyterian movement,[4] which found its

---

[1] A. F. Scott Pearson, *Thomas Cartwright*, p. 50; *Amer. Hist. Rev.*, v, 284, xxi, 484.

[2] Marguerite G. Campbell, *French Book of Discipline*, p. x, and 'Early English Presbyterianism and the Reformed Church of France' in *Journal of the Presbyterian History Society of England*, ii.

[3] *Puritan Manifestoes*, pp. 97, 107, 126.

[4] Gilby and Sampson are most nearly exceptions to this generalisation (cf. Strype, *Whitgift*, i, 55, and *Annals*, ii, i, 392–3), but the contrast between Gilby's works (*View of Antichrist* [1578] and *Dialogue betwene a Souldiour of Barwicke and an English Chaplaine* [1581]) and the typical presbyterian works of Cartwright and Travers is more marked than any resemblances.

supporters mainly in younger men who imbibed presbyterian ideas while they were undergraduates and who were characterised by inexperience of pastoral work and by a doctrinaire disregard for expediency. Cartwright and Travers were, in their own jargon, 'doctors' rather than 'pastors', and were still in their early twenties when they began to play their part in the revolt. Contemporaries were clearer about the development than most later writers have been: Bishop Sandys, who was aware that 'the author of these novelties, and after Beza their first inventor, is a young Englishman, by name Thomas Cartwright', referred to the presbyterians generally as 'foolish young men', and Grindal told Bullinger that 'they are young men who disseminate these opinions. . . . Humphrey and Sampson and some others, who heretofore moved the question about ceremonies, are entirely opposed to this party.'[1] Thus the presbyterian programme was formulated in England before it was heard of in Scotland.

The presbyterian missionary to Scotland was Andrew Melville. After being absent from his native country for ten years, the last five of which he spent at Geneva, Melville came back about the middle of 1574.[2] It seems possible that Beza and he had agreed on the line of action necessary in Scotland, for the Genevan had already expressed his distrust of the *pseudoepiscopi*, and he declared that his permission to Melville to leave Geneva was a sign of his good will to Scotland.[3] Besides, Melville's work was associated with the Geneva-inspired movement of Cartwright and Travers. He had almost certainly met Cartwright in Geneva,[4] and in 1575 he presented to the principal of King's College, Aberdeen, a copy of Travers's *Explicatio ecclesiasticae disciplinae*.[5] The continued Scottish association with the English presbyterians was strikingly illustrated

[1] *Zurich Letters*, I, 292, 295, 312. Cf. Burghley's remarks on 'rash young heads' (Strype, *Annals*, I, II, 158) and 'persons young in years but over-young in soundness of learning and discretion' (Strype, *Parker*, II, 350), and Bacon's description of the universities as 'the seat or continent of this disease' (Spedding, *Letters and Life of Bacon*, I, 82–3).

[2] James Melville, *Diary*, pp. 38–47.   [3] *Ibid.* p. 42; p. 188 above.

[4] Charles Borgeaud, *L'académie de Calvin 1559–1798*, pp. 107–10, 113, 119, 316, and 'Cartwright and Melville at the university of Geneva, 1569–74' in *Amer. Hist. Rev.* v, 284–90; Pearson, *op. cit.* pp. 47, 48, 53.

[5] Pearson, *op. cit.* p. 142.

in 1580, when Cartwright and Travers were invited to chairs at the university of St Andrews.[1] Nor did Melville lose touch with Geneva. Soon after his arrival in Scotland, he had letters from Beza, and he in turn reported to his master on the progress of the anti-episcopal and presbyterian movement.[2] The presbyterian campaign in Scotland also received direct support from Beza in a letter which became known as the *De triplici episcopatu*: probably in 1576, Lord Glamis, the Scottish chancellor, a statesman who saw clearly enough the implications for the civil as well as the ecclesiastical constitution of the presbyterian insistence on parity and on ecclesiastical independence, and the difficulties which would arise should a new polity be introduced, wrote to Geneva asking for an authoritative ruling on some of the matters at issue, and Beza's reply, which condemned episcopacy and recommended the presbyterian system of courts, was translated into English and became influential in England and Scotland alike.[3]

Presbyterianism was thus in no sense an indigenous Scottish movement. But whether Andrew Melville needed support from England and Geneva it might be hard to determine. He was clearly a man of outstanding energy, strong and determined will and great courage and tenacity. It must, indeed, have been his personal qualities which brought him fame and won him followers, for his list of published works is a very meagre one and he never committed to print any exposition of his principles. His renown as a scholar and teacher is said to have preceded him to Scotland, for on his arrival there was competition to obtain his services and when he was appointed principal at Glasgow 'the scholars frequented to the college in such numbers that the rooms were scarce able to receive them.'[4] It was not as an author, but as a teacher, by personal contacts, that Melville made his impression, and it was his position in the university world which gave him strength as a leader. And he was not

[1] Fuller, *Church History*, IX, VII, 52; Nat. Lib. Scot. Wodrow MSS. fol. vol. 42, No. 3.

[2] James Melville, *Diary*, p. 51; two drafts of letters, dated 1 Oct. 1578 and 13 Nov. 1579, in Wodrow MSS. fol. vol. 42, No. 3 (the second printed in Calderwood, *Vindiciae*, p. 41); cf. McCrie, *Andrew Melville*, pp. 71-2.

[3] See *S.H.S. Misc.* VIII, 89 f.

[4] James Melville, *Diary*, p. 47; Calderwood, III, 339.

alone: when he moved to St Andrews, he was succeeded at Glasgow by Thomas Smeton, who had made Melville's acquaintance on the continent and from 1577 had been a member of his staff at Glasgow; thus, with Melville's friend Arbuthnot at Aberdeen, all Scottish theological education was directed by men committed to the presbyterian programme. Whatever had been the real significance of Knox's warning against subjecting the church to the universities, it is a curious fact that within a few years of his death the leadership of the militant section of the Scottish clergy fell to a man who was no pastor—for Melville never in his life served as a full-time parish minister—but was of purely academic experience and outlook. A contemporary estimate of Andrew Melville's character described his ability as more suited to 'the schools' than to ecclesiastical or civil affairs; one Scottish archbishop described him as 'learned, chiefly in the tongues', and another, irritated by the presbyterians' display of their knowledge of Greek and Hebrew, retorted, 'In what school were Peter and Paul graduate?'[1] There were excellent reasons for Melville's demand that 'doctors' like himself should be acknowledged as an order in the church and be assigned a place in its courts.

To the extent and direction of Melville's influence there is ample testimony. The Regent Morton accused him and his followers of disturbing the peace of the church 'by their conceits and oversea dreams, imitation of Geneva discipline and laws', and Archbishop Spottiswoode, looking back on this period from the following century, remarked that in the year 1575, owing to Melville's arrival from Geneva, 'began the innovations to break forth which to this day have kept the church in a continual unquietness'.[2] The truth presented by those hostile commentators is corroborated by the admissions of those more friendly to Melville. James Melville, his nephew and colleague, acknowledged that before his uncle's arrival 'many knew not yet the corruption and unlawfulness of that invention of men' [i.e. episcopacy] and declared that several minis-

---

[1] Thomas Volusenus, *Vita Adamsoni* (1619), p. 4; Spottiswoode, *History*, II, 200; Calderwood, III, 579.
[2] James Melville, *Diary*, p. 68; Spottiswoode, *loc. cit.*

ters were 'informed more thoroughly by Mr Andrew of the unlawfulness of bishops, and the right manner of governing of the
kirk by presbyteries'.[1] A similar tribute to the work of Melville
comes from presbyterian historians who, somewhat inconsistently
with their reluctance to admit that the original polity of the Scottish reformed church was not presbyterian, yet acknowledge that
Melville effected a revolution in the opinions of his fellow-countrymen. Thomas McCrie, for instance, went out of his way to stress
that episcopal government was widely acceptable until Melville's
campaign began, and that his hero wrought a 'change of sentiment'
among his fellow-countrymen.[2]

Yet Melville's influence lay rather in the formation of a party of
younger men than in the conversion to his views of men who
had previously accepted reformation principles. In Scotland as in
England it is substantially true that the leading presbyterian divines
belonged to a new generation, their dates of birth separated by almost two decades from those of most of the reformers. It is not easy
to point to any minister, except perhaps Robert Pont, who had been
active in organising the reformed church in its earlier years and
who had a prominent place in the presbyterian movement. Not
only so, but some of the veterans of 1560 never gave Melville much
countenance and continued to support principles opposed to his.[3]
The truth is, of course, that the differences between the reformation
polity and Melville's programme were far too great to escape the
notice of contemporaries, however much later controversialists
have tried to efface them. It seems unlikely that Melville could have
approved of the first Book of Discipline, and it is certainly true that
the compilers of that book acquiesced in, and indeed pressed for,
modifications of their original programme which were not acceptable to Melville. It is easiest to explain the situation by stating that
Melville's opponents adhered to principles, accepted in 1560, to
which his proposals were contrary. Melville could never have sub-
scribed the statements, cited earlier,[4] in support of the *jus divinum*
of bishop or superintendent; while opinions not easy to distinguish

---

[1] James Melville, *Diary*, pp. 32, 48, 52. [2] McCrie, *Melville*, p. 64.
[3] P. 214 below. [4] Pp. 124–5 above.

from those statements were expressed by his opponents when they defended the episcopal order against his attacks.[1] The essential difference remains between a polity in which supervision is normally in the hands of individuals and one in which it is normally in the hands of committees or courts of ministers.

Although presbyterian thought was dominated by theory and theology, the movement had its practical side. There were problems in the church, there were abuses, connected mainly with finance, and to them the presbyterian programme offered a solution and a remedy. And with all Melville's advantages he might have found it harder to have his proposals accepted had this not been so.

The various devices introduced before the reformation whereby church revenues could be in effect alienated had not been checked, and the trend towards secularisation had continued. The monastic property, in this respect as in others, was the biggest problem. The proposals for the abbeys in 1572[2] were to operate only as vacancies occurred, and would therefore not take effect completely for a generation. Meantime the abbeys and priories remained in being as entities under successive lay commendators with virtually hereditary rights, while the surviving monks still enjoyed their portions and on a monk's decease his portion was granted by the crown to any favoured person. Whether the core of the monastic revenues would ultimately be annexed to the crown or be incorporated into hereditary secular lordships, that core was a dwindling one, constantly being diminished by the granting of feus of lands and tacks of teinds, and only very drastic action indeed could ever recover much of this ancient church property for ecclesiastical uses. The bishoprics were now mostly held by clergy of the reformed church, and to that extent their complete secularisation had been averted, but there was widespread dilapidation.[3] The example which had for so long been set by the possessors of the 'prelacies' was followed by the holders of other benefices, who too often set feus and tacks on terms disadvantageous to their successors. Indications of anxiety about the progress of dilapidation are to be

[1] Calderwood, III, 429; IV, 53–4, 499–501.
[2] P. 171 above. [3] P. 172 above.

found in the proceedings of the general assembly in 1574 and 1576.[1]

The second major evil was the continued possession of benefices by 'unqualified' persons who could not or would not serve in the reformed church. There was a heritage of unsatisfactory appointments made before 1560, things had been worse between 1560 and 1567, and the machinery set up since 1567 to control the actions of patrons and deal with the 'unqualified' had not yet been wholly successful. We have no ready-made reports for Scotland similar to those made by the English puritans in their great 'survey of the ministry', or the evidence for the proportion of non-preaching ministers, non-residents and pluralists to be found in other English sources,[2] and an analysis of the relevant Scottish registers has not been made, but there are glimpses of a desperate state of affairs in some areas. For example, on two pages of the Register of Stipends for 1586, where the names of nine ministerial charges are entered, each page bears the note 'All non residentis', and the names of only three readers are given. The struggle over the presentation of unsatisfactory candidates continued.[3]

Thirdly must be reckoned the continued failure to separate the teinds of appropriated churches from the other revenues of monastic houses, and the resultant unsatisfactory level of ministers' stipends.[4] The agitation for the separation of appropriated churches went on: a statute of 1581 provided that all annexed churches should have ministers whose stipends would in future be reserved on the appointment of a new holder of the 'prelacy'.[5]

There were three ways in which the presbyterian programme

---

[1] The ample evidence, in the shape of crown confirmations of feus, tacks and pensions, is in the Registers of the Great and Privy Seals and the Register of Presentations. Cf. *A.P.S.* III, 211, 355; *B.U.K.* I, 310, 373, II, 413–14, 417, 450, 479, 603, 632, 737, 776 (Calderwood, III, 338, 376–7, 411, 519, 686, IV, 686).

[2] The puritans, in 1586, could find only 472 preachers in 2,537 parishes (*Seconde Parte of a Register*, II, 88 ff.); ecclesiastical officials reported in 1603 that there were men licensed to preach (but not necessarily preaching) in only half the parishes of England (B.M. Add. MSS. 38,139, fo. 254v; cf. H.M.C. *Salisbury MSS.* xv, 390). Returns (for 1575) of persons holding more than one benefice show that 655 livings were held by 239 incumbents (*ibid.* XIII, 134).

[3] *B.U.K.* II, 582, 632, 659 (Calderwood, III, 628, 736, IV, 563); *A.P.S.* III, 212 c. 4, 309–10, 542–3, IV, 115; James Melville, *Diary*, pp. 347–8.

[4] See p. 93 above.   [5] *A.P.S.* III, 211 c. 2.

had a connection with the remedy of abuses. It was a direct and material point that the abolition of episcopal government would set free revenues which could be devoted to the purposes of the church generally, and especially to the maintenance of an efficient ministry and the relief of the poor. This idea was seldom absent from the minds of English[1] and Scottish presbyterians alike, and an Englishman remarked that 'out of one of their [the bishops'] livings may half a dozen learned preachers be sufficiently provided for'.[2] In Scotland, where episcopal wealth became less justifiable than ever as the presbyterian attack developed and the practical importance of the episcopal office dwindled, it was with equal frankness argued that the prelates had taken up 'for the maintenance of their ambition and riotousness, the emoluments of the kirk, which may sustain many pastors, the schools and the poor'.[3] The comments of the writer of the *Historie and Life of King James the Sext*, although he wrote of a period when the episcopate had become for the time almost wholly ineffective, are illuminating:

Becaus the Prelats had great rents that appertenit to the kirk be gude rycht, and that thay did na service or functioun thairin, bot levit at thair pleasure; And the saidis Bishopries and Prelaceis had certayne temporall lands annexit unto thayme, whereby ather of thayme are callit Lords. For thir twa cawsis, the ministers estemit thair estait sa odious, that thay preachit mikle aganis thayme; and besydis all this, they estemit thair awin ordinar stependis to litle, and evill payit, and tharefore devysit to put in the heid of the Prence that thais temporall lands could not, or sould not, justlie appertayne to the Prelats, bot rather to the Crown.[4]

The act of 1587 which appropriated the episcopal temporalities to the crown[5] was thus a victory for presbyterian principles.

A second link between the presbyterian programme and existing abuses lay in the method of conferring orders and giving admission to ministerial charges. It was argued that ordination or admission by a presbytery did not leave as wide a door open to possible abuse

[1] E.g. Whitgift, *Works*, II, 321; Cartwright, *Second Reply*, 649–50; *Seconde Parte of a Register*, II, 10, 75–6, 210; Travers, *Full and Plaine Declaration*, pp. 113–14, 123–4; *Puritan Manifestoes*, p. 95; *Zurich Letters*, I, 296, 299.

[2] *Seconde Parte of a Register*, I, 258.   [3] *B.U.K.* II, 425.

[4] *Historie and Life of King James the Sext*, p. 231.   [5] P. 217 below.

as ordination by an individual bishop or superintendent, and the presbyterians argued further against patronage and in favour of congregational election, which they thought would eliminate unsuitable men from the ministry. The works of English presbyterians frequently touch on this subject, and argue from the intrusion of unqualified men, as a result of collusion between a bishop and a patron, to a condemnation of a system of ordination which permitted such an abuse.[1] In Scotland, where there had been checks on the action of superintendents and bishops in instituting the nominees of patrons,[2] the evil must have been less serious, but there is evidence that some men unfit for spiritual office did hold benefices, that the introduction of the presbyterian system was advocated on the ground that it would bring about an improvement,[3] and that after presbyteries were erected they did take action to remedy the results of the abuse of patronage.[4]

The third connection between prevalent abuses and presbyterian theory is in the renewed stress on the diaconate. If lay finance officers, elected by and answerable to the congregations, had the management of ecclesiastical revenues, there would be an end to the possibility of dilapidation in the interests of individual benefice-holders, and the redistribution of the wealth of bishops and dignitaries would be facilitated. English presbyterians asserted that in primitive times, when the bishops held their property in trust, they committed it to the deacons, who made use of it for the benefit of the poor, inferior clerks, and strangers,[5] and Travers, in his *Full and Plaine Declaration*, arguing that 'the neede off a great nombre may be relieued by the aboundance and excesse off a fewe', suggest-

---

[1] *Zurich Letters*, II, No. liii, shows how one of Beza's earliest attacks on episcopacy concentrated on this issue. Cf. *Seconde Parte of a Register*, I, 71, 150, 170, II, 76; *Puritan Manifestoes*, p. 32.

[2] *B.U.K.* I, 294 (Calderwood, III, 308).

[3] Second Book of Discipline, caps. iii, iv, xii.

[4] J. Melville, *Diary*, pp. 347–8; *A.P.S.* III, 542–3; McCrie, *Andrew Melville*, p. 157 and note HH. McCrie over-simplifies the truth, both in suggesting that the evil arose in 'the period of the tulchan episcopacy' and in claiming that presbyteries showed peculiar solicitude in the matter. At points as far apart as 1584 and 1597 acts of parliament were concerned to restrict the arbitrary use of crown patronage (*A.P.S.* III, 309–10; IV, 115).

[5] E.g. *Seconde Parte of a Register*, II, 10.

ed that the deacons must 'enter an action' against the bishops for the recovery of revenues to which the poor have a right.[1] When a Scot wrote to Beza in 1584 to set before the Genevan the point of view of the Scottish ministers who had been exiled for their adherence to presbyterianism, he justified part of their policy thus:[2]

Quidam sunt in Scotia ecclesiastici ordinis homines beneficiorum decoctores, praecipue Episcopi, inter quos iste noster [i.e. Archbishop Adamson] primus est: patrimonium enim Episcopale quamvis valde opimum iam post quadriennium ad nihilum redegit: ut decoctoribus istis provideatur cupiunt ministri annuam saltem rationem diaconis fieri ne effraena epicureorum licentia ecclesiae bona profundat; quae partim pauperibus, partim ministris, partim scholis impendenda sunt.

The practical side of the presbyterian movement and what may be termed the inductive argument for its programme are amply represented in the literature of English puritanism from the Admonitions to Parliament down to the Millenary Petition. More than half of Travers's *Full and Plaine Declaration* is taken up with denunciation of abuses and the exposition of remedies for them; its discussion centred on the need for an efficient ministry and the means by which it could be secured and maintained. In Scotland there was no comparable literature, but the records of one general assembly after another reveal the constant concern over the fate of ecclesiastical property, and Melville's own interest in financial questions is indicated by his reference to the 'restoration of church revenues to their legitimate uses' in the report on the progress of the Scottish presbyterian movement which he sent to Beza in 1579.[3] Further, the second Book of Discipline was itself much concerned with practical matters: among enumerated grievances of which reformation was desired were the admission of men to 'papistical titles and benefices' having no function in the kirk, the existence of the chapters of abbeys and cathedrals (which 'serve for nothing now but to set feus and tacks, if anything be left of the kirk lands and teinds'), the survival of cathedral and diocesan dignitaries, 'who have no place in a reformed kirk', the continuance of

[1] Pp. 124, 154, 155.   [2] B.M. Add. MSS. 32,092 f. 43v.
[3] Calderwood, *Vindiciae*, p. 41.

appropriations, the continued allowance of two-thirds of their revenues not only to old possessors but to men 'as unmeet or rather unmeeter' recently appointed, and the setting of feus and tacks to the financial prejudice of the church.

At the heart of the Melvillian remedy for abuses lay a comprehensive claim to the ecclesiastical property. Melville proposed a policy in some respects even more radical than that of the first Book of Discipline, and completely at variance with developments since 1567. Benefices and patronage alike were to be dispensed with, and a claim was advanced to all ecclesiastical property, temporality as well as spirituality—lands, buildings and annuals as well as teinds. To use any of this patrimony for secular purposes is sacrilege, and the whole should be collected by deacons and disbursed to ministers and other church officials, the poor and the sick, and the schools (though acknowledgment is made that some may go to the 'common weal'). In these proposals lay ground for controversy, not indeed among churchmen, except in so far as the financial interests of bishops and dignitaries were threatened, but between the church on one side and the crown, the nobility and lairds on the other, for it was plainly not in the interests of the latter to further such a policy.

Among churchmen themselves, a programme which offered a comprehensive solution to so many outstanding problems, in ecclesiastical administration, in church-state relations and in endowment, was bound to attract very wide support. Yet the presbyterian campaign did not proceed without opposition even within the church. It is too soon, in the 1570s, to speak of two parties, but there certainly were two opinions, or rather, more than one opinion. The debates which must have taken place in successive general assemblies are not recorded, but the extant proceedings of the assemblies do indicate a division of opinion at two points—at the opening of the campaign against the bishops in 1575–6 and at its close for the time being in 1581. In 1575, when 'certain brethren' brought forward the question whether 'bishops, as they are now in the Kirk of Scotland, have their function of the Word of God or not', six ministers, three on each side, were appointed to debate this novel proposition.[1] Although Andrew Melville was one of

[1] B.U.K. I, 340 (Calderwood, III, 355).

their number, they came only to the lame conclusion that they thought 'it not expedient presently to answer directly' to the question, and even so their report was received only 'after reasoning and long disputation upon every article'.[1] And in 1581, after the assembly had 'all in ane voyce . . . , none opponing themselves in defending the said pretendit office', condemned the office of bishop as 'unlaufull in the selfe, as haveand neither fundament, ground nor warrant within the Word of God', some brethren had second thoughts, the precise nature of which does not appear, and the assembly had to repeat and clarify its decision.[2]

Apart from official record, we have all too little information. Yet it does appear that episcopal government was defended on both practical and theological grounds. There were those who argued that, quite apart from the place of the bishops in the civil constitution as one of the estates of the realm, consideration must be given to 'the character and unruliness of the people, who can only with difficulty, if indeed at all, be retained in their duty unless constrained by the authority of bishops'[3]—a remark which should perhaps be read along with Robert Baillie's comment on the English in the following century, that 'no people had such need of a presbytery'. But if episcopacy was thus defended on grounds of expediency, there were others who thought it defensible by the tests of scripture and apostolic example. The archbishop of Glasgow declared in 1578 that he 'understood the name, office and modest reverence borne to a bishop to be lawful and allowable by the scriptures', that it was proper for bishops to enjoy their 'livings and rents and other things granted by the prince' and that it was beneficial to the church that bishops should attend council and parliament and take part in 'the making of good laws and ordinances'; but he was prepared to submit himself to 'the honourable judgment of the kirk from time to time' and to be examined according to 'the canon left by the Apostle to Timothie, 1 Ep. cap. iii'.[4] This was no more than a state-

---

[1] *B.U.K.* I, 342, 352–3 (Calderwood, III, 355, 365–6).
[2] *Ibid.* II, 453, 474–5 (Calderwood, III, 469, 525).
[3] *S.H.S. Misc.* VIII, 101. For further evidence of arguments from expediency, see Melville's letters to Beza in 1580 (McCrie, *Melville*, pp. 71–2).
[4] *B.U.K.* II, 423 (Calderwood, III, 429).

ment of the conservative position, in loyal acceptance of the settlement of 1572, and it is hard to see how any of the first reformers
could have quarrelled with it. But as the presbyterian pressure intensified, it provoked the defenders of episcopal government to
make higher claims. Patrick Adamson, on his appointment as archbishop of St Andrews in 1576, had refused to submit to the trial and
examination of the general assembly or to hold his office on its conditions,[1] and a decade later he was asserting that 'the office of a
bishop, as he has it in his person, in all heads hath the ground of the
Word of God, and in purity hath continued from the days of the
apostles unto this time'. Adamson passed from defence to attack,
for when the assembly denounced as 'blasphemy' his 'fathering on
the scriptures the superiority of pastors above pastors', he retorted,
'Ye have mothered on the scriptures equality of pastors, which is
anabaptistry.'[2]

In England the defenders of the establishment against the puritans were for many years content on the whole to deny that there
was any divinely appointed form of church government, and sometimes even admitted that the order advocated by their opponents
had the better claim to be considered primitive or apostolic.[3] Indeed, when the contention that episcopacy had the better claim to
a scriptural foundation first became prominent, about 1590, it was
regarded by many contemporaries as a very singular novelty.[4] But
if it is thus true of England that a claim of a divine right for presbytery preceded by some years the corresponding claim to be made
for episcopacy, it is not so clear that it is true of Scotland. It would
certainly appear—and it is something of an historical curiosity—

[1] B.U.K. I, 377 (Calderwood, III, 371–2).   [2] Calderwood, IV, 499–501.
[3] E.g. Whitgift, Works, I, 378, 389, III, 175–6; Zurich Letters, I, 285. Cf. P. M.
Dawley, John Whitgift and the Reformation, pp. 139–41.
[4] Richard Bancroft, in his sermon at Paul's Cross on 9 Feb. 1588/9, implied a
claim of divine right by hinting that those who denied the superiority of bishops
were heretics. Cf. R. G. Usher, 'Bancroft and the divine right of bishops', in
Theology, I, and 'The supposed origin of the doctrine of the divine right of
bishops' in Mélanges d'histoire offerts à M. Charles Bémont. For contemporary comment, see Spedding, Letters and Life of Bacon, I, 86–7; letters from Sir Francis
Knollys to Walsingham (S. P. Dom. Eliz. ccxxiii, No. 23) and to Burghley
(Strype, Annals, IV, 7–8); letter from Reynolds to Knollys, and the speech of
Knollys in parliament, in Informations, or a Protestation (1608).

that whereas the presbyterian programme was formulated in England before it was in Scotland, on the other hand the emergence in Scotland of a claim for *jure divino* episcopacy preceded its emergence in England.

CHAPTER IX

THE SEARCH FOR A 'SETTLED POLITY'

THE opposition to Melville within the church was not in the end wholly ineffective, as the history of later generations has shown, but at the time it was far too weak to prevent the approval of his programme by general assembly decisions which were formally unanimous. The second Book of Discipline, which was adopted by the general assembly in April 1578, was emphatic enough on theory: the 'power ecclesiastical flows immediately from God..., not having a temporal head on earth'; the offices of pastor, bishop and minister are identified, and it is declared contrary to scripture that bishops should be 'pastors of pastors, pastors of many flocks'; and the diversion of any part of the ecclesiastical patrimony from the service of the church is 'detestable sacrilege'. But, although negatively there was denunciation of specific abuses which existed in Scotland,[1] there were gaps in the positive and practical application of the new polity. In particular, while mention was made of a national assembly, of the assembly of a province and of the eldership (which might, especially in rural districts, be for three or four congregations jointly), there was no word of the presbytery; nor was anything said of the manner in which the functions of oversight, previously exercised by bishops and superintendents, were to be carried out in the future. Even when the assembly which approved the Book of Discipline 'concluded that no bishops shall be elected or admitted hereafter, before the next general assembly', and the next assembly (June 1578) 'concluded and provided that the said act shall be extended to all times to come',[2] there was still silence about the transfer of the powers of oversight. But the development of the presbytery as the complement to the suppression of the episcopate was implied when the assembly of October 1578 declared that 'they [the bishops] usurp not the power of presby-

---

[1] Pp. 198–9 above.
[2] *B.U.K.* II, 408–9, 413 (Calderwood, III, 403–4, 411).

teries';[1] it would, however, have been more candid had the assembly defined its policy as the erection of presbyteries to usurp the power of bishops.

The transition from the existing polity to a presbyterian polity need not in practice have been very difficult. The eldership was already established in many Scottish parishes and required no alteration save the supersession of annual election of elders by appointment for life. The provincial synod needed only to lose its permanent president (bishop or superintendent). A general assembly, too, already existed, but it required some not unimportant changes in composition: the ministers who were to attend would have to be elected, and elders would have to be substituted for 'barons' and burgh commissioners; the second Book of Discipline proposed that the members of assembly should be chosen by the synods, and this proposal was adopted in a scheme drawn up by the assembly in 1581.[2] A body intermediate between the kirk session and the provincial synod—in the place, that is, to be occupied by the presbytery—already existed (though with ministerial members only) in the 'exercise'.

Weekly meetings, for 'prophecy' and 'interpretation', of ministers and readers in and near the larger burghs had been prescribed in the first Book of Discipline.[3] Virtually nothing is known about their operation, but it would seem that, while enthusiasm was so far from universal that there was at times a danger that they might lapse altogether, yet there is some indication that exercises may sometimes have provided opportunities for discussing synod and general assembly business.[4] Additional strength would undoubtedly attach to the exercise in some large burghs from its association with the 'general kirk' of the burgh, a united consistory composed of the ministers and elders of the several congregations in the burgh;[5] this body, in itself weighty, had formed the superinten-

---

[1] B.U.K. II, 425 (Calderwood, III, 431–2).
[2] Ibid. 480 (Calderwood, III, 520).
[3] Laing, II, 242–5 (Dickinson, II, 315).
[4] B.U.K. I, 265, 321, 366 (Calderwood, III, 279, 344, 375).
[5] It is not impossible that there was some conception of such a 'general kirk' as the body intermediate between the 'particular kirk' or congregation and the 'universal kirk' or general assembly (cf. Maitland Club, Misc. I, I, 97). It may be

dent's court for the district and was also the kernel of the local exercise. It was not, therefore, a very radical departure when such an exercise began to perform administrative and judicial functions. For example, in August 1578, when the 'brethren of the exercise of Edinburgh, being convened with the commissioner of Lothian', appointed two of their number to attend on 'the lords lately departed out of this town',[1] the distinction between the exercise, the commissioner's court and possibly the 'general kirk' of Edinburgh had become blurred. Certainly wherever an exercise had a vigorous life it provided the beginnings of something very like a presbytery, and recognition was given to such a development when the general assembly of July 1579 pronounced that in places where an exercise was in existence 'the exercise may be judged a presbytery'.[2] Again, in 1580, when the general assembly gave authority to the 'brethren of the exercise of Edinburgh' to report on certain offences alleged against a minister',[3] it was recognising the exercise as an executive organ.

But even if this somewhat meagre evidence does suggest that the exercise could be transformed, by almost imperceptible stages, into the presbytery, it is quite unnecessary to postulate a deliberate intention that this should take place, at least at any date earlier than the later 1570s. Later controversialists[4] fostered the idea that the exercise was from the first designed to develop into a presbytery, but this view appears to be quite untenable, not only because of the silence of the first Book of Discipline on the subject and the fact that such a development was directly contrary to the whole character of the polity of the Scottish church in the 1560s, but also be-

---

added that there is no mystery about the use of 'universal' to mean no more than 'whole'. We find 'universal rowme of Scotland' in 1516 (Morton Papers, Eccl. [Kinross and Urwell]), 'tota et universalis ecclesia Scoticana' c. 1520 (*Formulare*, I, p. 85) and 'universalis ecclesia Scoticana' in 1547 (*R.M.S.* IV, 159). Cf. Patrick, *Statutes of the Scottish Church*, p. 151.

[1] *Wodrow Soc. Misc.* I, 407–8.   [2] *B.U.K.* II, 439 (Calderwood, III, 450).
[3] *Ibid.* 465 (Calderwood, III, 477).
[4] E.g. Scot, *Apologetical Narration* (Wodrow Soc.), p. 10: 'The presbiteries or classicall meetings could not be constitut for discipline and government at the first, because of the rarity of ministers; yet we had weekly meetings of ministers, and others aiming at the ministry, for the exercise of prophesieing from the very beginning'.

cause a precisely parallel development took place in England, where bishops who had at first encouraged exercises for the intellectual and spiritual profit of their clergy found to their dismay that the meetings were apt to be transformed into the illegal *classes* or presbyteries advocated by Cartwright and his followers. The second *Admonition to parliament* (1572), which contained a description of the complete presbyterian platform, had given the following description of 'conferences' or *classes:*

> A conference I call the meeting of some certain ministers, and other brethren, . . . to confer and exercise themselves in prophesying, or in interpreting the scriptures, after the which interpretation, they must confer upon that which was done, and judge of it, the whole to judge of those that spake. . . . At which conferences, any one . . . of the brethren, are at the order of the whole, to be employed upon some affairs of the church. . . . The demeanours also of the ministers may be examined and rebuked, . . . sundry causes within that circuit . . . may be decided.[1]

Anyone reading this passage, or anyone familiar with the 'colloquies' of the French protestants, which were at once exercises and administrative units,[2] could see the possibility of developing exercises into bodies laying down rules which bound their members, and even of using them as opportunities for ordinations after the presbyterian fashion.[3] The danger from the exercises as gatherings which provided the nonconforming party with an organisation was fully realised by some of the bishops in 1576, and the bishop of Hereford, who understood the character of the polity advocated by the presbyterian leaders, wrote 'I feared that might happen in my diocese, which I hear to have happened in some others: where some platform of Cartwright's church, under colour of such exercises, hath been laid. And if it be not well and wisely looked unto will creep *ut Gangrenae morbus.*'[4] Episcopal disapproval did not prevent the development which this bishop foresaw, and the exercises, continuing unofficially and even secretly after official recognition was withdrawn in 1577, were gradually turned into the *classes* or presbyteries of the next decade.[5]

---

[1] *Puritan Manifestoes*, pp. 107–8.   [2] Campbell, *French Book of Discipline*, p. 25.
[3] *Seconde Parte of a Register*, I, 71.   [4] B.M. Add. MSS. 29,546 f. 52v; cf. 56v.
[5] The 'orders' drawn up for the meetings of the Dedham *classis* were in effect those of an exercise (R. G. Usher, *Presbyterian Movement*, p. 25).

Although, in the Scotland of 1580, exercises were here and there beginning to undertake executive functions, and although the assembly of April 1581, which reaffirmed and clarified the resolution of the previous July condemning the office of bishop, also drew up a scheme for organising the parishes of the country in fifty presbyteries,[1] anything like a system of presbyterian government was still remote. Even when the assembly took the more modest step of appointing that 'a beginning be had of the presbyteries instantly' at thirteen towns in central and southern Scotland, 'to be exemplars to the rest which may be established hereafter',[2] it must have been aware, though its records hardly reveal the fact, that however simple it might seem to be to transform the existing polity into a presbyterian system there was a major obstacle to be overcome. That obstacle lay in the relations of the church with the state. Claims could be advanced to ecclesiastical independence, but until these claims were admitted by the state they were valueless. Thus, while the church could go so far in its substitution of presbytery for episcopacy, it could not complete the process without the alteration of statute law. The second Book of Discipline had been submitted to parliament in July 1578 in the hope that it would be 'confermit be act of parliament and have the strenth of ane law',[3] but the hope was not realised. Not only had parliament declined to sanction the book, but the book was incompatible with existing statute law: a statute of 1567 had given the power of collation to benefices to superintendents and commissioners, and several other acts of parliament and council had given authority in a variety of matters to bishops, superintendents and commissioners; until these acts were repealed or modified, collation by a presbytery could hardly give a legal title to a benefice. In practice, too, bishops and commissioners were still, in 1579, 1580 and 1581, receiving presentations, giving collation, presiding over synods and dealing with recusant clergy,[4] and even at St Andrews, one of the places where

---

[1] *B.U.K.* II, 480 (Calderwood, III, 520).
[2] *Ibid.* 482–7 (Calderwood, III, 523).　　[3] *A.P.S.* III, 105.
[4] Register House Charters, No. 2523; Mey Papers, No. 188; *Laing Charters*, No. 1019; Breadalbane Papers, 29 Aug. 1581 and 13 Aug. 1583; Reg. Pres. II, 38.

the assembly appointed a model presbytery in April 1581, the arch-bishop was still acting in association with the kirk session and the 'exercise' at various dates between December 1581 and August 1583.[1] Evidently, although the assembly could order the bishops to demit office, as it did in 1580, its command was disregarded. Further, although the assembly could forbid fresh elections of bishops, as it had done as early as 1578, it could hardly in practice prevent the crown from operating the machinery for episcopal appointments; and even if it did, the crown had a further card to play, for it was always in the power of the government to appoint a bishop *quoad civilia*. And the government, at the very time when the assembly was condemning the episcopal office and proceeding to plans for the erection of presbyteries, resorted to the advantage which that power gave it, for it in effect accepted the assembly's challenge by making a new appointment to the archbishopric of Glasgow. The answer by church courts was to threaten the new archbishop with excommunication, and the privy council, which a few months before had shown signs of some readiness to further plans for the erection of presbyteries,[2] now forbade 'presbyteries, elderships and general and synodal assemblies' to proceed against him for 'aspiring to the bishopric'.[3] The conflict between ecclesiastical proceedings and statute law became still plainer when, in November 1581, parliament passed an act confirming several statutes which gave authority to bishops and superintendents.[4]

When the assembly's proceedings did receive a measure of official countenance, it came, almost fortuitously, as a result of political developments in themselves irrelevant to the controversy over the machinery of ecclesiastical administration. The over-throw of the earl of Morton, the ascendancy over the boy king of Esmé Stewart (created earl of Lennox in March 1580) and the activities of Roman catholic and Marian agents, led to a 'Popish Scare'.

[1] *Reg. K. S. St A.*, pp. 461, 464, 482, 489, 508.   [2] *R.P.C.* III, 383.
[3] *Ibid.* III, 476–7. Cf. *Historie and Life of King James the Sext*, pp. 186–7: 'At the beginning of [1582] . . . it pleased the members of court to give ear to certain informations made against a new erected society of ministers, called The Presbytery: so that their moderators were summoned to compear before the king and council to produce the books of their proceedings, to be seen and considered'.
[4] *A.P.S.* III, 210–11.

The ultra-protestant feeling of the time was expressed in the Negative Confession, signed early in 1581, which denounced 'all kinds of papistry', including the pope's 'blasphemous priesthood . . . , his manifold orders, . . . his worldly monarchy and wicked hierarchy'. Any who felt that an episcopal regime savoured of papistry would certainly be confirmed in their opposition. Then, when the Lennox administration, suspected of a Romanising policy and certainly committed to the maintenance of an episcopate, was overthrown by the *coup d'état* known as the Ruthven Raid (August 1582), the new government almost at once issued a proclamation favourable to the presbyterian campaign: after referring to 'the privilege granted to God's kirk, and in all ages observed, and specially since our coronation, in the convocation of general, synodal and particular assemblies', it was declared that it was not the royal will to stop the convention of such assemblies.[1] But this did not expressly mention presbyteries, and, while it guaranteed freedom to meet, it said nothing of the powers of the 'assemblies'. The general assembly, for its part, pushed on busily with plans for presbyteries,[2] but the government disregarded its petition for the transfer from bishops to presbyteries of such powers as giving collation to benefices, designating manses and glebes and taking action for the repair of churches.[3]

Not for the first or the last time in its post-reformation history, the organisation of the Scottish church was far from uniform, if indeed the situation did not verge on anarchy. Here and there presbyterial administration must have been firmly established, and well on the way to superseding the rule of superintendent or bishop. We find the presbytery of Edinburgh exercising the function of visitation in June 1583,[4] and in that year the presbytery of Linlithgow was sufficiently well established to have its seal, the matrix for which still exists.[5] In Glasgow, David Wylie, who had in earlier days been clerk to the superintendent of the west and his court,[6]

---

[1] Calderwood, III, 650–1 [4 Sept. 1582].
[2] *B.U.K.* II, 586–7 (Calderwood, III, 680–1).
[3] *Ibid.* 601 (Calderwood, III, 684).   [4] *Wodrow Soc. Misc.* I, 459.
[5] J. H. Stevenson and M. Wood, *Scottish Heraldic Seals.*
[6] *Thirds of Benefices*, p. 262.

had latterly become clerk 'of the ministry and presbytery of Glasgow', and after his death the king, on 20 March 1583/4, appointed his son as his successor, 'willing that the same presbytery shall not be destitute of a sufficient and qualified person for using of the said office'.[1] In the *Register of the Kirk Session of St Andrews* the presbytery appears from time to time in 1583 and the beginning of 1584 as an organ to which the session was subordinate.[2] Yet presentations continued to be directed normally to bishops, superintendents and commissioners; a presbytery was occasionally named as a possible alternative to one of those officials, but very rarely indeed was a presentation directed simply to a presbytery.[3] Equally, bishops, superintendents and commissioners continued normally to exercise their power of deprivation; only one instance is on record of deprivation by a presbytery in this period.[4]

The continued recognition accorded to bishops and commissioners must have arisen from doubts about the legality of presbyteries: the statutory constitution of the church remained episcopal, the presbyterian experiment now being conducted was unofficial, and the first appearance of the presbytery in the Acts of the Parliaments of Scotland is in a reference in 1584 to the 'pretended presbyteries'.[5] Clearly the presbyterian achievement was at this time very limited; the presbyterian leaders themselves did not claim that the polity they advocated was in full operation, but only that their 'whole form of church government . . . was growing and increasing . . . and did grow and increase until it came to a reasonable perfection'.[6]

And no doubt presbyterial administration would have con-

---

[1] Reg. Pres. II, 102.   [2] *Reg. K. S. St A.*, pp. 494–5, 500, 503, 520, 523.
[3] The following presentations mention presbyteries:
9 Dec.   1581   —archbishop of St Andrews, commissioner of Lothian, or presbytery and eldership of Haddington (Reg. Pres. II, 64).
30 May 1582   —presbytery, superintendent or commissioner (R.S.S. XLIX, 3).
24 Jan. 1583/4—'commissioner over the kirks within the presbytery of Dalkeith' (Reg. Pres. II, 95).
10 Apr. 1584   —presbytery or commissioner (R.S.S. L, 116).
9 May   1584   —presbytery (R.S.S. L, 129).
May   1584   —commissioner or moderator of the presbytery of Aberdeen (Reg. Pres. II, 102).
[4] R.S.S. LI, 137.   [5] *A.P.S.* III, 312 c. 31.   [6] Calderwood, IV, 75.

tinued to 'grow and increase', as it did later between 1586 and 1592,[1] but for an interruption arising from another palace revolution—James's escape from the 'Raiders' in August 1583 and the subsequent rout of the Ruthven faction after their abortive attempt to regain power in April 1584. The administration which followed, under James Stewart, earl of Arran, has been called an 'anti-presbyterian dictatorship', but its resolute legislation against Melvillian proceedings was only one aspect of a powerful and many-sided reaction against the radical tendencies of late years.

One of the 'Black Acts' of May 1584 ordained that the bishops and commissioners were to 'direct and put order to all matters and causes ecclesiastical within their dioceses, visit the kirks and state of the ministry within the same, reform the colleges therein, receive his highness's presentations to benefices and give collations thereupon'.[2] While this was the first statute which in such summary and comprehensive terms gave authority to an episcopate in the reformed church, it amounted to no more than a reaffirmation of the system which had operated since 1560 and which already had parliamentary and conciliar sanction in detail. To that extent it represented no innovation. Another of the 'Black Acts', narrating that during the 'troublous times' of the preceding twenty-four years 'sundry forms of judgments and jurisdictions as well in spiritual as temporal causes are entered in the practice and custom whereby the king's majesty's subjects are ofttimes convocate and assembled together' without approval of parliament, discharged the said 'judgments and jurisdictions' and forbade any of the king's subjects to assemble 'for holding of councils, conventions or assemblies to treat, consult and determine in any matter of estate civil or ecclesiastical .... without his majesty's special commandment, express licence had and obtained to that effect'.[3] This was sweeping in its terms, but the *Declaration of the king's majesty's intention and meaning towards the late acts* stated that synods twice yearly, and exercises for spiritual purposes, were expressly sanctioned, and that the act was aimed especially at 'that form lately invented in this land, called the presbytery', which 'usurped all the whole ecclesiastical jurisdic-

---

[1] Pp. 217–19 below.   [2] *A.P.S.* III, 303 c. 20.
[3] *Ibid.* 293 c. 4.

tion'.[1] The general assembly, although it was criticised, was not condemned outright, and some kind of national assembly, by which bishops could be censured, was envisaged[2]—possibly something like the 'great council of the church' of which the first Book of Discipline had made mention, possibly something like the 'national synod' which was proposed in the Restoration period in the following century. As to the kirk session, the archbishop of St Andrews gave an assurance in June 1584 that it was not the government's intention 'to inhibit the convening of the elders and deacons of any congregation within this realm, nor to inhibit any good order established within the same for punishment of vice, but only to inhibit the new erected presbyteries',[3] and at a meeting of the kirk session of Perth on 10 August 1584, a letter was produced on the king's behalf 'giffing licence to the assemblie particular off Perth to convein thame selffis oulkly for the distributioun of the almis to the puir and to mantein vertew and punische vyce'.[4] The legislation on 'assemblies' was, therefore, like the legislation on bishops, in the main a restoration or reaffirmation of old practice rather than an innovation.

Where the 'Black Acts' did represent a real innovation was in church-state relations. The second of the acts was an act of supremacy, affirming 'the royal power and authority over all estates, as well spiritual as temporal, within this realm' and ordaining that the king and his council should be 'judges competent to all persons his highness's subjects, of whatsoever estate, degree, function or condition that ever they be of, spiritual or temporal, in all matters wherein they or any of them shall be apprehended, summoned or charged to answer to such things as shall be inquired of them by our said sovereign lord and his council'.[5] With that act should be read the third, against impugning the dignity and authority of parliament or seeking the diminution of its powers; and that the issue was civil as well as ecclesiastical emerges in yet another act ordering that George Buchanan's *History* and his *De jure regni* should be purged.[6] But what it all meant in the ecclesiastical sphere was pointedly

---

[1] Calderwood, IV, 258–60, 265, 266.   [2] *Ibid.* 266.
[3] *Reg. K. S. St A.*, II, 529.   [4] Perth Kirk Session Records (MS.).
[5] *A.P.S.* III, 292 c. 2.   [6] *A.P.S.* III, 293 c. 3, 296 c. 8.

expressed in the act in favour of the bishops, which referred to 'the king's majesty's commissioners in ecclesiastical causes', so in effect turning the bishops into crown commissioners, and in the oath to be taken by all clergy and teachers, which included this clause: 'We shall show our obedience to our ordinary bishop or commissioner appointed or to be appointed by his majesty to have the exercise of spiritual jurisdiction in our diocese'.[1] In spite of the language of the *Declaration*, it would seem that the intention was to suppress the general assembly—which in fact did not meet while Arran's regime lasted—and to subject the bishops not, as before, to it, but to the crown. In this respect, but perhaps in this respect alone, the Black Acts represented a departure from the practice of the years after 1572, when the general assembly had been preserved.[2]

Yet, while the assertion of crown supremacy in such direct terms was a novelty in Scotland, it is not easy to argue that such an assertion was in principle contrary to the thought of the reformers. Indeed, it is possible to go further and say that in the 'Black Acts' we have the logical development of the principles of the reformation. The king's claim that he had a special duty to see vice punished and virtue maintained[3] recalls the appeals of the reformers to the magistracy; and the condemnation at this point, as a popish error, of Melville's claim to ecclesiastical independence[4] recalls one of John Knox's most forcible exhortations.[5] It would seem that the general assembly had, in due time, been superseded by the godly prince; superintendents and commissioners under the assembly had been superseded by bishops under the crown—and was a bishop commissioned by the king so very different from a superintendent commissioned by the lords of council? That it is not absurd to

---

[1] *Ibid.* p. 303 c. 20, 347 c. 2.

[2] It must be kept in view that from 1585, if not earlier, it was proposed that the parliament, which since 1572 had included representatives of the reformed church in the persons of the bishops, should be further strengthened by the addition of shire commissioners: should this addition be made—as it was in terms of a statute of 1587—it would become still more difficult, on reformation principles, to justify the continued existence of a general assembly alongside a parliament fully representative of the 'godly estates'.

[3] Calderwood, IV, 256.   [4] *Ibid.* 257.   [5] Pp. 132–3 above.

identify the 'Black Acts' with the principles of the reformation is proved by the fact that, while Andrew Melville and about a score of his disciples fled to England, most of the older ministers evidently considered that episcopal administration and crown supremacy were not inappropriate in the conditions now prevailing. Erskine of Dun not only resumed his functions as a superintendent and was regarded by Archbishop Adamson as his assistant in the northern parts of the diocese of St Andrews, but he also exerted his influence on the ministers north of the Tay to accept the new regime.[1] David Lindsay, minister of Leith, was another of the veterans of 1560 who welcomed the reaffirmation of an episcopal polity;[2] and John Craig, yet another, was successful in devising a formula whereby the government's requirements were rendered acceptable to tender consciences, and he 'inveighed against' the ministers who had abandoned their charges and gone to England.[3] As the great majority of the rank and file of the ministers throughout the country were acquiescent, it would seem indisputable that although the Melvillian faction, when active in the general assembly, had prevailed, Melville had not won the adherence of the whole body of the clergy.

If the policy represented in the 'Black Acts' is regarded as in some sense the royal and episcopal response to the Melvillian challenge, then it may be said that by 1584 two extreme points of view have emerged, two irreconcilable theories have been defined, each of them one which persisted as long as the presbyterian–episcopalian controversy continued within the Church of Scotland, and each of them one which always in future commanded some support among clergy and laity alike. All the elements were now present which went to shape the future evolution of the Scottish reformed polity. But although there were extremes which were irreconcilable, and although it is true that ever since the outbreak of controversy in the 1570s the Scots have not been unanimous on the issues then raised,

---

[1] *Spalding Club Misc.* IV, 69–72; H.M.C. *Report*, V, 636; *Wodrow Soc. Misc.* I, 432, 436. On Erskine's conservatism generally, see *B.U.K.* II, 745, 783, and cf. Spottiswoode, II, 412.

[2] *Wodrow Soc. Misc.* I, 434. See 'David Lindsay' in *Fathers of the Kirk* (ed. R. S. Wright).

[3] Calderwood, IV, 246, 466.

yet it is equally true that not all Scots have been irreconcilables on either one side or the other. And in practice most of the history of the period from 1575 to 1690—that is, down to the point when it at last proved impossible to retain both presbyterians and episcopalians in one church—is not a history of the pursuit of extremes, not a history of a series of violent oscillations between two irreconcilable polities. It is rather the history of a series of attempts at compromise, with a view to satisfying the theories of ecclesiastics—especially the presbyterians—and at the same time providing machinery which would solve practical problems in endowment, church-state relations and ecclesiastical administration. The problem to which such a variety of solutions was to be offered during the next century and more was not unsuitably defined as early as March 1574/5: the estates of the realm, on the narrative that there was not yet a 'perfect polity' in the church, appointed a commission to frame such an ecclesiastical constitution as would be 'maist aggreabill to the trewth of Goddis word and maist convenient for the estate and people of this realme'.[1] But whereas in 1572 it had proved possible, or so it seemed, to reconcile the traditional ecclesiastical structure and the just claims of the crown with the reformers' opinions on church order, it was to prove much more difficult, and in the end impossible, to reconcile that structure and those claims with the opinions on church order enunciated by Andrew Melville.

In the early stages of the presbyterian campaign, before opinion had crystallised, there had been made the first of many attempts at a compromise, based on a reconciliation of presbyterian theory with administrative convenience. The commission which thought 'it not expedient presently' to adjudicate on the scriptural foundation of episcopacy suggested that although 'the name of bishop is common to all them who have a particular flock, over the which they have a peculiar charge, as well to preach the Word as to minister the Sacraments', yet 'out of this number may be chosen some to have power to oversee and visit such reasonable bounds beside their own flock as the general kirk shall appoint, and in these bounds to appoint ministers, . . . to appoint elders and deacons . . . and to suspend ministers', with the advice of the ministers of the 'province'

[1] *A.P.S.* III, 89.

and of the people of the congregations.[1] When the assembly accepted this suggestion, in April 1576, it ordained that each bishop should receive the charge of 'a particular congregation'.[2] This compromise was evidently acceptable to some, for certain bishops agreed to undertake a congregational ministry, and Erskine of Dun indicated his assent by being inducted to a parochial benefice, whereas other bishops, and apparently also the superintendent of Fife, declined.[3] There was probably less disposition on the other side to accept such a scheme as a final settlement, because it did not secure the substitution for episcopal oversight of administration by courts of ministers, at which Melville aimed.

A second attempt at a compromise was made when the presbyterian leaders and their lay allies, after the reverse they had suffered in the episode of the 'Black Acts', were in a position to renew the contest. Another *coup d'état* had brought about the dismissal of Arran (December 1585), whereupon Andrew Melville and most of the other presbyterian exiles returned from England. The experiment was then tried, somewhat as in 1572, of a settlement arrived at by a conference of ministers and councillors, which in February 1586 agreed on what was designed as a compromise. The existence of presbyteries was accepted and their erection was to proceed systematically; bishops, nominated by the king and admitted by the assembly (to which they were answerable for life and doctrine), were to be permanent moderators of the presbyteries meeting in their places of residence, but were to have each his particular congregation and were to act in visitation, examination and collation only with the advice of a committee of ministers—a 'senate or presbytery'—chosen by the general assembly.[4] In the month of May following, the general assembly, after long discussion and with some hesitation, accepted this arrangement, and drew up a fresh scheme of fifty-two presbyteries and sixteen synods.[5]

---

[1] *B.U.K.* I, 342–3 (Calderwood, III, 355–6).
[2] *Ibid.* 352–3 (Calderwood, III, 365–6).
[3] *R.S.S.* VII, 266; *B.U.K.* I, 358–60, 378–9 (Calderwood, III, 367–8, 370–1).
[4] Calderwood, IV, 491–4.
[5] *B.U.K.* II, 652–4, 665 ff. (Calderwood, IV, 558–9, 571 ff.)

A comparison of this compromise with the suggestions made in 1575 is a measure of the Melvillian achievement of the intervening ten years. Now the bishops or commissioners must not only have their congregational charges and be responsible to the assembly, but their day-to-day work in administration is to be strictly controlled; further, the presbytery, although still without statutory authority, had now arrived and was never again to be completely set aside in the established church. Such a compromise had much to commend it: in some ways it anticipated the system which was to work during part of the following century, and it represents something very like the concept of the bishop-in-presbytery. But whether any compromise would have worked in the circumstances of that time may be doubted. The assembly, controlled by the Melvillians, made no serious effort to make the plan work or to reach a *modus vivendi* with the bishops, and no means had as yet been discovered, as was later to be discovered by the ingenuity of James VI, whereby an assembly could be curbed, or gained to compliance. There may have been more disposition to compromise on the other side, for Archbishop Adamson made a formal submission to the assembly,[1] but a state of affairs in which the archbishop of St Andrews and some of the Fife ministers had been excommunicating each other hardly provided a suitable atmosphere for concord. Further, an examination of the record evidence shows that while administration was being carried out by individuals (no doubt with the advice of ministers), there was a clear preference for commissioners rather than bishops. Nor did the assembly show any readiness to co-operate in making fresh appointments to vacant sees,[2] and the act of annexation of 1587, which deprived the bishops of their temporality, leaving them only their castles, 'yards' and teinds, went a long way towards the eclipse of the episcopate.

Between 1587 and 1592, although no enactment bearing on ecclesiastical administration was passed—for the act of annexation was purely secular and financial in its scope—there were many changes in practice, and what ultimately emerged was a presbyterian system operating over the greater part of the country.

[1] *B.U.K.* II, 662–3 (Calderwood, IV, 553).
[2] *Ibid.* 690, 693, 697–8 (Calderwood, IV, 621, 622, 625–6).

Legally, the bishops and other 'commissioners of the king in ecclesiastical causes' were still alone entitled to receive presentations,
to give collation and to carry out deprivations, and in general they
continued to do so until about 1588 (although, as mentioned above,
there was a preference for commissioners rather than bishops).[1]
Alongside them, however, the growing recognition of the presbytery is conspicuous. As early as November 1586 a presentation
was directed to 'the presbiterie of Cunynghame',[2] and by 1588
nearly a quarter of the crown presentations make mention of a
presbytery, though nearly always along with or as an alternative to
a bishop or commissioner. In the two following years the proportion of presentations mentioning a presbytery steadily increased,
and 1591 marks the substantial triumph of the presbytery: no less
than 85 per cent of presentations in that year mention a presbytery,
and the number which mention only a presbytery, though no more
than five in the first half of the year, rises to thirteen in the second
half. Yet commissioners were still active[3] and a presentation could
still be directed to 'the reverend father in God, the bishop of Dunkeld, or the superintendent or commissioner in these bounds'.[4] By
1592 the ascendancy of the presbytery is all but complete: 96 per
cent of presentations mention a presbytery and approximately half
of them mention no alternative.

Other evidence likewise shows the increasing importance of
presbyterial organisation. Apparently as early as 1589 a presbytery
might appoint commissioners to the general assembly.[5] When, in
December 1590, the king appointed two commissioners to 'plant
ministers' in the presbytery of Dunblane and assign them stipends,
their work was to be subject to review by the presbytery.[6] In the
account of the collector general of thirds for 1590 (audited 3 January 1591/2) the term 'presbytery' is for the first time used to denote
a district. Deprivation, like collation, was passing out of the hands
of the bishops and commissioners into those of presbyteries.[7] The
depression of the episcopate is correspondingly conspicuous not
only in the increasing rarity of the direction of presentations to

---

[1] E.g. Reg. Pres. II, 155; R.S.S. LVII, 139, 172.   [2] Reg. Pres. II, 159.
[3] R.S.S. LXI, 134.   [4] Ibid. LXII, 53.   [5] Wodrow Soc. Misc. I, 527–8.
[6] R.S.S. LXI, 99.   [7] Reg. Pres. II, 174; R.S.S. LIX, 20, LXII, 26, 35.

bishops—three in 1591 and two in 1592—but also in Aberdeen records which show that 'Bishop David Cunningham, minister' was now nothing more than the senior member of the clergy of the city.[1]

By 1592, therefore, current practice in the admission of ministers and in administration generally was manifestly no longer in accordance with statute law, and the consciousness that this was so may be implied by the tendency for presentations either to omit any reference to the taking of an oath of obedience to the ordinary or to substitute an oath for 'due obedience to the kirk' or an oath to 'the kirk, his ordinary'.[2] Thus the act of parliament of 1592[3] which for the first time gave official authorisation to the presbyterian polity amounted to no more than a step to bring law into line with practice, little more than a recognition of a *fait accompli.*

Nor did the statute of 1592 represent either a comprehensive settlement or capitulation to Andrew Melville, many of whose proposals were passed by. It did not proceed on any allusion to the divine right of the presbyterian system, or on any general acknowledgment of ecclesiastical independence. The general assembly was to meet once a year or oftener *pro re nata,* but at each meeting it was the king or his commissioner, if present, who was to name time and place for the next meeting—the assembly being free to appoint time and place if neither king nor commissioner was present, but no machinery being provided to ensure that the assembly would meet if the crown declined to summon it. While no specific provision was made for the representation of a presbyterian church in parliament, the general assumption was that clerical representation of some kind was to continue. Synods, presbyteries and kirk sessions received express recognition, and it was provided in particular[4] that in order to deal with the 'abussis quhilkis ar laitlie croppin in the kirk throw the misbehaviour of sic personis as ar providit to ecclesiastical functionis' sentence of deprivation by a presbytery, synod or general assembly was to be effective in rendering the benefice vacant. The second of the 'Black Acts' of 1584 was modified so that spiritual office-bearers should be independent in spiritual

[1] *Spalding Club Misc.* II, 67–8.   [2] R.S.S. LXII, 39; LXIV, 179.
[3] *A.P.S.* III, 541.   [4] *Ibid.* 542–3.

affairs, including the appointment and deprivation of ministers, and the twentieth of those acts was annulled, so that episcopal powers, including collation, were transferred to presbyteries, which thus at last received statutory authority.

However, at the top of the structure, nothing was done to transform the general assembly into the clerical body demanded by Andrew Melville. It would appear that in practice the ministerial members of the assembly were by this time sometimes being commissioned by the synods or the presbyteries, which, here as elsewhere, had been taking over the functions of bishops and superintendents.[1] But the law of representation was not settled until 1597,[2] when the assembly ordained that three ministers and one 'baron' should go to the assembly from each presbytery, along with two representatives of Edinburgh and one from each of the other royal burghs.[3] The reference to the 'baron' and the provision for burghal representation show that the conception of the three estates was not extinct and that the assembly was not, even now, to be a mere gathering of ministers and elders.

Further, the office of bishop, although eclipsed, was not abolished in 1592, or at any point before 1638. Some sees, it is true, were vacant, others held by mere titulars, but some were held by men exercising ecclesiastical functions, if only as ministers, and the tenure of a see still conferred the right to a place in parliament. 'Bishops' of a kind there still were, and the bishoprics (though deprived of their temporality since 1587) remained in being. The cathedral and diocesan dignities, too, survived, and, although they were merely titular, it was not easy to reconcile them with presbyterian theories of parity. Not only so, but presbyterial administration did not yet prevail throughout the whole country. In 1593 presentations to benefices in the diocese of the Isles were directed to the king's commissioner in ecclesiastical causes in the diocese or to the superintendent, visitor or commissioner there, and resort was once had to the presbytery of the Chanonry of Ross 'becaus the

[1] *Wodrow Soc. Misc.* I, 527–8; Perth Kirk Session Register (MS.), 6 May 1594, 30 June 1595.
[2] *B.U.K.* III, 906, 935 (Calderwood, v, 590–1, 706).
[3] *Ibid.* 947 (Calderwood, v, 709).

sait of the Illis is vacand'.[1] In Argyll, a presentation went to the visitor, commissioner or presbytery in July 1594 and to the bishop or commissioner in August 1595.[2] Nor is it perhaps very remarkable that in Caithness, Shetland and Annandale commissioners were regarded as the appropriate persons to receive presentations.[3] It would be more surprising that we find commissioners or 'superintendents' at work in Aberdeen, Glasgow, Dundee, Fife, Stirling and other places in the Lowlands,[4] were it not for the fact that the general assembly's records themselves suggest that presbyteries were not operating with entire success or were not regarded as wholly adequate for the tasks of oversight and administration. The assembly of April 1593 declared that in addition to visitation by presbyteries there should be commissioners, appointed by the assembly, to 'visit and try the doctrine, life and conversation, diligence and fidelity of the pastors', to seek out non-residents and dilapidators and to proceed, with the advice of the presbytery, against unfit ministers.[5] An act of March 1596 clearly implies that presbyteries had not yet been set up everywhere, because it appointed commissioners for all the outlying parts of the country, with power to try pastors *within presbyteries where they were established* and also elsewhere, to discover non-residents and dilapidators and to proceed against delinquent clergy, adjoining to them some of the presbytery *where one existed*.[6] In May 1601 commissioners with power to 'try' ministers and 'plant kirks' were appointed for the entire country, and in November 1602 commissioners were appointed with power to 'try' not only ministers and congregations but also presbyteries themselves.[7] There is little indication that presbyterial organisation was becoming any more effective with the passage of years, or that there would be any rude interruption should the pendulum begin to swing towards episcopacy once more.

Even at congregational level, the programme of Andrew Mel-

[1] R.S.S. LXV, 18, 99; LXVII, 54.   [2] *Ibid.* LXVI, 180; LXVII, 184.
[3] *Ibid.* LXV, 12, 19, 92; LXVIII, 46.
[4] *Ibid.* LXV, 56; LXVI, 125; LXVII, 23, 101; LXVIII, 3, 83, 168.
[5] B.U.K. III, 800–1 (Calderwood, v, 246).
[6] *Ibid.* 862–3 (Calderwood, v, 419–20).
[7] B.U.K. III, 972–3, 986–7, 992–4 (Calderwood, VI, 122–3, 168–70, 171–3).

ville, or for that matter the programme of the first Book of Discipline, was not yet in operation. The expansion of kirk sessions throughout the country is not easy to trace, and it is especially difficult to ascertain what provision, if any, was made for discipline in the many parishes which did not have ministers. In large towns the ministers and elders of the various churches met in a single consistory, and a similar arrangement may have been made in some rural areas, to enable the kirk session of a parish which had a minister to exercise the oversight of adjacent parishes which had only readers, but there is no evidence to show that this was so. The statute of 1592 authorising the presbyterian system referred to 'particular kirkis, gif they be lauchfullie reulit be sufficient ministeris and sessioun',[1] and in 1596 the general assembly found it necessary to issue instructions that every minister 'have a session established of the meetest men in his congregation, ... and this to be a universal order throughout the realm'.[2] And where there were kirk sessions, they still consisted of elders holding office for a year at a time and not for life.[3] The deacons, it may be added, had never acquired that comprehensive control over church property which both the first Book of Discipline and the second had claimed for them, and the most they can have done in most parishes was to administer the funds available for the relief of the poor; the office never fulfilled the expectations of the reformers. The claim that congregations should elect their ministers had never yet been admitted, and presentations by the crown and by lesser patrons[4] make no reference to congregational rights. The assembly of March 1596 indeed protested that as presentations resulted in the thrusting of unwanted ministers on congregations, no one should seek a presentation without the ad-

---

[1] *A.P.S.* III, 542.   [2] *B.U.K.* III, 865 (Calderwood, V, 403).

[3] This appears to have been the rule until well through the seventeenth century. A general assembly act of 1642 'anent the choosing of sessions' implies that annual election was usual. The Corstorphine Kirk Session Register, on 23 Sept. 1656, discloses that the session was held to have remained in office too long, contrary to the 'order and practice' of the church, which was that either every year or every second year there should be a new election and a change of elders. (I am indebted to Dr. C. T. McInnes for this reference.) P. Hateley-Waddell, *An Old Kirk Chronicle*, p. 73, shows that in the middle of the seventeenth century elders were often appointed for only a year or a term of years.

[4] E.g. *Wodrow Soc. Misc.* I, 534–5.

vice of the presbytery,[1] and there is evidence that in the early seventeenth century, after the restoration of episcopacy, there was in practice a good deal of flexibility;[2] but the full rights of the patron were still maintained by law, for presbyteries were 'bund and astrictit to ressave and admitt quhatsumevir qualifiet minister presentit be his majestie or uther laic patrounes'.[3]

It would seem, therefore, that the constitution of 1592—the first statutory presbyterian constitution—was deliberately and consciously a compromise between the claims of the presbyterians and those of the crown; but it was also, and perhaps more conspicuously, an incomplete and inadequate settlement which left many problems still to be solved. It is appropriate to compare it with the settlement arrived at a century later, when parliament again prescribed a presbyterian polity for the Church of Scotland. This settlement was professedly based on a revival of the statute of 1592, and it was still in some respects a compromise: there was still no recognition of ecclesiastical independence; the presbyterian polity was prescribed by parliament not because of its claims to be founded on the word of God but on the purely secular ground that it was said to be in accordance with the wishes of the generality of the people; contemporaries were in no doubt that what one parliament had conceded another parliament could withdraw; it was demonstrated again and again in later generations that the Church of Scotland was still subject to the crown-in-parliament. But 1690 represented a settlement of many problems left unsolved in 1592. The office of bishop, name and thing, was now formally abolished, and the door by which episcopacy had been re-insinuated a century earlier was now closed (as it had been closed for a time by an act of assembly in 1638), at the cost of relinquishing clerical representation in parliament; while the royal right to name time and place for the assembly's meetings was for a few years still asserted (resulting in a dispute with King William which recalls the dispute with King James a century earlier), it was soon abandoned in practice; presbyterial organisation, though restricted to a small part of the country in 1690, soon spread, and the commissioners and visitors so familiar

[1] *B.U.K.* III, 864 (Calderwood, v, 402).
[2] McCrie, *Andrew Melville*, pp. 434–5.   [3] *A.P.S.* III, 542.

in earlier generations became a thing of the past; although congregational election of ministers was still not admitted, the rights of individual patrons were abrogated; barons no longer attended the assembly—unless they happened to come as elders—but the burgh commissioners still appeared. Thus the solution of 1690, though still a compromise, was a more distinctly presbyterian settlement than the constitution of 1592 had been.

The triumph of Andrew Melville, it may be remarked, was deferred until much later times. Patronage was abolished in 1874; in 1921 the Church of Scotland's right to determine its own doctrine, worship, discipline and government was conceded by parliament; in 1926 the crown's claim to be able to determine the time and place of the general assembly's meetings was finally abandoned; and in 1929 the commissioners of the royal burghs disappeared from the general assembly. At some undetermined point, probably in the late seventeenth century, it had come to be the practice to 'ordain' elders for life. Thus the concept of the clerical oligarchy in the end prevailed, and laymen, properly so called, were excluded from any part in the management of the affairs of the Church of Scotland, whether in parliament, general assembly or kirk session.

During the century which intervened between the attempts of 1592 and 1690 at a settlement on a presbyterian foundation, there had been two periods of a compromise on an episcopalian basis. The initiation of the first of them, under James VI, undoubtedly arose mainly from practical, or at least non-theological, considerations. One of the problems left unsolved in 1592 had been that of adequate clerical representation in parliament, and it was the need to provide for such representation that opened the door to a revival of the episcopate, through the appointment of ministers to the episcopal titles so that they could vote in parliament; but the imperfections of the 1592 settlement meant also that, as presbyterial oversight was inadequate, commissioners had still to act, and the existence of the office of commissioner made it possible for bishops to be endowed with administrative functions without causing any dislocation to the established polity. The next step—the appointment of bishops as permanent moderators of presbyteries and synods—was a reversion to one of the features of the compromise proposed in 1586. The episcopate thus revived, even when restored to its ancient endowments and even when reintegrated into the normal episcopal succession through the consecrations carried out in England in 1610, was not fatal to the general assembly, for throughout most of the reign of James VI, although the administration was in the hands of bishops, there was still a general assembly which was recognised as the highest authority in church affairs and which might be manipulated by the king but could not be ignored. And so far from the existence of bishops being detrimental to the rest of the presbyterian system, the evidence suggests that in administration the combination of bishops with presbyteries worked well, while under their joint direction the kirk sessions operated more widely and effectively than ever before. It is a striking illustration of the persistence of reformation principles that just as the first care of the superintendents, on their appointment in 1561, had been the constitution of kirk sessions, so the first care of the bishops, on their reappointment after the Restoration, was the constitution of kirk sessions.[1] And if administration was thus conducted without friction, the episcopate was introduced and developed without needlessly offending presbyterian susceptibilities, for there was no general reordination of men in presbyterian orders either after 1610 or after 1661; there was no 'threefold ministry', for ministerial deacons were extremely rare; and the rite of confirmation by bishops was all but unknown. Presbytery and episcopacy are no doubt based on irreconcilable principles—ordination and superintendence by a corporate body on the one hand and by an individual on the other—but if a reconciliation between the two can be achieved it was achieved in seventeenth-century Scotland. The initiation of the compromise had arisen, as was said above, mainly from practical factors, and those who worked it out may not have had the deliberate intention of combining the merits of the two systems, but that happy result was undoubtedly achieved in practice. No one familiar with Scottish church history views with any surprise most of the elements in schemes of reunion like that of South India, and several recent proposals have introduced nothing which had not previously occurred to the fertile brain of King James VI.

[1] Appendix A(2); W. R. Foster, *Bishop and Presbytery*, p. 61.

Ia MANDATE TO JOHN SPOTTISWOODE AS SUPERINTENDENT OF LOTHIAN

Apud Edinburgh. 10 Martii a.d. 1560[61]

The lordis of secreit counsale, understanding that conforme to the kirk [*rectius* buik] of reformatioun and discipline of the kirk approvit and affirmit be the saidis lordis, thai have elected maister Jhone Spottiswode, persone of Calder, superintendent of the dyocesy of Lowtheane, quha hes acceptit the office thairof upon him, to quhom the saidis lordis hes promisit to assist, mantayne and defend him and to caus him be ansuerit in all thingis concerning the said office, that thairby the kirk of God may be sett in ordour, vice punishit and vertue nurishit, to the increase of Christis kyngdome and suppressing of Sathan, Antichrist and his king-dome: Thairfor the saidis lordis ordanis lettiris to be direct to charge the said maister Jhone Spottiswod, superintendent foirsaid, to exercise his said office within the said dyocesy treulie and faythfullie and to appoynt and se that within every parochin thairof elders, deacones and utheris officiaris be appoyntit and how every ane of thame dischargis thair offices. And alse to se that every minister within his said dyocesye be qualifeit and abill to use his office to his flok and parochinaris. And that thai be sufficientlie provydit of thair levingis, that without care thai may gif attendence to thair vocatioun. And that the mansis [and] yardis be red to thame and thai enterit to the possessioun thairof and to se that every paroche kirk be sufficientlie reparit in all thingis that the people may thairin convene to heir the word of God precheit and the sacramentis treulie ministrate, and all thingis apperteyning thairto sett in cumlye and decent ordour. And that the parochinaris resort and repair to the hering of Goddis worde, and to trye all faltis committit within his said dyocesye and the samin to cause be redressit and reformit. And inlike-maner to take inquisitioun quhat persones sen the last parliament aganis the tenour of the actis and statutis maid thairin hes said mess or hard mess or that ministrate the sacramentis nocht being admittit thairto and report the samin to the saidis lordis, that the panes contenit in the saidis actis may be execute upon thame for contemptioun thairof. And inlikmaner that the saidis officiaris charge all our soverane ladeis liegis dwelland within the boundis of the said dyocesye to answer and obey to the said maister Jhone thair superintendent in all and syndry thingis concerning the said office and to do thair detfull reverence to him. And that nane of thame resist, ganestand or make impediment to him in using the said office and all thingis concerning the samin nor yit absent thame fra the preching of the word at the dayis appoyntit thairto be thair ministeris.

James
James Hamylton   Mortoun
James Stewart   Glencarn
Lyndesay   Setoun

Warrender Papers, vol. A, fo. 93

Ib CIRCULAR LETTER SENT BY JOHN SPOTTISWOODE, SUPERINTENDENT OF LOTHIAN

Maister Jhonne Spottiswod, superintendent of Lautheane, to the perrochinaris of N., desyris grace, mercy and peace from God the Father of Our Lorde Jesus Christ, with the perpetuale increise of vertew and godlines.

It is nocht unknawin onto yow, belovit brethrene, that be the consent of the kirkis of Lautheane and be the commandement of the nobilitie I am appoynttit superintendent oure the same and be vertew thareof be the lordis of secreit consale I am straitlie chargeit to visey the kirkis for establissing of ane uniforme and godlie ordour in the same, as by thare charge, quhilk heirwith I send you, mair evidentlie may appeir: quhairfoir I hartlie require you and in the name of God and of the secreit consale, oure present and lauchfull magistratis, I command you to nominate and cheise sum from amangis you maist godlie, prudent and able to beir charge in the kirk to be elderis and diacones in your kirk, quhais office and dewtie sal be mair evidentlie declarit onto thame selfis the day of thare electioun other be me or ellis be sum uthir godlie and leirnit minister appoyntit for that purpose, quhilk day of electioun because I wald nocht poynt without your knawlege and consent I have directit onto you this my requeist and charge to the effect ye being advertist may be your messingeir or writtin lat me understand the day that you will that I sall visey you for the purpose forsaid; and in the meyntyme I require and charge you to repair your kirk as it becummis ane house into the quhilk the wourde of God suld be precheit and his blissit sacramentis

ministrat, and sufficient stipend be preparit for the ministeris, and also
that ye note sike persones as leif ane ungodlie lyfe, to wit that ar knawin
drunkardis, huremongaris, oppressouris of the pure, sweiraris, blas-
phemaris of God, evil speikaris of his worde and ministeris, contemp-
naris of the samin, sike also as ar mayntenaris of ydolatrie, heiraris or
sayaris of mess, abusaris or prophanaris of the sacramentis, or sik as dois
take upoun thame to ministir thame nocht being callit to the office of
ministerie, that thai may be punissit, as mair expreslie is contenit in the
actis of parliament and in the buke of discipline, and last that the manse
be maid fre to the minister, all uther personis removit from it with possible expeditioun, and that the glebe assignit onto it without delay, to wit
sex aikaris of land, gif the glebe extend thairto, nixt adjacent to the
manse, that it may be maid fre and that he may peaceabillie joy and possess the same, as the buik of reformatioun laitlie admittit mair fullie dois
report, assuring you that gif in ony of thir premissis ye be ather negligent
or disobedient that I will nocht onlie complane to the lordis of secreit
consale bot also will proceid aganis yow with sik ordour of justice as my
conscience may be dischargeit befor God and my dewtie befor man. And
thus I committ you to the protectioun of the Omnipotent. From Edinburgh the xxii day of Marche 1560.

Warrender Papers, vol. A, fo. 98v.

IIa NOMINATION OF A BISHOP

ENGLISH	SCOTTISH
Trusty and well-beloved, we greet you well.	*Trustie and weillbeloved, we greete you weill.*
Whereas *the bishopric of H.* is now void, *by the* death *of the late incumbent of the same,*	Forsamekle as *the bishoprick of S.* presentlie vaiketh, *by* deceasse *of the late incumbent of the same;*
we let you wit that, *calling to our remembrance the virtue, learning,*	and, *calling to our remembrance the vertue, learning,* good conversatioun
and other good *qualities of our trusty and well-beloved* A.B., *we have thought* good,	*and other* godlie *qualiteis of our trusty and weillbeloved* A.B., preacher of the word of God, *we have thought,*

by these our letters, to name	*by thir oure letters, to name*
and recommend *him unto you*	him, and commend *him to you,*
to be elected and *chosen*	*to be chosin*
to the said bishopric of H.	*to the said bishoprick of S.*
Wherefore we require	*Wherefore we require*
and pray you forthwith,	you indilatlie,
upon the receipt hereof,	*upon the recept heerof,*
to proceed to your election,	*to proceed to your election,*
according to the laws of	*according to the lawes of*
this *our realme*	*our realme*
and our congé d'élire	*and our* licence to choose
sent unto *you herewith,*	*sent* to *you heerwith,*
and the same election so made	*and the same election so made*
to certify unto *us*	*to certifie* to us
under your common seal.	*under your common seale.*
Given under our signet, etc.	*Givin under our signet, etc.*

G. W. Prothero,
Select Statutes, pp. 242–3.

Calderwood, III, 181
(*B.U.K.* I, 217).

II*b* ROYAL ASSENT TO ELECTION, WITH MANDATE TO CONSECRATE

ENGLISH	SCOTTISH
Regina etc. reverendissimo in	Jacobus etc.
Christo patri domino Mathaeo	
archiepiscopo Cantuariensi,	
totius Angliae primati et	
metropolitano, salutem.	
Cum *vacante nuper sede* epis-	Quia *vacante nuper sede* epis-
copali E. per legitimam depri-	copatus R. ob processum . . . con-
vationem ultimi episcopi ejusdem	tra J. olim R. episcopum rite
	deductum, nos
ad humilem petitionem decani	*ad humilem petitionem decani*
et capituli ecclesie nostre	*et capituli ecclesie*
cathedralis E. predicte,	*cathedralis* R.
iisdem *per literas nostras*	*per* alias *nostras literas* nostro
patentes *licentiam* concesserimus	sub magno sigillo *licentiam*
alium sibi eligendi in	nostram *alium sibi eligendi in*

episcopum et pastorem
sedis predicte;
iidemque decanus et capitulum
vigore et obtentu licentie
nostre predicte dilectum nobis
in Christo magistrum R.C.
sacre theologie professorem
sibi et ecclesie predicte
elegerunt in episcopum et pastorem
prout per literas suas patentes
sigillo eorum communi sigillatas

nobis inde directas plenius
liquet et apparet.

Nos
electionem illam acceptantes
eidem electioni
regium nostrum assensum
adhibuimus pariter et favorem
et hoc

vobis
tenore presentium significamus:

rogantes ac in fide et di-
lectione quibus nobis tene-
mini firmiter precipiendo
mandantes quatenus eundem
magistrum R.C.
in episcopum et pastorem
ecclesie cathedralis E. predicte
sic ut prefertur electum

episcopum et pastorem
sedis predicte concessimus;
cujus nostre licentie vigore
iidem decanus et capitulum
predilectum nostrum magistrum
A.H., verbi dei predicatorem

ipsis in episcopum et pastorem ecclesie prescripte
elegerunt
prout per eorum literas
sigillo suo communi et sub-
scriptionibus manualibus
corroboratas nobis inde
directas plenius liquet et
apparet.
Nos ideo cum . . . consensu . . .
Regentis electionem illam
acceptantes eidem electioni
regium nostrum assensum
adhibimus pariter et favorem
et hoc reverendissimo
reverendisque in Christo
patribus N. N. et N. superintendentibusque N. et N. aut
aliquibus eorum duobus
presentium tenore significamus:
cum mandato seu directione
in eisdem prefatis
archiepiscopo episcopis
superintendentibusque eorumve
aliquibus duobus, ipsos
rogantes ac in fide et di-
lectione quibus nobis tenen-
tur firmiter precipiendo
mandantes quatenus prefatum
magistrum A.H.
in episcopum et pastorem
dicte ecclesie
sic ut premittitur electum

electionemque predictam confirmare et eundem magistrum R.C.
episcopum et pastorem ecclesie
predicte *consecrare ceteraque*
omnia et singula peragere quas
vestro *in hac parte incumbunt*
officio pastorali juxta formam
et effectum statutorum in ea
parte editorum et provisorum
velitis *cum effectu.*

consecrare electionemque
predictam confirmare

ceteraque omnia et singula
que eorum
in hac parte incumbunt
officio pastorali peragere
velint *juxta formam* legum
regni nostri *cum* omni
diligentia favore et *effectu.*

Prothero, op. cit. pp. 243–4.

R.S.S. XLII, 124

III THE STATUTE 13 ELIZ. CAP. XII AND THE SCOTTISH STATUTE OF JANUARY 1573 (CAP. 3)

ENGLISH

That the Churches of the
Queenes Majesty's Domynyons
maye *be served* with Pastors
of sounde Religyon,

SCOTTISH

. . . that the kirk within
this Realme
be servit be Godly persounis
of sound Religioun obedient to
the authoritie of the Kingis
Maiestie our Soverane Lord. It
is thairfoir concludit statute
and ordanit be his Maiestie
with auise of his said Regent
thre Estatis and haill body
of this present
Parliament That euery
persoun

be it enacted by the
aucthoritie *of thys present*
Parlyament, That every
person under the degree
of a Bysshop which doth or
shall pretend to be a Priest
or *Minister of Godes* holy
Word and Sacraments, by
reason of any other fourme
of Institution . . .
shal in the presence of the
Bysshop or Gardian of the

           quha *sall*
pretend to be ane
Minister of Goddis
word and Sacramentis, Or quha
presently dois or sall pretend
. . .
sall in the presence of the
Archebischop, *Bischop*

231

Spyritualties *of some one Diocesse where he hath or shall have* Ecclesiastical Lyving declare *his Assent and subscribe* to all *the Artycles of Religion* which onely concerne the Confession of the true Christian Faithe . . . *And shall bryng* from such Bysshop or Gardyan *in Wryting* under his Seale autentike, *a testimoniall* of such Assent and Subscription, *and openly on some Sunday in the tyme of the publique* servyce afore noone *in every Churche where by reason of* any Ecclesiastical Lyving *he ought to attende*	Superintendent or Commissionar *of the Diocie* or Province *quhair he hes or sall haue* the *Ecclesiasticall leuing* gif *his assent and subscriue the articklis of Religioun* contenit in the actis of our Soverane Lordis Parliament. . . *and sall bring ane testimoniall in wryting* thairupon. *And oppinly on sum Sonday in tyme of* Sermone or *publict* prayeris *in the* Kirk *quhair be ressoun of* his *ecclesiasticall leving* he aucht to attend or of the frutes quhairof he ressauis commoditie *reid baith the* Testimoniall and Confessioun . . .
reade both the said *Testimonial* and the said Artycles; . . . *And that yf any person Ecclesiastical or which shall have Ecclesiastical Lyving shall* advysedly *maynteyne* or affyrme *any Doctrine directly contrarie or repugnant to any of the said Articles, and being convented* before the Bysshop . . . *shall persist therein* or *not revoke his Errour, or after* such *Revocation* eftsoones *affyrme* such *untrue Doctryne, such maynteyning* or *affyrming*	*and gif ony persoun Ecclesiasticall or quhilk sall haue Ecclesiasticall leuing sall* wilfully *mantene ony doctrine directly contrair or repugnant to ony of the saidis articklis and being conuenit* and callit as foliowis *sall persist thairin* and *not reuoke his errour, or efter* his *reuocatioun* sall of new *affirme sic vntrew doctrine sic mantening affirming*

232

and persisting or such
eftsones affyrming, *shalbe
just cause to depryve* such
person *of his Ecclesiasticall*
promotions; *And it shalbe
lefull to* the Bisshop of the
Diocesse or Thordynarie, or
the said Commissioners, *to
deprive* suche person so
persisting . . .

*and persisting
       salbe
Just caus to depriue* him
       of his ecclesiasticall
leuing. *And it salbe
lauchfull to* thame befoir
quhome he is callit and
conuenit *to
depriue* him . . .

INDEX

Abbacies: at disposal of crown before reformation, 37–9; appointments to, after 1560, 155–6; proposal to dissolve (1567), 159; arrangements for (1572), 171; after 1572, 194.

Abell's Chronicle, cited, 9, 44, 105, 116.

Aberdeen: burgh of, progress of reformation in, 30; diocese of, reform in, 34–5.

Adamson, Patrick, archbishop of St. Andrews: dilapidated see, 198; defended episcopacy, 201; submitted to general assembly, 217.

Admonition to parliament, the second, 189.

A Lasco, John, cited, 109.

Annexation, act of (1587), 217.

Ante-Communion service, 83.

Anti-clericalism: before reformation, 11; in reformed church, 84, 130–1.

Appropriations, *see* Parishes.

Argyll, reformed church in, 89.

Augustinian canons regular, reform among, 3, 32.

Aylmer, John, cited, 109.

Ayr, reformation in, 50–1.

Bailies of prelacies, 41–2.

Baptism: administered by readers, 84; administered privately, 180.

'Barons' in general assembly, 141, 220; to be excluded, 204.

Benefices: litigation over, 17; hereditary succession in, 17–18, 20, 39–40; admission to, before reformation, 18–19, 33; thirds of, *see* Thirds; remain in being after 1560, 72, 149; disposal of, after 1560, 73–4, 150; admission of reformed clergy to, 93, 164; secured to reformed church, 152–3; held by 'unqualified'

men, 195; presentations to, 210, 217–19, 220–1.

Betoun, James (II), archbishop of Glasgow: and reform, 34; in France from 1560, 55, 60.

Beza, Theodore: views of, 187–8; condemned episcopacy, 187–8; his *De Triplici Episcopatu*, 191; Scottish correspondence with, 198.

Bible in vernacular, 30.

Bishoprics: appointments to, before reformation, 20, 26, 38–9; at disposal of crown, 37–9; revenues of, 64; appointments to, 1560–7, 155–6; pensions from, 38–9, 155; between 1567 and 1572, 159–60; after 1572, 172–3, 194; their temporalities annexed to crown, 217.

Bishops: attitude of reformers to, 54–5, 102–11, 166–8; negotiations with, in 1560, 55–8; some support reformation, 58–60, 157–8; their powers after 1560, 72–4; to preach, 102, 109; 'false' and 'true', 103–11; 'godly' or reformed, 108–11, 115–16; their morals, before reformation, 104; arrangements for appointments (1572), 163–5, 228–31; their jurisdiction (1572), 164; relations with superintendents, after 1572, 173–5; functions of (1581), 207–8; receive presentations to benefices, 207, 210; their authority reaffirmed, as king's commissioners (1584), 211–13; to have particular congregations, 215–16; subject to general assembly, 216; to be permanent moderators, 216, 224–5; to act with advice of ministers, 216; decline of their powers after 1587, 217–19; their office not abolished in 1592, 220; abolished in 1638 and 1690, 223.

234